# BLOCK SCHEDULING:
# A CATALYST FOR CHANGE IN HIGH SCHOOLS

Robert Lynn Canady
and
Michael D. Rettig

EYE ON EDUCATION
P.O. BOX 3113
PRINCETON, N.J. 08543
(609) 395-0005
(609) 395-1180 fax

Production services provided by Richard H. Adin Freelance Editorial Services,
9 Orchard Drive, Gardiner, NY 12525 (914-883-5884)

ISBN 1-883001-14-5

**Library of Congress Cataloging-in-Publication Data**

Canady, Robert Lynn.
    Block scheduling: a catalyst for change in high schools / by Robert
Lynn Canady and Michael D. Rettig.
        p.   cm.
    Includes bibliographical references.
    ISBN 1-883001-14-5
    1. Schedules, school—United States. 2. High schools—United States—
Administration. 3. School year—United States. I. Rettig, Michael D., 1950- .
I. Title.
LB3032.C36  1995
371.2'42'0973—dc20                                          93-7773
                                                              CIP

10 9 8 7 6

*Available from Eye On Education:*

## THE LIBRARY OF INNOVATIONS

**Innovations in Parent and Family Involvement**
by William Rioux and Nancy Berla

**The Directory of Innovations in High Schools**
by Gloria G. Frazier and Robert N. Sickles

**Research on Educational Innovations**
by Arthur K. Ellis and Jeffrey T. Fouts

**Research on School Restructuring**
by Arthur K. Ellis and Jeffrey T. Fouts

---

## THE LEADERSHIP AND MANAGEMENT SERIES

**The Principal's Edge**
by Jack McCall

**The Administrator's Guide to Personal Productivity
with the Time Management Checklist**
by Harold L. Taylor

**Quality and Education: Critical Linkages**
by Betty L. McCormick

**Transforming Education Through Total Quality
Management: A Practitioner's Guide**
by Franklin P. Schargel

**The Educator's Guide to Implementing Outcomes**
by William J. Smith

**The School Portfolio:
A Comprehensive Framework for School Improvement**
by Victoria L. Bernhardt

**Schools for All Learners: Beyond the Bell Curve**
by Renfro C. Manning

**The Administrator's Guide to School-Community Relations**
by George E. Pawlas

# DEDICATION

We could never have completed this undertaking without the support and patience of our wives, Marjorie and Sally, and our children--Carol, Donna, Robert, and Sarah Canady; and Danny, Anne, and Alison Rettig.  Thank you.

# ACKNOWLEDGMENTS

Our greatest fear in attempting to name the many individuals who have inspired and assisted us in the completion of this book is that we will miss someone who deserves our thanks. So we first thank the many teachers, administrators, parents, students, and colleagues with whom we have worked and whose ideas and words have helped shape this book. Specifically, we wish to thank John Sessoms for his research on the history of school scheduling and Brenda Tanner for her work in the area of staff development. We thank Dr. Thomas Shortt, Dr. Thomas DeBolt, Clarence (Skip) Edwards, Dr. Dale Baird, Dr. Marian Stephens, and Dr. Alfred R. Butler for their inspirational leadership in the scheduling reform movement in the Commonwealth of Virginia.

At the University of Virginia we thank Drs. Jay Chronister and James M. Cooper for their encouragement and support and Paula Price and Donna Farnum for their valuable assistance. At James Madison University we wish to thank graduate students Jennifer Briggs, Robbie Higdon, and Jennifer Whitehair for their research and editing; Judy Patterson and Judy Richardson for their assistance and patience; and Drs. Alvin Pettus and Elizabeth D. Morie for their support and encouragement. We also express our appreciation to Robert Sickles, our publisher, for tenaciously urging us to complete this project.

Finally we wish to thank several of our public school teachers who were instrumental in helping us as students to develop and to succeed:

From Dickson (TN) High School: Mrs. Joe B. Weems, "Miss Dockie" to her students; Mrs. Floyd Williams, "Miss Annie Lee" to her students; and Mrs. Garner Harris, "Miss Karene" to her students; together who gave more than 100 years of dedicated service and who were an inspiration to thousands of students in Dickson County, Tennessee.

From the Commack (NY) Public Schools: Miss Dubitsky, who danced the "Hora" with her students in 5th grade; Miss Keely, who allowed you to be different; and Mr. Griffin, who encouraged, appreciated, and accepted divergent thinking and writing.

# ABOUT THE AUTHORS

**Dr. Robert Lynn Canady** is Professor and former Chair, Department of Educational Leadership and Policy Studies at the University of Virginia. He received his Ed.D. degree from the University of Tennessee. His major publications have been in the area of grading practices, implementing programs for at-risk students, and restructuring schools. He has worked extensively with school districts in 28 states.

Dr. Canady has taught in grades 4 through 12, served as principal of elementary, middle, and junior high schools in Tennessee and Kentucky, and in central offices in Tennessee. In addition to receiving the Phi Delta Kappa Distinguished Service Award and the Outstanding Professor Award in the School of Education, University of Virginia, he has received two university-wide awards for distinguished teaching and service.

**Dr. Michael Rettig** is assistant professor of Education at James Madison University in Harrisonburg, Virginia. He received his Ph.D. from the University of Virginia, where he was named outstanding graduate student in 1991 through Phi Delta Kappa. He taught for ten years in the Syracuse City schools and served as a school administrator in Virginia for six years.

During the past five years, Dr. Rettig has presented on the topic of school scheduling at over ten national state conferences and workshops. In addition, Dr. Rettig has served as a consultant on school scheduling issues in over twenty states and over fifty school districts.

Readers may be interested in a video entitled HIGH SCHOOL ALTERNATIVE SCHEDULING, presented by Robert Lynn Canady, available from The Video Journal of Education, 549 West 3560 South, Salt Lake City, Utah 84115–4225. Phone (800) 572–1153.

# PREFACE

Why write about scheduling? What we began to realize as early as the 1960s when Lynn began his work with elementary school scheduling, and what we continue to believe more each day, is that school scheduling is far more important than the simple mechanical assignment of students to teachers in rooms for the school day. Within the school schedule resides **power**: the power to address problems, the power to facilitate the successful implementation of programs, and the power to make possible the institutionalization of effective instructional practices. As well, those who design the school schedule also have the power to create mass confusion, to waste resources, and to cause unnecessary stress. A bit of research will confirm that, with few exceptions, discussions about high school scheduling in the past have focused primarily on the "mechanics": minimizing schedule conflicts, making room assignments, collecting students' choices, assigning teachers to sections, meeting contractual requirements, etc. Too little thought and action have been given to the educational and emotional impact of a school schedule on the lives of students and teachers. It is to that purpose we have written this book.

During the two years it has taken us to write this text, we have worked with hundreds of high schools in 32 states across the country. We have come to believe if the American high school is to educate the students of the present and the future, as successfully as we were educated in the past, it must change! If high schools do not change, we fear the continued erosion of public schooling and the polarization of educational opportunity in our country, a process which is well underway today. While not a panacea, we strongly believe that a well-designed school schedule **can be** a catalyst for critical changes needed in high schools across America.

Finally, we invite your comments and suggested improvements; we, too, are still searching for the perfect high school schedule!

Lynn and Mike
April, 1995

# TABLE OF CONTENTS

ACKNOWLEDGMENTS . . . . . . . . . . . . . . . . . . . . . . . . . . . . . . . . . . . . vii
ABOUT THE AUTHORS . . . . . . . . . . . . . . . . . . . . . . . . . . . . . . . . . . ix
PREFACE . . . . . . . . . . . . . . . . . . . . . . . . . . . . . . . . . . . . . . . . . . . . . . . xi

1  RE-EXAMINING THE AMERICAN HIGH SCHOOL SCHEDULE . 1
   A National Critique . . . . . . . . . . . . . . . . . . . . . . . . . . . . . . . . . . . . . 1
   Problems with High School Schedules . . . . . . . . . . . . . . . . . . . . . 4
      Single-Period Schedules Contribute to the Impersonal
         Nature of High Schools . . . . . . . . . . . . . . . . . . . . . . . . . . . . 5
      Single-Period Schedules Exacerbate Discipline Problems
         in High School . . . . . . . . . . . . . . . . . . . . . . . . . . . . . . . . . . 6
      Single-Period Schedules and Increased Graduation
         Requirements Have Cut the "Time Pie" Very Thinly . . . 7
      Single Period High School Schedules Limit
         Instructional Possibilities for Teachers . . . . . . . . . . . . . . 8
      Single-Period Schedules Do Not Permit Flexible Time
         for Teaching and Learning . . . . . . . . . . . . . . . . . . . . . . . 9
      Single-Period Schedules Do Not Result in
         User-Friendly Workplaces for Teachers . . . . . . . . . . . . . 11
   Goals of the High School Scheduling Reform Movement . . . . . 12
   A Brief History of High School Scheduling . . . . . . . . . . . . . . . . 13
      Block Scheduling in the Context of High School
         Restructuring . . . . . . . . . . . . . . . . . . . . . . . . . . . . . . . . . . 15
   Block Scheduling and the Change Process . . . . . . . . . . . . . . . . . 18
   Models of Block Scheduling: An Introduction . . . . . . . . . . . . . . 22
   Why Focus on Scheduling? . . . . . . . . . . . . . . . . . . . . . . . . . . . . . 29

2  ALTERNATE DAY BLOCK SCHEDULES . . . . . . . . . . . . . . . . . . . 31
   The Basic Plan . . . . . . . . . . . . . . . . . . . . . . . . . . . . . . . . . . . . . . . 31
      Discussion . . . . . . . . . . . . . . . . . . . . . . . . . . . . . . . . . . . . . . . 37
   Developing the Models . . . . . . . . . . . . . . . . . . . . . . . . . . . . . . . . 42
      Six-Course Models . . . . . . . . . . . . . . . . . . . . . . . . . . . . . . . . 42
      Seven-Course Models . . . . . . . . . . . . . . . . . . . . . . . . . . . . . . 52
      Modifications . . . . . . . . . . . . . . . . . . . . . . . . . . . . . . . . . . . . . 56

        Alternate Day: Modification 1 ...................... 59
        Alternate Day: Modification 2 ...................... 62
        Alternate Day: Modification 3 ...................... 63
   Conclusion .......................................... 66

3  THE 4/4 SEMESTER PLAN ............................. 67
   The Basic Plan ........................................ 68
        Discussion ........................................ 68
   Developing the Model .................................. 73
   Critical Issues Regarding the 4/4 Semester Plan ............ 85
        Instructional Issues .............................. 86
             Retention of Learning ......................... 86
             Minutes per Course ............................ 88
             Curriculum Organization ........................ 90
             Course Sequencing and Foreign Language .......... 90
             Music Programs ................................ 93
             Special Education ............................. 95
             Cooperative Work Programs ..................... 96
             Advanced Placement Courses ................... 100
             Community College Dual-Enrollment ............ 101
        Student Issues ................................... 101
             Transfer ..................................... 101
             Credits Required for Graduation ................. 104
             Student Choice ............................... 105
             Schedule Balance ............................. 105
             Attendance Policies ........................... 106
             Athletic Eligibility ........................... 106
             Discipline ................................... 107
        Teacher Issues ................................... 107
             Planning Time ............................... 107
             Course Preparation ........................... 108
             Contractual Issues ........................... 108
        Cost ............................................ 109
   Conclusion .......................................... 113

4  MORE INTENSIVE SCHEDULING: QUARTER-ON/
   QUARTER-OFF, TRIMESTER, AND SINGLE-COURSE
   PLANS ............................................. 115
   The Quarter-On/Quarter-Off Plan ....................... 118
   Trimester Model ..................................... 121
        Trimester Schedule with Two Extended
             Learning Time (ELT) Periods ................... 125
   Intensive Scheduling ................................. 129

The Copernican Plan .................................. 130
Conclusion .......................................... 132

5   INSTRUCTIONAL TERMS WITHIN THE 180-DAY
    SCHOOL YEAR ..................................... 133
    Short Terms Scheduled in the Middle of Courses ........... 134
        Alternate Day Block Schedule with a 30-Day
            Middle Term ................................. 134
            Discussion .................................. 136
        The 4/4 Semester Plan with Five-Day Middle Terms .... 140
    Short Terms Scheduled After the Completion of Courses .... 142
        The 75–75–(30) Plan ............................. 146
            Discussion .................................. 149
            Adaptations ................................. 152
    Schedules that Provide Short Terms Both During and
        After the Completion of Courses .................... 153
        Semester Block Schedule with Middle Terms
            and End Terms ............................... 154
        Alternate Day Block Schedule with a Middle Term
            and an End Term ............................. 156
    Conclusion ........................................ 158

6   BLENDING SCHEDULING MODELS .................... 159
    Adding the Alternate Day Twist to the 4/4 Semester Plan
        and Other Intensive Schedules ..................... 159
    Extending the School Day ............................ 164
    Scheduling the Four-Day Week ....................... 170
    The Five-Block, Ten-Course, Semester Plan Schedule ....... 176
    Conclusion ........................................ 179

7   SCHEDULES THAT EXTEND TEACHER PLANNING AND
    PROFESSIONAL DEVELOPMENT OPPORTUNITIES ......... 181
    Scheduling Extended Teacher Planning Time During the School Day
        Without Sending
            Students Home .............................. 184
            Daily Period Models ......................... 184
            Alternate Day Models ........................ 192
            Staff Development Time in the 4/4 Semester Plan ....... 193
    Scheduling Short Instructional Terms into the School
        Calendar to Provide Full Days for Teacher Planning
            and Staff Development ........................ 197
    Conclusion ........................................ 203

**8    TEACHING IN THE BLOCK** ......................... 205
   Three-Part Lesson Design: Explanation, Application,
      and Synthesis ...................................... 206
      Explanation  ..................................... 206
      Application  ..................................... 207
      Synthesis ........................................ 209
   Instructional Strategies for the Block Schedule ............. 210
      Cooperative Learning .............................. 210
         Class Building .................................. 211
         Team Formation ................................ 212
         Team Building and Team Identity .................. 213
         Cooperative Learning Structures .................. 214
         Group Processing and Evaluation ................. 215
         Some Quick Cooperative Starters ................. 216
      Paideia Seminar Teaching ......................... 218
         The Seminar ................................... 220
         The Students .................................. 220
         The Teacher ................................... 220
         The Question .................................. 221
         The Text ...................................... 222
      The "Other" Models of Teaching .................... 222
         Concept Development ........................... 224
         Concept Attainment  ........................... 225
         Inquiry ....................................... 227
         Synectics  .................................... 228
         Simulations ................................... 231
         Technology  ................................... 233
         Learning Centers or Stations  ................... 233
         Lectures ...................................... 235
   Designing a Staff Development Plan ..................... 237
      Day One  ....................................... 237
      Days Two and Three ............................. 239
      Days Four and Five .............................. 239
      Days Six to Ten  ................................ 239
   Conclusion ........................................ 240

**REFERENCES**  ........................................ 241
**APPENDIX A: EVALUATION MATRIX** ...................... 251
**APPENDIX B: PLANNING CHECKLIST FOR ALTERNATIVE**
   **SCHEDULING FOR HIGH SCHOOLS** .................... 257
**APPENDIX C: INDICATORS OF ACHIEVEMENT FOR**
   **HIGH SCHOOL RESTRUCTURING EFFORTS** ............. 261

# 1

# RE-EXAMINING THE AMERICAN HIGH SCHOOL SCHEDULE

*Learning in America is a prisoner of time. For the past 150 years, American public schools have held time constant and let learning vary. The rule, only rarely voiced, is simple: learn what you can in the time we make available. It should surprise no one that some bright, hard-working students do reasonably well. Everyone else—from the typical student to the dropout— runs into trouble.* **Time is learning's warden.**

[National Education Commission on Time and Learning, 1994, p. 7]

## A NATIONAL CRITIQUE

Nowhere is the observation that "time is learning's warden" more true than in the assembly line we call the American high school with its six-, seven-, or eight-period daily schedule. Members of the National Education Commission on Time and Learning, which was established in 1991 by Congress to conduct a comprehensive study of the relationship between learning and scheduled time in America's schools, reported that "the degree to which today's American school is controlled by the dynamics of clock and calendar is surprising, even to people who understand school operations" [1994, p. 7]. In addition, the Commission made the following observations regarding the rigidity of time schedules in public schools:

- With few exceptions, schools open and close their doors at fixed times in the morning and early afternoon—a school in one district might open at 7:30 a.m. and close at 2:15 p.m.; in another, the school day might run from 8:00 in the morning until 3:00 in the afternoon.

- With few exceptions, the school year lasts nine months, beginning in late summer and ending in late spring.

- According to the National Center for Education Statistics, schools typically offer a six-period day, with about 5.6 hours of classroom time a day.

- No matter how complex or simple the school subject—literature, shop, physics, gym, or algebra—the schedule assigns each an impartial national average of 51 minutes per class period, no matter how well or poorly students comprehend the material.

- The norm for required school attendance, according to the Council of Chief State School Officers, is 180 days. Eleven states permit school terms of 175 days or less; only one state requires more than 180.

- Secondary school graduation requirements are universally based on seat time—"Carnegie units," a standard of measurement representing one credit for completion of a one-year course meeting daily.

- Despite the obsession with time, little attention is paid to how it is used: in 42 states examined by the Commission, only 41 percent of secondary school time must be spent on core academic subjects [p. 7].

"The results are predictable," according to the Commission, "The school clock governs how families organize their lives, how administrators oversee their schools, and how teachers work their way through the curriculum. Above all, it governs how material is presented to students and the opportunity they have to comprehend and master it" [p. 8].

During the early 1980s and again during the early 1990s, school personnel were bombarded with reports on the inefficient and ineffective use of school time. One of the most important concerns expressed in the 1984 report, *A Nation At Risk*, was related to how time was used in America's schools. The following questions were posed: How do we use time? How do we allocate time? How do we account for time [National Commission on Excellence in Education, 1984]? In response to concerns arising from the report, many state legislators argued that schools should increase both the length of the school day and the school year. Many educators, however, were resistant to such suggestions, contending that a mere extension of school time was not necessarily a solution and would be very costly. In fact, one administrator reported that the extension of the school day would translate to a need for additional duplicating paper so teachers could prepare more busy work!

The argument that educators should become more efficient in their use of currently allocated time was supported by research of the early '80s. For example, Rossmiller [1983] reported that observations by a number of researchers suggest that only about 60 percent of the school day is actually available for instruction. Gilman and Knoll [1983] calculated that "a fair estimate of the average time devoted to instruction during a school day is probably less than 30 percent" [p. 44]. Justiz [1984] reported that 16 percent, or approximately one hour, of instructional time each school day was lost on the average "in the process of organizing the class and by distractions resulting from student conduct, interruptions, and administrative processes" [p. 483]. Karweit [1985] has reported research findings that suggest students engage in productive academic activities only 38 percent of the school day. One teacher described the problem as follows: "Time is the currency of teaching. We barter with time. Every day we make small concessions, small tradeoffs, but, in the end, we know it's going to defeat us" [Boyer, 1983a, p. 30].

The most recent addition to the school time controversy came in the report issued by the National Education Commission on Time and Learning [1994]. One of the Commission's recommendations which made headlines was that the **"ACADEMIC DAY SHOULD BE NEARLY DOUBLED"** [Sommerfeld, 1994, p. 12]. Other specific recommendations of that commission having implications for school scheduling practices include the following:

♦ Schools should be reinvented around learning, not time.

♦ State and local school boards should work with schools to redesign education so that time becomes a factor supporting learning, not a boundary marking its limits.

♦ Schools should provide additional academic time by reclaiming the school day for academic instruction.

♦ Teachers should be provided with the professional time and opportunities they need to do their jobs well [Sommerfield, 1994].

## PROBLEMS WITH HIGH SCHOOL SCHEDULES

Increasingly, there is no typical high school schedule in the United States. Prior to the current "block scheduling" reform movement, however, schedules did have many commonalities. In general, schools operated with six, seven, eight, or sometimes even nine daily periods. Six-period schools operated classes somewhere between 50 and 60 minutes in length; seven-period schools had classes of 45 to 52 minutes; eight-period schools ran sessions of 40 to 48 minutes; and the few schools operating nine-period schedules generally had classes of 42 minutes or less. In six- and many seven-period schools, lunch was a separate, shorter session built around instructional periods. In nine-period, many eight-period, and some seven-period schools, lunch consumed one of the periods. In general, schools provide three to five minutes of passing time between classes.

Since the demise of the earlier "flexible modular" scheduling reform attempt of the '60s and '70s, it has repeatedly been reported in the literature that the traditional schedule did not support many of the changes that needed to be made in high schools across the country; in fact, it was often lamented that "the schedule was the problem!"

A variety of specific criticisms have been leveled against single-period models of high school scheduling in America. This next section will discuss these problems at length.

## SINGLE-PERIOD SCHEDULES CONTRIBUTE TO THE IMPERSONAL NATURE OF HIGH SCHOOLS

It is doubtful that most adults could survive the impersonal, hectic pace expected of students in a typical single-period high school schedule. Imagine adults going to work each day and having to work for seven or more supervisors, often in eight or more workplaces, in seven or more areas of expertise. Carroll [1990] stated that "at no other time, whether at school or at work, is anyone placed in such an impersonalized, unproductive, frenetic environment" than in the typical high school [p. 365]. He also commented that we must question "whether the American high school is responding to the alleged innate, hyperactive characteristics of teenagers or exacerbating those characteristics" [p. 365].

Joining the attack on traditional high school schedules and their depersonalizing characteristics are teachers who contend that they cannot prepare adequately for and interact with the large number of students being assigned to them on a daily basis. Most teachers prepare for five or six different groups of students daily. If we assume class sizes of between 20 and 30, each high school teacher must instruct between 100 and 180 students daily. We ask the question: "Who among us can begin to understand and address the intellectual and emotional needs of 100 to 180 students every day?" Is it any wonder that high school teachers get a reputation for being "subject-centered?" Who, but Mother Teresa, could be "child-centered" under such circumstances? High school teachers are under tremendous stress simply trying to deal with the large number of students passing through their classrooms each day. As a result, many teachers report they are unable to teach using more effective, active learning methods; in the interest of survival, instructional compromises are made. As Ted Sizer [1984] argued, though, "Horace Smith should not have to compromise; he should be responsible for only 80 students at a time, not 120 or 150 or 175 as is common today in many public and parochial schools" [p. 197].

From a student's perspective, current schedules present an equally impersonal experience of schooling. We ask students to prepare for six, seven, or eight classes daily. We ask them to adapt to the teaching styles, academic expectations, and classroom management techniques of six, seven, or eight teachers every day.

We ask students to change desks and chairs six, seven, or eight times a day. We ask students to adapt to different lighting and different heating and cooling systems six, seven, or eight times per day. We ask students to work with six, seven, or eight different groups of students daily. What teacher (or adult for that matter) would stand for such a system? Imagine changing offices (or classrooms), desks, chairs, computers, colleagues, and bosses six, seven, or eight times daily! The very idea is ludicrous.

## SINGLE-PERIOD SCHEDULES EXACERBATE DISCIPLINE PROBLEMS IN HIGH SCHOOL

Nationwide concern regarding discipline and violence [Fulong & Morrison, 1994; National Educational Goals Panel, 1994] in schools has been an important aspect of the current critique of traditional high school scheduling practices. Traditional schedules create at least three situations which may result in an increase in school discipline problems.

Any assistant principal in charge of discipline will verify that a preponderance of disciplinary referrals emanate from scheduled transitions, when large numbers of students spill into the hallways, congregate in lunch rooms and commons areas, or are herded into locker rooms to change clothes for physical education classes. If students are not sent to the office directly from the transition area, whatever problem has occurred often carries over into the classroom, where the teacher must deal with it at the beginning of the period. While we realize that class changes and other transitions are a welcome release for students from the classroom, often this time is not well-supervised by staff. A reduction in the number of transitions during the school day nearly always has a positive effect on a school's disciplinary climate.

In the previous section we discussed the assembly-line traditional period schedule and the manner in which it contributes to the depersonalizing nature of high schools. When teachers are responsible for 100 to 180 students daily, and students must answer to six, seven, or eight teachers a day, it is nearly impossible for them to develop close relationships. We know that students and teachers who know each other better are less likely to be disrespectful of each other when potentially explosive situations arise. Avoiding unnecessary "in your face" challenges is a key aspect of school discipline. Perhaps if teachers saw fewer students, there would be a greater likelihood of improved student-teacher relations.

Short instructional periods may also contribute to a negative disciplinary climate. Teachers instructing in a 40- to 60-minute period feel powerful pressure to cover the curriculum—to get their lesson taught. When disciplinary situations arise in the classroom and the offending student does not respond immediately to a quick correction by the instructor, the typical reaction of many teachers is to send the student to the office. When only 40 to 60 minutes of instructional time are available, any time taken away from classwork is seen as unacceptable. In block classes, teachers report a greater willingness to ask the student in question to step out into the hall, give the class a question or some other assignment to focus on, and then spend a few minutes with the student discussing the issue in private.

## SINGLE-PERIOD SCHEDULES AND INCREASED GRADUATION REQUIREMENTS HAVE CUT THE "TIME PIE" VERY THINLY

During the 1980s, graduation requirements in most states were increased. In some cases students were required to earn up to 24 units for their academic diploma, which became a major problem for students attending high schools operating under a six-period daily schedule. Such a schedule offered little room for any electives for large numbers of students; hence, enrollments in performing arts and vocational classes began to drop [Association for Supervision and Curriculum Development, 1985]. To address these issues, many high schools added periods within each school day simply by dividing the "time pie" differently. Generally, the total amount of time in the school day was not increased; in fact, in some states the school day was shortened during the late '70s and '80s! As a result of these actions, class periods in many high schools became shorter, and the school day became even more hectic and fragmented for both teachers and students. During 1994 we have worked in at least three states where high schools scheduled periods of just 40 minutes, which means teachers must "fight" to deliver even 25 or 30 minutes of instruction each class period. No wonder teachers begin to say, "All I do is direct traffic"! Imagine trying to complete a worthwhile science lab, conduct a Paideia seminar [Adler & Van Doren, 1984], play a volleyball game, or teach an electronics class in a time period of 40 minutes!

Thus, in our attempt to satisfy expanded graduation requirements and still maintain student elective choice, we caused many students to become overwhelmed trying to adjust to eight or more teachers each day, multiple notebooks, homework assignments, and tests. In those schools in which additional periods were not added, students were often squeezed out of elective programs, such as music, vocational education, and fine arts, because there wasn't "room in the schedule" for those classes. A good description of the student in a traditional high school schedule was offered by Carroll: "Americans typically view teenagers as hyperactive, frenetic individuals who are difficult to understand. The American high school deals with this hyperactivity by placing teenagers in a state of perpetual motion and interrupted attention. Today, typical high school students are in seven different classes, a homeroom, and a cafeteria—nine different locations—in a 6½-hour day. In addition, if they have physical education, these young people may change clothes twice and shower once. This is certainly not a schedule that fosters deep reflection" [pp. 364-365].

## SINGLE PERIOD HIGH SCHOOL SCHEDULES LIMIT INSTRUCTIONAL POSSIBILITIES FOR TEACHERS

Teachers have also played a significant role in promoting scheduling changes because, as many of them moved away from the lecture teaching format, they became frustrated with the single-period scheduled day and began to seek changes. Boyer [1983a] reported that ". . . the sense of the clock ticking is one of the most oppressive features of teaching" [p. 30].

The short single periods offered by most scheduling models limit flexibility in terms of the kinds of instructional strategies that can be accomplished. When teachers are faced with only 45 minutes, they often feel pressed to at least expose children to curriculum. The most efficient way to provide "exposure" to content is the lecture. Unfortunately, the lecture is probably not the most effective means for students to learn material. Often in our work with groups in the area of Cooperative Learning [Johnson & Johnson, 1987; Kagan, 1990; Slavin, 1990], high school and middle school teachers have commented: "Yeah, cooperative learning is pretty good, but I don't have time for it." When teachers instruct in longer blocks, most are unable to lecture effectively for long periods of time and they may see the benefit of other instructional strategies.

Short instructional periods make the accomplishment of laboratory work very difficult. It is nearly impossible for science teachers to involve students in active experimentation in a 40- to 60-minute period. Setup and take-down reduce the available instructional time to such an extent that approximately 20 to 35 minutes is all that remains for classwork. Similarly, it is difficult to implement other creative teaching techniques in short time blocks, for example, Paideia seminars [Adler & Van Doren, 1984], simulations, and other creative models of teaching such as synectics, concept development, concept attainment, role-playing, and inquiry [Gunter, Estes, & Schwab, 1990; Joyce, 1992].

Current schedules also affect the manner in which curriculum is organized and delivered. Students traveling through the six-, seven-, or eight-period day are exposed to six, seven, or eight pieces of unconnected curriculum each day. They rarely if ever have time to study anything in depth. To each teacher in his or her discipline, work may make sense; but to students who receive a fragmented, piecemeal education, the relevance of their efforts is sometimes lost. Ted Sizer comments, "The subjects come at a student...in random order, a kaleidoscope of words: algebraic formulae to poetry to French verbs to Ping-Pong to War of the Spanish Succession, all before lunch. Students are to pick up these things. Tests measure whether the picking up has been successful" [p. 81].

## SINGLE-PERIOD SCHEDULES DO NOT PERMIT FLEXIBLE TIME FOR TEACHING AND LEARNING

Perhaps the most critical (and unsolved] issue facing schools regarding the allocation of time is the indisputable fact that some students need more time to learn than others. Secondary schools' reliance on the Carnegie Unit as a seat-time measure of credit has ensured that all students become "Prisoners of Time":

> High-ability students are forced to spend more time than they need on a curriculum developed for students of moderate ability. . . . Struggling students are forced to move

with the class and receive less time than they need to master the material. . . . [Average] students get caught in the time trap as well. Conscientious teachers discover that the effort to motivate the most capable and help those in difficulty robs them of time for the rest of the class. [National Education Commission on Time and Learning, 1994, p. 15]

High schools across the country experience this problem, especially in late January. After the semester grades have been calculated, it becomes pointedly obvious to a number of students that it will be mathematically impossible to pass for the year—regardless of their performance during the second semester. These students become behavior and attendance problems. They rarely react positively to teachers' advice to "Work hard! It'll help you next year" [Canady & Hotchkiss, 1989].

In a way, we have created a system to handle students who need more time to learn and master course content and skills; we grade students with an "F" and then require them to repeat the course during summer school or the next academic year! This is a punitive system for students who need more time to learn; it is also an ineffective system for students whose problem is motivation.

On the other end of the spectrum, the possibilities for acceleration in the American high school are very limited. In most districts there is, however, one celebrated occasion for possible advancement. At the end of 7th grade in middle and junior high schools throughout the nation, a decision must be made as to whether or not a student should enroll in algebra during the 8th grade. This decision determines if it will be possible for a student to be accelerated in mathematics and possibly take calculus in the senior year. If a student takes algebra in 8th grade, the option remains open; if not, calculus is ruled out in many high schools. We would argue that this is an unreasonably inflexible system. Although the National Council of Teachers of Mathematics recommends otherwise, math courses prior to algebra predominately focus on arithmetic skills; therefore, this decision must be made when instructors know more about students' abilities in *arithmetic* than their abilities in *mathematics*. If the school schedule were not as rigid, perhaps the decision to accelerate could be made at different and more appropriate times for students.

We need a more continuous K-16 approach to education in the

United States. All too often, we focus only on "high" school or "middle" school or "college" or "vocational" school. What is needed is a K-16 vision in which "tech-prep" [Bottoms, Presson, & Johnson, 1992], college prep, dual enrollment, and "work prep" are interwoven to provide opportunities for students. An ideal system would punish students neither for needing more time to learn nor for needing less time to learn. Several schedules presented later in this book begin to address this difficult issue.

## SINGLE-PERIOD SCHEDULES DO NOT RESULT IN USER-FRIENDLY WORKPLACES FOR TEACHERS

Current high school schedules not only provide a frenetic, stressful environment for students, but also for teachers and administrators as well. How well can we expect teachers to prepare for lessons if they must plan for three, four, five, or sometimes even six lessons daily? How well can we expect teachers to know children, if they must work with 150 each day? How accurate and meaningful can we expect teachers' assessments of student progress to be when 150 grades must be computed? How realistic is it for schools to expect teachers to provide extra help for students who need more time to learn, when that time must come before school, after school, during lunch, or in lieu of a planning period? How reasonable is it to expect teachers to provide focused, connected learning experiences for students, when they have five "starts" a day? As class size [National Center for Education Statistics, 1993, p. 74] and accountability mandates [p. 149] have increased during the early '90s, how reasonable is it to ask teachers to meet the intellectual and emotional needs every student brings to the classroom, not to mention the paperwork? As our student population increases in diversity and we attempt to address their diverse needs in increasingly heterogenous classes, how reasonable is it to ask teachers and their students to continue on this treadmill? We would argue that it is not reasonable for schools to continue operating with schedules which may have made sense 90 years ago, but are now obsolete. We would argue, as has one teacher in Maine, that "The problem with our schools is not that they are *not* what they used to be, but that they *are* what they used to be" [National Education Commission on Time and Learning, 1994, p. 21].

## GOALS OF THE HIGH SCHOOL SCHEDULING REFORM MOVEMENT

The upswell of criticism has sparked a nationwide review of high school scheduling practices and a search for models better able to meet the needs of teachers and students. This reform effort is attempting to create high school schedules which are designed to:

♦ Reduce the number of class changes and movements that large groups of students are required to complete during any one school day;

♦ Reduce the duplication and inefficiency reportedly documented in many high schools using the daily, single-period high school schedule;

♦ Reduce the number of students for and with whom teachers must prepare and interact each day and/or each term;

♦ Reduce the number of courses for which teachers must prepare each day and/or term;

♦ Reduce the number of classes, and the accompanying assignments, tests, and projects, that students must address during any one day or term;

♦ Reduce the fragmentation inherent in single-period schedules, a complaint that is especially pertinent to classes requiring extensive practice and laboratory work;

♦ Provide teachers with blocks of teaching time that allow and encourage the use of active teaching strategies and greater student involvement; and

♦ Allow students variable amounts of time for learning, without lowering standards, and without punishing those who need more or less time to learn.

# A Brief History of High School Scheduling[1]

The rigid American high school schedule did not always exist in its current state. Prior to 1892 and the work of the National Education Association's Committee of Ten, early high schools and their predecessors, Latin Grammar Schools and Academies, showed some flexibility in their school schedules [Gorman, 1971]. "The academies, for example, and the high schools prior to about 1910 offered many subjects on two, three or four-day a week schedules" [p. 112]. The report of the Committee of Ten was the seed for the formation of the rigidly structured high school schedule as we know it today. The result "was to encourage every high school...to center the work of each student upon five or six academic areas in each of the four high school years" [p. 114]. With the development of the "Carnegie Unit" in the early 20th century, the every-day-period schedule became standardized:

> The Carnegie Foundation proposed a standard unit to measure high school work based on time. A total of 120 hours in one subject—meeting 4 or 5 times a week, for 40 to 60 minutes, for 36 to 40 weeks each year—earns for the student one "unit" of high school credit. "The Carnegie Unit," became a convenient, mechanical way to measure academic progress throughout the country. And, to this day, this bookkeeping device is the basis on which the school day, and indeed the entire curriculum is organized. And at some schools, adding up Carnegie units seems to be the main objective. [Boyer, 1983b, p. 60]

The every-day-period high school schedule, which developed from the recommendations of the Committee of Ten and the development of the Carnegie Unit, has remained remarkably unchanged for the past 70 years, except for the addition in some schools of an extra period or two. There was, however, one attempt, during the '60s and early '70s, to break away from this lockstep format: the flexible modular schedule. Because of its striking

---

[1] We are indebted to John C. Sessoms, formerly a high school principal in Virginia and currently a doctoral candidate at the University of Virginia, for his research and assistance in the development of this section.

similarity to the "block scheduling" reform movement of the 1990s, a closer look at flexible modular scheduling is warranted.

J. Lloyd Trump [1959] is credited with the original design of the flexible modular schedule (FMS). The Trump Plan, as it came to be known, sought to eliminate the rigid class schedule of the traditional high school and replace it with instructional sessions of varying lengths. Based upon the time needs of individual subjects and different instructional strategies, some classes might have short meetings of one "module" or 20 minutes, while other subjects might convene for longer classes of 40, 60, 80, or 100 minutes. For example, a biology class might meet for two 40-minute lectures, one 100-minute lab, and one 20-minute help session weekly. Students would spend their time in a variety of instructional formats—large group (100 or more), small group, and individual study—depending on the needs of students and subjects [Trump, 1959]. Trump also recommended frequent regrouping of students as their educational needs required. During its zenith in the late '60s and early '70s, Goldman [1983] estimates that 15 percent of American high schools were utilizing modular scheduling.

Initially, early attempts at FMS were viewed positively, especially by teachers and students. Based on a synthesis of over two dozen studies, Goldman [1983] reported that both teachers and students preferred flexible modular high school schedules over traditional schedules of six or seven single daily periods; however, parents and community members tended to offer a greater range of opinions concerning the plan. In addition, Goldman reported that student achievement in schools operating FMSs was at best mixed and probably was no better than in traditionally scheduled schools.

Ultimately, most high schools returned to traditional schedules primarily because of a number of problems with flexible modular scheduling—most related to student discipline. A popular notion of the '60s was the individualization of learning; hence, a major feature of FMS was the allocation of 30 to 40 percent of the school day to unscheduled student time to be used for independent study and individual tutorials. The problems that resulted from unscheduled student time were cited as the major factor for discontinuation of FMS systems [Goldman, 1983]. Another leading objection was the issue of teaching methods and teacher behavior. Teachers often found it difficult to tailor their teaching practices to the varying lengths of time [Goldman, 1983]; hence, for a variety of reasons, not the least of which was blaming scheduling and other school innovations for all the real and imagined ills of education in the 1960s, most large-scale experiments with various high school scheduling models were short-lived [Grinsel, 1989]. Goldman's final comment regarding the demise of FMS was prophetic:

> Some form of flexible, adapted scheduling is a sophistication which we probably cannot afford to overlook; the lesson to be learned from the FMS experience is that such flexibility must be real, must produce significantly better results than any system it replaces, and must not cause more problems than it solves. [1983, p. 209]

By the late 1980s and early 1990s the experience of FMS had faded, and many high schools again began to re-examine high school scheduling practices with the intention of eliminating or reducing the dependency on the lock-step, daily, single-period schedule and in search of Goldman's "adapted scheduling." In fact, scheduling became a critical factor in the restructuring efforts of schools across America.

## BLOCK SCHEDULING IN THE CONTEXT OF HIGH SCHOOL RESTRUCTURING

Cawelti [1994], in *High School Restructuring: A National Study*, provides a broad national picture of the overall high school restructuring movement and the place of the innovation known as "block scheduling" within that movement. Five major components of high school restructuring were identified: curriculum/teaching, school organization, community outreach, technology, and monetary incentives. Within each of these categories, 36 specific indicators of restructuring activity were classified (see Figure 1.1).

FIG. 1.1. MAJOR COMPONENTS AND ELEMENTS OF HIGH SCHOOL
RESTRUCTURING

♦ **Curriculum and Teaching**
Cooperative Learning
National Mathematics
   Standards
Staff Development in
   Teaching Strategies
Thinking Skills
Outcome-Based Education
School-to-Work Transition
Alternative-Assessment
   Techniques
Interdisciplinary Teaching

♦ **School Organization**
Shared School Governance
Site Based Management
Teacher Team
   Responsibilities
Transition to Upper
   Grades
Teacher-Advisee System
School-Within-A-School
*Block Schedule*
Total Quality Management
Divisional Organization
Extended School Year

♦ **Community Outreach**
Community Use of School
Allied Youth Services
Business/Industry Alliances
School/College Partnerships
Adult Volunteer Program
Community Service

♦ **Technology**
Video Instructional Materials
Word Processing
   Applications
CD ROM Technology
Computer Literacy
Modems
Multimedia Systems
Distance Learning
Integrated Learning Systems

♦ **Monetary Incentives**
Career Ladder Plan
Administrator Incentive Pay
Teacher Incentive Pay
Group Incentive Pay

*Note: Adapted from Cawelti (1994, p. 7).*

During the spring of 1993, all regionally accredited public and
private high school principals in the United States were surveyed
regarding the extent to which their schools had implemented each
of the elements listed in the figure. Approximately 33 percent of

the schools responded to the survey.[2] National and state-by-state summaries were produced.

"Block scheduling" was defined in the study as the following: "At least part of the daily schedule is organized into larger blocks of time (more than 60 minutes, for example) to allow flexibility for varied instructional activities" [p. 23]. Almost 11 percent of responding high schools reported that block scheduling, as defined, was "in general use;" 12 percent stated that it was "partially implemented;" 15 percent reported that block scheduling was planned for next year; and 61 percent of the responding schools reported that it was "not planned for next year".

Cawelti identified block scheduling as one of seven primary indicators of major restructuring occurring at the high school level [Cawelti, 1994]. These elements were as follows: outcome-based teaching; alternative assessment; interdisciplinary teaching work; site-based management; block scheduling; business/industry alliances; and the use of modems [Cawelti, 1994].

Because of the definition used in the study we believe that the use of *school-wide* programs of block scheduling may be far less for the time period indicated [1992-93 school year or planned for the 1993-94 school year]. Many already existing high school programs have "at least part of the daily schedule . . . organized into larger blocks of time (more than 60 minutes, for example)." For years, many vocational classes have operated in double and even triple periods. In addition, it is not uncommon for an interdisciplinary humanities or American Civilization course to be offered by an English and history teacher in a two-period block. Principals responding to the survey definition easily could have responded "in general use" or "partially implemented" if their school operated similar programs.

Case in point: Through the "Study of Innovative High School Scheduling in Virginia" [Rettig, 1994], we are aware of no more than five of 287 schools in the state who were operating school-wide

---

[2] Cawelti [1994] notes the following: "Readers are cautioned, however, that the data reported here could be subject to possible *non-response* bias to the extent that non-responding schools are different from the responding schools. Except for the possibilities of non-response differences, the results of this survey can be generalized to the entire population of accredited public and private high schools in the nation" [p. 6].

block schedules during the 1992-93 school year; however, the ERS study reported that block scheduling was "in general use" by 21 percent of the schools in Virginia.

Two years later, however, because of its rapid spread across the country, the level of adoption of block schedules far surpasses ERS estimates made in 1992-93. For example, in Virginia fully 33% of the high schools in the state were operating a school-wide block schedule during the 1994-95 school year [Rettig, 1994].

There is much evidence that a number of divergent programmatic changes were encouraged during the 1990s that had an impact on traditional high school schedules. For example, options were explored in relation to varying the length of courses, offering an increased number of electives within a given time frame, integrating curriculum, providing authentic learning environments, and building in professional growth opportunities for teachers. To accommodate many of the programmatic changes and the changing clientele in America's high schools, alternative scheduling models were designed to create a more manageable work load and work day that was believed to be in the best interest of both teachers and students.

We also believe that during the '90s, scheduling became a major catalyst for change in the restructuring plans of high schools across America. Attempts are being made, however, not to repeat the mistakes of the '60s; therefore, most of the schedules we will discuss were designed primarily to provide large blocks of time where classes meet on a **consistent** basis; also, little, if any, unscheduled school time is available for students.

## BLOCK SCHEDULING AND THE CHANGE PROCESS

Although the focus of this book is on innovations in school scheduling, a new schedule often constitutes a profound educational change for a school community. Much research has been reported during the past 40 years regarding efforts to implement innovations in education; schools contemplating scheduling changes should understand the many mistakes and few successes of the past. These efforts are synthesized in Michael Fullan's [1991] book, *The New Meaning of Educational Change*.

Fullan defines a change in educational practice as a change in materials, teaching approaches, and/or beliefs [Fullan, 1991, p. 37]. Central to the change process is the belief that change "ultimately is a problem of the smallest unit" [McLaughlin, 1987, p. 174]. Or, as Fullan [1982] comments, " . . . it is what *people develop* in their minds and actions that counts" [p. 62].

The process of change can be subdivided into three interacting and overlapping stages: initiation, implementation, and continuation.

The *initiation* of an innovation is dependent upon a combination of three factors: relevance, readiness, and resources. *Relevance* refers to a perceived need for a change, the clarity in which the innovation is understood by potential practitioners, and the practical utility of the innovation. *Readiness* for the initiation of change includes a number of organizational and individual factors. Organizationally, is there a school culture and resource infrastructure (facilities, materials, equipment, etc.) in place to support the effort? Are other change efforts in progress? Do individuals see a need which they believe can be met by the change? Do they possess appropriate knowledge and skills? Do they have time for implementation? Simply put, what is the school's capacity for change? Finally, are there *resources* available to both begin and to continue the change effort [Fullan, 1991, p. 63]?

During the initiation or study phase, as a school investigates the possibilities of block scheduling, a number of activities would be advisable. In addition to creating a representative study committee who deliberate on the details of various plans and brings a proposal to the entire faculty, we recommend that all parties with a vested interest be provided opportunities to learn about this innovation by engaging in many of the following activities:

- A general presentation regarding the pros and cons of various models of block scheduling;
- School visits by teachers, students, parents, and school board members;
- Panel presentations by teachers from schools operating block schedules;
- Faculty discussion meetings;
- Faculty vote or faculty consensus;
- Parent community meetings;

+ Assemblies for students conducted by students from other schools or by their peers who have visited other schools;

+ Distribution of relevant research data and implementation procedures;

+ School board presentations and approval; and

+ Staff development as to the appropriate design of curriculum and use of extended blocks of time for instruction.

Ideally, meeting the conditions of relevance, readiness, and resources should improve the likelihood of success; however, in the real world of schools, change efforts which seem to have been perfectly initiated can fail, and the clumsiest of beginnings can become a wild success. While successful initiation is important, implementation is where the action is. For it is the process of implementation which determines the success or failure of a change effort.

Fullan describes nine factors affecting implementation. The following four characteristics of the innovation itself are important: need, clarity, complexity, and the quality and practicality of the program. The existence of a perceived *need* for change has been important for successful implementations [Rosenblum & Lewis, 1979; Emrick & Peterson, 1978; Louis & Sieber, 1979]. Lack of *clarity* in terms of both the goals and means of change has been linked to unsuccessful implementations [Fullan, 1991, p. 70]. The *complexity* of the change attempted also affects success, but often in counter-intuitive ways. Logically, it would seem that small, simple change efforts would have a greater likelihood of success than major restructuring efforts. However, stakeholders may view a minor change as not worth their attention, while a more complex and ambitious program may inspire more enthusiasm and commitment. In general, larger efforts accomplish more change, but people may risk massive failure by attempting too much. Finally, the *quality* and *practicality* of the program itself affects implementation. The choice of a program can be made for the wrong reasons; for example, politics, availability, existence of supportive resources, and ease of implementation may exert undue influence on the decision. Only those programs that pass the "practicality ethic" of teachers can be successful. That is, the change must address a need, fit the teachers' situation, be focused, and include concrete strategies [Doyle & Ponder, 1977–78 in Fullan, 1991, p. 72].

In addition, a variety of local and external contextual factors affect implementation. Local influences include the school district, the school board and community, the principal, and the teachers. Factors related to the *school district* can influence success. A history of botched change attempts often results in a skeptical audience for the next change effort. When superintendents and the central office actively support implementation, efforts are more successful than when no support or more general support is provided. While *school board* and *community* characteristics influence the success of implementation, it is difficult to generalize regarding their effects. School districts sometimes ignore the community and/or school board when attempting change; this can be disastrous, if the innovation is controversial and later precipitates a community outcry. Certainly, widespread board and community support can be seen as aiding implementation [Fullan, 1991]. Active involvement of the *principal* is also a positive influence on the implementation of change; teacher-initiated or district-initiated efforts are unlikely to be successful without this active support. In the final analysis, because the success of a change effort involves individual learning, *teachers* have a central role. Schools with the greatest success in implementing change have a culture of collegiality which supports " . . . open communication, trust, support and help, learning on the job, and getting results . . . "[p. 77]. Teachers and administrators in successful schools engage in frequent discussions about teaching improvement; observe each other teaching and provide feedback; plan, design, research, evaluate, and prepare teaching materials together; and finally, teach each other the practice of teaching [Little, 1981, pp. 12–13]. External governmental agencies also have an impact on implementation.

We believe that many of the same activities listed for the initiation phase are also crucial for successful implementation. After a program has been adopted, a school's efforts should focus on ensuring that all details of the schedule are addressed and that all relevant interest groups are made aware of these details. Most important, however, teachers should be provided time to alter their curriculum appropriately and get training in suitable instructional strategies that will be effective in the block. (See Appendix A for "Evaluation Matrix for Selecting an Alternative High School Schedule." See Appendix B for "Planning Checklist for Alternative Scheduling for High Schools.")

The research on *continuation* of successfully implemented programs provides further insight into the change process. Lack of funding for staff development, especially for new teachers or administrators who had not participated in the original initiation and implementation processes, and lack of staff support were key reasons given in the research for noncontinuance. Central to these issues was the role of the principal who, through active support, could influence continuation. Evidence of continuance or institutionalization included policy, budgets, timetables, and procedures for continuing assistance and training of new teachers and administrators [Fullan, 1991, pp. 88–90].

We predict that the single most important factor in determining the success or failure of block scheduling programs will be the degree to which teachers successfully alter instruction to utilize extended time blocks effectively (see Chapter 8). If instructional practices do not change, the block scheduling movement of the 1990s, like the flexible modular scheduling movement of the 1960s and 1970s, will be buried in the graveyard of failed educational innovations.

Finally, any program a school implements should be evaluated. If a school opts for an alternative schedule, a variety of data should be collected to provide documentary support for this evaluation (see Appendix C for a list of "Indicators of Achievement for High School Restructuring Efforts").

The following section serves as an introduction to the basic models of block scheduling; each of these models is developed in greater detail in subsequent chapters.

## MODELS OF BLOCK SCHEDULING: AN INTRODUCTION

In reviewing the high school schedules being implemented or considered for implementation during the '90s, we find five basic designs:

♦   *Single-period daily schedules.* Students typically participate in six, seven, or eight classes every day, varying in length between 40 and 60 minutes. Teachers instruct five or six of these classes. Little discussion is needed of this model; it has been the predominant form of high school scheduling for the last 70 or 80 years.

♦ *Plans that alter periods within the day or week: for example, alternate day plans (also called "A-B" and "Day 1, Day 2") or "slide" schedules.* In general, rather than classes meeting daily, students and teachers meet their classes every other day for extended time "blocks" or at different times during the day on a rotating basis.

For example, Figure 1.2 illustrates an alternate day six-course schedule. Students and teachers meet half of their classes one day and the other half the next day. We discuss this plan and its many variations in detail in Chapter 2.

| FIG. 1.2. BLOCKED ALTERNATE DAY SCHEDULE BUILT FOR 6 COURSES | | | | | | | |
|---|---|---|---|---|---|---|---|
| Days | | M Day 1 A | T Day 2 B | W Day 1 A | R Day 2 B | F Day 1 A | M Day 2 B |
| P | Block I | 1 | 2 | 1 | 2 | 1 | 2 |
| E | | 1 | 2 | 1 | 2 | 1 | 2 |
| R | Block II | 3 | 4 | 3 | 4 | 3 | 4 |
| I | | 3 | 4 | 3 | 4 | 3 | 4 |
| O | Block III | 5 | 6 | 5 | 6 | 5 | 6 |
| D | | 5 | 6 | 5 | 6 | 5 | 6 |

Figure 1.3 shows a slide schedule in which periods in a seven-period school "slide" through the day meeting at different times on a seven-day cycle.

| | | | | | | | |
|---|---|---|---|---|---|---|---|
| **FIG. 1.3. SEVEN PERIOD SLIDE SCHEDULE** | | | | | | | |
| Days | M Day 1 | T Day 2 | W Day 3 | R Day 4 | F Day 5 | M Day 6 | T Day 7 |
| P | 1 | 2 | 3 | 4 | 5 | 6 | 7 |
| E | 2 | 3 | 4 | 5 | 6 | 7 | 1 |
| R | 3 | 4 | 5 | 6 | 7 | 1 | 2 |
| I | 4 | 5 | 6 | 7 | 1 | 2 | 3 |
| O | 5 | 6 | 7 | 1 | 2 | 3 | 4 |
| D | 6 | 7 | 1 | 2 | 3 | 4 | 5 |
| | 7 | 1 | 2 | 3 | 4 | 5 | 6 |

◆ *The 4/4 semester plan; also called the "4 by 4" or "accelerated" plan.* Students enroll in four courses which meet for approximately 90 minutes every day for 90 days. Teachers teach three courses each semester. A formerly "year-long" course is completed in one "semester." Students enroll in four new courses (teachers teach three) for the second semester. This college-like plan is illustrated in Figure 1.4. The 4/4 semester plan is detailed in Chapter 3.

| FIG. 1.4. BASIC 4/4 SEMESTER BLOCK SCHEDULE (8 COURSES) | | | |
|---|---|---|---|
| | | Semester 1 | Semester 2 |
| P | 1 | Course 1 | Course 5 |
| E | 2 | | |
| R | 3 | Course 2 | Course 6 |
| | 4 | | |
| I | 5 | Course 3 | Course 7 |
| O | 6 | | |
| D | 7 | Course 4 | Course 8 |
| | 8 | | |

♦ *Trimester, quarter-on-quarter-off, and other intensive scheduling models.* Several additional scheduling models being implemented around the country offer shorter, more intense courses of instruction. For example, several schools are operating trimester plans in which students take two core courses and related subjects every 60 days, as shown in Figure 1.5. Trimester plans, the quarter-on-quarter-off plan, and single-course plans are discussed in Chapter 4.

| FIG. 1.5. TRIMESTER PLAN | | | | | |
|---|---|---|---|---|---|
| Period | 60 days | Period | 60 days | Period | 60 days |
| 1 | Course 1 | 1 | PE/ Health | 1 | Course 5 |
| 2 | | 2 | Arts/ Vocational | 2 | |
| 3 | Course 2 | 3 | Individual Assistance | 3 | PE/ Health |
| 4 | | 4 | Course 3 | 4 | Arts/ Vocational |
| 5 | PE/ Health | 5 | | 5 | Individual Assistance |
| 6 | Arts/ Vocational | 6 | Course 4 | 6 | Course 6 |
| 7 | Individual Assistance | 7 | | 7 | |

♦ *Various reconfigurations of the 180-day school year.* Some districts across the nation are investigating the possibility of reconfiguring the 180-day school year into a combination of long terms and short terms for the purpose of providing instructional time for remediation and enrichment for students and professional growth and development time for teachers. One example, the 75(15)–75(15) plan, is illustrated in Figure 1.6. Innovations of this nature are detailed in Chapters 5 and 7.

| FIG. 1.6. 75–15–75–15 PLAN | | | | |
|---|---|---|---|---|
| | Fall Term 75 Days | **Middle Term 15 Days** | Spring Term 75 Days | **End Term 15 Days** |
| Block I Per. 1 & 2 112 min | Science | **Enrichment, Elective, Community Service, Remedial Work, etc.** | English | **Enrichment, Elective, Community Service, Remedial Work, etc.** |
| Block II Per. 3 & 4 112 min | Health/ Physical Education | | Art | |
| Period 5/L 48 min + 24 for lunch | Band & Lunch | **Band & Lunch** | Band & Lunch | **Band & Lunch** |
| Block III Per. 6 & 7 112 min | Math | **Enrichment, Elective, Comm. Serv., etc.** | Social Science | **Enrichment, Elective, Comm. Serv., etc.** |

Among the purported benefits of block scheduling, Calwelti [1994] notes the following:

- Increases length of class periods;
- Enables teachers to use a variety of instructional approaches;
- Decreases the number of class changes;
- Saves time;
- Limits the number of preparations for teachers;
- Provides the opportunity for interdisciplinary teaching;
- Decreases the number of students taught each day by a teacher;
- Increases planning time for teachers;
- Helps teachers to develop closer relationships with their students;
- Provides the opportunity for project work; and
- Provides additional opportunities for teachers to help students [1994].

Canady and Rettig [1993] indicated that at least one form of block scheduling—the 75–75–30 plan—offers the following advantages:

- It facilitates variety in the use of instructional approaches;
- Students see fewer teachers each term and teachers see fewer students;
- Discipline problems are reduced;
- Instructional time is increased;
- Teachers and students are able to focus on fewer subjects;
- The benefits of summer school can be offered to all students at no additional cost to students or the school district;
- Possibilities for acceleration are provided at least twice during the regular school year; and
- Students can repeat a failed course during the regular school year.

## Why Focus on Scheduling?

We realize that "block scheduling" alone is not a panacea for the many problems of the American high school. A school schedule can, however, have an enormous impact on a school's instructional climate. The schedule is not merely a means of moving teachers and students to various spaces during selected periods of time.

- ◆ A schedule can be viewed as a **resource**; it is the schedule that permits the **effective utilization of people, space, time, and resources** in an organization.

- ◆ A schedule can help **solve problems** related to the **delivery of instruction**; or a schedule can be a major source of problems.

- ◆ A schedule can **facilitate** the **institutionalization** of **desired programs and instructional practices**.

We strongly believe that scheduling is an untapped resource which can serve as a catalyst for school improvement. The models that follow only hint at the power of scheduling to address problems and implement needed programs. With open minds and equal doses of creativity and technical expertise, school administrators, teachers, parents, and students can harness this power to escape the paralysis of the single-period every-day lockstep high school schedule.

# 2

# ALTERNATE DAY BLOCK SCHEDULES

A simple way to increase teaching time and reduce many of the management problems associated with moving thousands of high school students in hallways throughout the day is to create an ALTERNATE DAY BLOCK SCHEDULE. The plan creates few political issues, and its major cost is the staff development needed to assist teachers in developing teaching strategies appropriate for longer instructional blocks. The alternate day block schedule is often a "first move" or transitional step from single instructional periods. This scheduling plan is also referred to as a "Day 1, Day 2" or an "*A* Day, *B* Day" schedule.

We begin this chapter by illustrating and discussing the basic mechanics and reasoning behind the alternate day block schedule. Second, we add to the basic plan by inserting lunch or activity periods to create a variety of different bell schedules. We then discuss modifications of this plan which have come from our work with schools across the country. Finally, we offer a number of suggestions for school personnel considering the implementation of the alternate day block schedule.

## THE BASIC PLAN

The alternate day block schedule may be adapted to meet the needs of schools that offer six, seven, or eight courses (credits). In schools where students take six or eight courses, half of the classes meet in double instructional blocks one day, while the other three or four classes meet in double blocks the next day. In seven-period schools, six courses meet in double blocks every other day; one course, called a singleton, meets daily in the traditional single-period format. Thus, if a school wishes to offer six courses, on Day 1 odd-period courses 1, 3, and 5 might meet in double periods, and even courses 2, 4, and 6 would follow the same format on Day 2 (see Figure 2.1). This pattern repeats throughout the 180-day school year, resulting in an equal number of Day 1's and Day 2's regardless of the number of holidays or school days within a week. In the example given, there would be 90 Day 1's and 90 Day 2's.

### FIG. 2.1. BASIC ALTERNATE DAY BLOCK SCHEDULE BUILT FOR 6 COURSES

| Days | M<br>Day 1<br>A | T<br>Day 2<br>B | W<br>Day 1<br>A | R<br>Day 2<br>B | F<br>Day 1<br>A | M<br>Day 2<br>B |
|------|------|------|------|------|------|------|
| P | 1 | 2 | 1 | 2 | 1 | 2 |
| E | 1 | 2 | 1 | 2 | 1 | 2 |
| R | 3 | 4 | 3 | 4 | 3 | 4 |
| I | 3 | 4 | 3 | 4 | 3 | 4 |
| O | 5 | 6 | 5 | 6 | 5 | 6 |
| D | 5 | 6 | 5 | 6 | 5 | 6 |

Figure 2.2 shows how separate periods are put together to create longer instructional blocks.

| | | M<br>Day 1<br>A | T<br>Day 2<br>B | W<br>Day 1<br>A | R<br>Day 2<br>B | F<br>Day 1<br>A | M<br>Day 2<br>B |
|---|---|---|---|---|---|---|---|
| **FIG. 2.2. BLOCKED ALTERNATE DAY SCHEDULE BUILT FOR 6 COURSES** | | | | | | | |
| Days | | | | | | | |
| P | Block I | 1 | 2 | 1 | 2 | 1 | 2 |
| E | | 1 | 2 | 1 | 2 | 1 | 2 |
| R | Block II | 3 | 4 | 3 | 4 | 3 | 4 |
| I | | 3 | 4 | 3 | 4 | 3 | 4 |
| O | Block III | 5 | 6 | 5 | 6 | 5 | 6 |
| D | | 5 | 6 | 5 | 6 | 5 | 6 |

A similar alternate day plan based on seven periods, with period 5 remaining a single period every day, is shown in Figure 2.3.

| | FIG. 2.3. BASIC ALTERNATE DAY BLOCK SCHEDULE BUILT FOR 7 COURSES | | | | | |
|---|---|---|---|---|---|---|
| Days | M Day 1 A | T Day 2 B | W Day 1 A | R Day 2 B | F Day 1 A | M Day 2 B |
| P | 1 | 2 | 1 | 2 | 1 | 2 |
| E | 1 | 2 | 1 | 2 | 1 | 2 |
| R | 3 | 4 | 3 | 4 | 3 | 4 |
| I | 3 | 4 | 3 | 4 | 3 | 4 |
| O | 5 | 5 | 5 | 5 | 5 | 5 |
| | 7 | 6 | 7 | 6 | 7 | 6 |
| D | 7 | 6 | 7 | 6 | 7 | 6 |

Again in Figure 2.4, we join periods to form blocks; however, in this model a singleton class (period five) meets every day.

| FIG. 2.4. BLOCKED ALTERNATE DAY SCHEDULE BUILT FOR 7 COURSES | | | | | | | |
|---|---|---|---|---|---|---|---|
| Days | | M<br>Day 1<br>A | T<br>Day 2<br>B | W<br>Day 1<br>A | R<br>Day 2<br>B | F<br>Day 1<br>A | M<br>Day 2<br>B |
| P | Block I | 1 | 2 | 1 | 2 | 1 | 2 |
| P | Block I | 1 | 2 | 1 | 2 | 1 | 2 |
| E | Block II | 3 | 4 | 3 | 4 | 3 | 4 |
| R | Block II | 3 | 4 | 3 | 4 | 3 | 4 |
| I O | Period 5 | 5 | 5 | 5 | 5 | 5 | 5 |
| D | Block III | 7 | 6 | 7 | 6 | 7 | 6 |
| D | Block III | 7 | 6 | 7 | 6 | 7 | 6 |

Figure 2.5 depicts a similar alternate day plan based on eight periods.

| | FIG. 2.5. BASIC ALTERNATE DAY BLOCK SCHEDULE BUILT FOR 8 COURSES | | | | | |
|---|---|---|---|---|---|---|
| Days | M<br>Day 1<br>A | T<br>Day 2<br>B | W<br>Day 1<br>A | R<br>Day 2<br>B | F<br>Day 1<br>A | M<br>Day 2<br>B |
| P | 1 | 2 | 1 | 2 | 1 | 2 |
| E | 1 | 2 | 1 | 2 | 1 | 2 |
| R | 3 | 4 | 3 | 4 | 3 | 4 |
| I | 3 | 4 | 3 | 4 | 3 | 4 |
| O | 5 | 6 | 5 | 6 | 5 | 6 |
| D | 5 | 6 | 5 | 6 | 5 | 6 |
| | 7 | 8 | 7 | 8 | 7 | 8 |
| | 7 | 8 | 7 | 8 | 7 | 8 |

Finally, we combine the eight-course schedule into four blocks in Figure 2.6.

## FIG. 2.6. BLOCKED ALTERNATE DAY SCHEDULE BUILT FOR 8 COURSES

| Days | | M<br>Day 1<br>A | T<br>Day 2<br>B | W<br>Day 1<br>A | R<br>Day 2<br>B | F<br>Day 1<br>A | M<br>Day 2<br>B |
|---|---|---|---|---|---|---|---|
| P | Block I | 1 | 2 | 1 | 2 | 1 | 2 |
| E |  | 1 | 2 | 1 | 2 | 1 | 2 |
| R | Block II | 3 | 4 | 3 | 4 | 3 | 4 |
| I |  | 3 | 4 | 3 | 4 | 3 | 4 |
| O | Block III | 5 | 6 | 5 | 6 | 5 | 6 |
| D |  | 5 | 6 | 5 | 6 | 5 | 6 |
|  | Block IV | 7 | 8 | 7 | 8 | 7 | 8 |
|  |  | 7 | 8 | 7 | 8 | 7 | 8 |

## DISCUSSION

Compared to schedules in which students meet for all classes for a single period every day, both students and teachers working in alternate day plans have several advantages.

♦ **All teachers benefit from increased useable instructional time.** In our conservative estimates, an alternate day schedule results in an annual increase of 1170 minutes per year (the equivalent of 23 50-minute periods) of "quality instructional time" for each block course in comparison to courses in every-day schedules. Previous research has shown that a great deal of instructional time is lost in secondary classrooms to proced--
and interr-----'-   '-

nominal minutes in a period or block minus the number of minutes lost to these procedures, routines, and interruptions. One study found that instructional activities accounted for an average of only 28 minutes (54.2%) of each 55-minute class period [Seifert and Beck, 1984]. This finding translated to 27 minutes of lost instructional time every period because of class openings, closings, and various interruptions.

We chose to be extremely conservative in determining the average number of instructional minutes lost because of these routines, because we realize that time will be lost changing activities in longer block classes. Therefore, in our calculations we subtracted only 13 minutes from each class period (less then half of the 27 minutes indicated above) and designated the remainder of the scheduled time for each class to be "quality instructional time." Our computations are summarized in Figure 2.7 and are based upon this assumption and a 420-minute school day.

If we translate a six-period plan into a three-block plan, "quality instructional time" will be gained at the rate of 13 minutes for each of the 90 blocks met annually, an increase of 1170 minutes (13 months x 90 days). The same amount of "quality instructional time" per course is gained when changing from seven periods to three blocks and a singleton and from eight periods to four blocks.

Of more interest, perhaps, is the fact that if we changed from a six-period every-day schedule to a seven-period alternate day plan, the addition of the seventh course would result in a net loss of only 450 minutes of quality instructional time per year for blocked courses (8460m vs. 8010m); the singleton course would be only 180 minutes shorter (8460m vs. 8280m). This seems a small price to pay in instructional time for the addition of another offering for students. Even more surprising is the result of a move from the single seven-period every-day schedule to a four-block alternate day (or 4/4 semester) schedule. Eight block courses actually provide 90 minutes more quality instructional time annually than do seven single-period every-day courses (6930m vs. 6840m). *Thus an additional offering may be provided for students without lengthening the school day or adversely affecting the amount of quality instructional time per course.*

FIG. 2.7. NOMINAL VS. QUALITY INSTRUCTIONAL TIME AVAILABLE:
EVERY DAY VS. ALTERNATE DAY
(OR ALTERNATE SEMESTER) SCHEDULES

| | | Annual Minutes of Instructional Time | | |
|---|---|---|---|---|
| Number of Courses | | Every Day Single Periods | Alternate Day Blocks | Gain per Course over Every Day Plans |
| 6 Courses | Nominal Minutes | 10800 minutes 180d x 60m | 10800 minutes 90d x 120m | 0 |
| | Quality Minutes | 8460 minutes 180d x 47m | 9630 minutes 90d x 107m | 1170 minutes |
| 7 Courses | Nominal Minutes | 9180 minutes 180d x 51m | Block 9180 minutes 90d x 102m | 0 |
| | | | Singleton 10620 minutes 180d x 59m | 1440 minutes |
| | Quality Minutes | 6840 minutes 180d x 38m | Block 8010 minutes 90d x 89m | 1170 minutes |
| | | | Singleton 8280 minutes 180d x 46m | 1440 minutes |
| 8 Courses | Nominal Minutes | 8100 minutes 180d x 45m | 8100 minutes 90d x 90m | 0 |
| | Quality Minutes | 5760 minutes 180d x 32m | 6930 minutes 90d x 77m | 1170 minutes |

Key: d = Days; m = Minutes per Period or Block

Surprisingly, the change from seven every-day courses to eight alternate day (or semester) courses may be made without any additional faculty (This point is developed at the end of Chapter 3).

♦ **Teachers are able to plan extended lessons.** This is especially beneficial in subjects that require extensive set-up and clean-up. Science teachers can complete entire labs during the double block. Students enrolled in art classes can devote extensive uninterrupted time to their projects; set-up and clean-up time would be cut in half. English teachers can engage their classes in the complete writing process by leading the group through a prewriting activity, a first draft, proofreading and revision, and perhaps even traveling to the computer lab to create the final polished copy. The band or orchestra director has more useable playing time; students spend less time unpacking their instruments, tuning up, warming up, and repacking their instruments.

♦ **The number of class changes is reduced.** Time used for moving between classes can be absorbed into instructional periods. In addition, fewer transitions result in an automatic reduction in the number of tardies and usually reduce disciplinary referrals as well. It has been our observation that most discipline problems do not occur during actual class time but during transitions such as class changes, lunch, and before and after school. In addition, many teachers report that when a discipline problem does occur, meeting classes every other day provides "cooling-off" time for both students and teacher. School hallways seem much quieter; however, classrooms may not be quieter because of the increased active learning both possible and necessary in the longer instructional blocks. Custodial staffs report that schools are cleaner and experience less vandalism.

♦ **Teaching with a variety of instructional models is encouraged.** Teachers occasionally express concern regarding students' abilities to maintain attention for 90 or 100 minutes. It has been our observation, however, that it is not the length of the block which determines whether or not students will pay attention but what is done during the class session. Maintaining student interest by using the traditional lecture/discussion mode of instruction is nearly impossible for a 90-minute period. Teachers have the opportunity, and probably find it necessary in order to be effective, to provide a variety of activities during the block. The use of alternate models of instruction, including cooperative learning, inquiry, group discussion, concept development, role-playing, exploration of feelings, conflict resolution, Paideia seminars, and synectics, is possible [Gunter, Estes, & Schwab, 1990; Adler & Van Doren, 1984; Joyce, 1992]. We discuss the instructional uses of "the block" in greater detail in Chapter 8.

♦ **The alternate day plan permits concentrated work in specialized programs.** Vocational schools, schools for the gifted or talented, and cooperative education programs typically offer half-day programs. A more efficient use of school time is possible for such programs using the alternate day scheduling model. For example, vocational classes could meet a full day at the vocational center on Day 1 and on the alternating day, or Day 2, for a full day at the regular school. In addition to allowing students to wear appropriate clothes for an all-day activity, such as working on a car motor, the plan maximizes students' time on the task. If the task is to practice bricklaying, the student does not have to prepare mortar each day and clean up just to practice laying bricks for a relatively short period of time.

Such a practice also can cut transportation costs. For example, if a school district has four high schools which share one vocational or technology center, two of the schools could send students on Day 1 and the other two high schools on Day 2. Travel between the base school and the vocational-technical center also would be eliminated during the day.

♦ **Compared to every-day models, students have fewer classes, quizzes, tests, and homework assignments on any one day.**

♦ **Work missed because of a student absence is easier to gather and monitor.** If a student misses a day, make-up work is required in fewer classes, and the task of seeing teachers for make-up assignments is reduced. It is also true that students miss more work in classes from which they were absent. Seeing teachers and making up this works gains increased importance.

♦ **Itinerant teacher schedules can be simplified.** If itinerant teachers are assigned to schools sharing the same alternating period schedule, they can work in School A on Day 1 and in School B on Day 2. Such a plan prevents teachers from having to travel to both schools each day, thus saving both time and transportation costs. Typically, when a teacher serves two schools each day, at least one instructional period is lost to travel time.

## DEVELOPING THE MODELS

The major purpose of this section is to develop further the basic models described briefly in the section above. Accordingly, we now begin to add details, including a bell schedule with a homeroom time and several options for lunch. We hope the reader notices our bias: we always begin our planning by thinking about what is best for the academic program, and then we add lunch—not the reverse!

As we proceed through the book, each scheduling plan developed will be based on a seven-hour (420 minutes) school day. We realize that schools in different states and districts have shorter and (rarely) longer school days; consequently, we also offer several suggestions for ways to accommodate these differences.

## SIX-COURSE MODELS

We begin with a more detailed structure for an alternate day, six-course schedule, as shown in Figure 2.8.

FIG. 2.8. ALTERNATE DAY BLOCK SCHEDULE BUILT FOR
6 COURSES (1 LUNCH PERIOD; EARLY START)

| | Blocks and Times | M Day 1 A | T Day 2 B | W Day 1 A | R Day 2 B |
|---|---|---|---|---|---|
| **P** | Block I & HR 8:00–10:06 am | 1 | 2 | 1 | 2 |
| | | 1 | 2 | 1 | 2 |
| **E** | Block II 10:14 am–12:14 pm | 3 | 4 | 3 | 4 |
| **R** | | 3 | 4 | 3 | 4 |
| **I** | | | | | |
| **O** | Lunch 12:22–12:52 pm | L U N C H | | | |
| **D** | Block III 1:00–3:00 pm | 5 | 6 | 5 | 6 |
| | | 5 | 6 | 5 | 6 |

This schedule includes three instructional blocks of 120 minutes each; eight minutes are allowed for class changes; and six minutes are added to Block I for homeroom routines. Only one lunch has been scheduled after Block II; this might be appropriate for a small school that begins relatively early in the morning. This lunch period is effectively 46 minutes long because it includes two eight-minute class changes. The model illustrated in Figure 2.9 is prepared for a school that starts later in the morning; in this case, the one lunch period is placed immediately following Block I.

| | FIG. 2.9. ALTERNATE DAY BLOCK SCHEDULE BUILT FOR 6 COURSES (1 LUNCH PERIOD; LATE START) | | | | |
|---|---|---|---|---|---|
| | Blocks and Times | M<br>Day 1<br>A | T<br>Day 2<br>B | W<br>Day 1<br>A | R<br>Day 2<br>B |
| P | Block I & HR<br>8:45–10:51 am | 1<br>—<br>1 | 2<br>—<br>2 | 1<br>—<br>1 | 2<br>—<br>2 |
| E | Lunch<br>10:59–11:29 am | L U N C H | | | |
| R | | | | | |
| I | Block II<br>11:37–1:37 pm | 3<br>—<br>3 | 4<br>—<br>4 | 3<br>—<br>3 | 4<br>—<br>4 |
| O | | | | | |
| D | Block III<br>1:45–3:45 pm | 5<br>—<br>5 | 6<br>—<br>6 | 5<br>—<br>5 | 6<br>—<br>6 |

We understand that most schools are forced to serve lunch during more than one period. Figure 2.10 shows one way to accomplish two lunch periods.

The obvious problem that occurs in Figure 2.10 is the fact that the two lunch periods are separated by more than an hour and a half. This may be unacceptable to some schools, mainly because of the inefficient use of cafeteria staff; although, if the cafeteria were shared by two schools operating on different schedules, as is customarily the case in most 7-12 situations, the hour-and-a-half

| | Blocks and Times | M<br>Day 1<br>A | T<br>Day 2<br>B | M<br>Day 1<br>A | T<br>Day 2<br>B |
|---|---|---|---|---|---|
| | | **FIG. 2.10. ALTERNATE DAY BLOCK SCHEDULE BUILT FOR 6 COURSES (2 LUNCH PERIODS; LATE START)** | | | |
| | | ½ of School<br>Follows This<br>Schedule | | ½ of School<br>Follows This<br>Schedule | |
| **P** | Block I & HR<br>8:45–10:51 am | 1 | 2 | 1 | 2 |
| **E** | | 1 | 2 | 1 | 2 |
| **R** | Lunch and<br>Block II<br>10:59–1:37 pm | Lunch 30 min | | 3 | 4 |
| **I** | | 3 | 4 | 3 | 4 |
| **O** | | 3 | 4 | Lunch 30 min | |
| **D** | Block III<br>1:45–3:45 pm | 5 | 6 | 5 | 6 |
| | | 5 | 6 | 5 | 6 |

break could be used to schedule lunch for the second school. Two additional possibilities exist for ameliorating this difficulty in the three-block plan. One adaptation involves providing activity periods that meet opposite the lunch periods, as shown in Figure 2.11.

A variety of uses can be made of the Activity Period. Clubs can meet; students can receive tutoring; instructors can maintain office hours; an occasional advisory period could be conducted for guidance activities; students can receive assistance in the resource room; and school-wide seminars or mini-courses can be conducted. In addition, lunch-time detention could be held.

FIG. 2.11. ALTERNATE DAY BLOCK SCHEDULE BUILT FOR
6 COURSES (2 LUNCH PERIODS; ACTIVITY PERIOD)

| | Blocks and Times | M Day 1 A | T Day 2 B | M Day 1 A | T Day 2 B |
|---|---|---|---|---|---|
| | | ½ of School Follows This Schedule | | ½ of School Follows This Schedule | |
| P | Block I & HR 8:00–9:56 am | 1 / 1 | 2 / 2 | 1 / 1 | 2 / 2 |
| E | | | | | |
| R | Block II 10:04–11:56 am | 3 / 3 | 4 / 4 | 3 / 3 | 4 / 4 |
| I | 12:00–12:30 pm | Lunch | | Activity Period | |
| O | 12:34–1:04 pm | Activity Period | | Lunch | |
| D | Block III 1:10–3:00 pm | 5 / 5 | 6 / 6 | 5 / 5 | 6 / 6 |

The second adaptation involves breaking one of the blocks in half to accommodate a lunch period, as illustrated in Figure 2.12.

The change illustrated in Figure 2.12 forces a break in courses 3 and 4 for half the students and teachers in the school; a continuous hour of instructional time, however, is still available both before

| Blocks and Times | M Day 1 A | T Day 2 B | M Day 1 A | T Day 2 B |
|---|---|---|---|---|
| FIG. 2.12. ALTERNATE DAY BLOCK SCHEDULE BUILT FOR 6 COURSES (2 LUNCH PERIODS; BROKEN BLOCK) | | | | |
| | ½ of School Follows This Schedule | | ½ of School Follows This Schedule | |
| Block I & HR 8:45–10:51 am | 1 | 2 | 1 | 2 |
| | 1 | 2 | 1 | 2 |
| Lunch and Block II 10:59–1:37 pm | Lunch 30 min | | 3 | 4 |
| | 3 | 4 | Lunch 30 min | |
| | 3 | 4 | 3 | 4 |
| Block III 1:45–3:45 pm | 5 | 6 | 5 | 6 |
| | 5 | 6 | 5 | 6 |

(P E R I O D)

and after the lunch block. Students could be grouped for lunch by grades, houses, or teams; and, if deemed necessary, half of the school could follow each of the lunch schedules for one semester and then switch. A third manner in which to provide two lunch periods is to create a schedule in which not all periods meet in blocks, as depicted in Figure 2.13.

### FIG. 2.13. ALTERNATE DAY BLOCK SCHEDULE BUILT FOR 6 COURSES (2 LUNCH PERIODS; 2 SINGLETON CLASSES)

| Blocks and Times | M Day 1 A | T Day 2 B | M Day 1 A | T Day 2 B |
|---|---|---|---|---|
| | ½ of School Follows This Schedule | | ½ of School Follows This Schedule | |
| **P** Block I & HR 8:45–10:51 am | 1 / 1 | 2 / 2 | 1 / 1 | 2 / 2 |
| **E R I** Lunch and Block II 10:59–1:37 pm | Lunch 30 min | | 3 | |
| | 3 | | Lunch 30 min | |
| | 4 | | 4 | |
| **O D** Block III 1:45–3:45 pm | 5 / 5 | 6 / 6 | 5 / 5 | 6 / 6 |

(Left vertical label: P E R I O D)

In this plan, courses 1, 2, 5, and 6 meet in double periods on alternate days; courses 3 and 4 meet every day as single classes. Some instructors prefer to meet daily, especially for first-year foreign languages, band and chorus (if they insist), keyboarding, and selected math classes. We suggest that laboratory sciences, physical education, vocational courses, and fine arts selections be given first priority for block classes.

We could dictate a specific lunch period for each grade. For example, 9th and 10th grade students could be assigned to eat lunch from 10:59 to 11:29 a.m., while 11th and 12th grade students eat from 12:03 to 12:33 p.m. As shown, period 3 would be scheduled at different times for students assigned to either lunch. A problem occurs, however, when lunch periods are assigned by grade level; students from grades 9 and 10 would not be able to mix with students from grades 11 and 12 in period 3 classes. This would eliminate the possibility of placing courses with membership that crosses these grade levels during third period.

Schools requiring three lunch periods can be accommodated by adding a late lunch period at the end of the second block (see Figure 2.14, p. 50). One-third of the school must split a block.

Courses 3 and 4 could also be scheduled as singletons, as shown in Figure 2.15 (on p. 51), to accomplish the same three lunch periods.

Thus, students and teachers would meet for courses 1, 2, 5, and 6 on alternate days in double periods, and courses 3 and 4 would meet in single periods every day.

(*Text continues on page 52*)

FIG. 2.14. ALTERNATE DAY BLOCK SCHEDULE BUILT FOR 6 COURSES
(3 LUNCH PERIODS; LATE START; BROKEN BLOCK)

| Blocks and Times | M Day 1 A | T Day 2 B | M Day 1 A | T Day 2 B | M Day 1 A | T Day 2 B |
|---|---|---|---|---|---|---|
| | ⅓ of School Follows This Schedule | | ⅓ of School Follows This Schedule | | ⅓ of School Follows This Schedule | |
| Block I & HR 8:45–10:51 am | 1 | 2 | 1 | 2 | 1 | 2 |
| | 1 | 2 | 1 | 2 | 1 | 2 |
| Lunch and Block II 10:59–1:37 pm | Lunch 10:59–11:29 am | | 3 | 4 | 3 | 4 |
| | 3 | 4 | Lunch 12:03–12:33 pm | | 3 | 4 |
| | 3 | 4 | 3 | 4 | Lunch 1:07–1:37 pm | |
| Block III 1:45–3:45 pm | 5 | 6 | 5 | 6 | 5 | 6 |
| | 5 | 6 | 5 | 6 | 5 | 6 |

P E R I O D

FIG. 2.15. ALTERNATE DAY BLOCK SCHEDULE BUILT FOR 6 COURSES
(3 LUNCH PERIODS; 2 SINGLETON COURSES)

| Blocks and Times | M Day 1 A | T Day 2 B | M Day 1 A | T Day 2 B | M Day 1 A | T Day 2 B |
|---|---|---|---|---|---|---|
| | ⅓ of School Follows This Schedule | | ⅓ of School Follows This Schedule | | ⅓ of School Follows This Schedule | |
| Block I & HR 8:45–10:51 am | 1 | 2 | 1 | 2 | 1 | 2 |
| | 1 | 2 | 1 | 2 | 1 | 2 |
| Lunch and Block II 10:59–1:37 pm | Lunch 10:59–11:29 am | | | | | |
| | 3 | | 3 | | 3 | |
| | 4 | | Lunch 12:03–12:33 pm | | 4 | |
| | | | 4 | | Lunch 1:07–1:37 pm | |
| Block III 1:45–3:45 pm | 5 | 6 | 5 | 6 | 5 | 6 |
| | 5 | 6 | 5 | 6 | 5 | 6 |

P E R I O D

## SEVEN-COURSE MODELS

Similar modifications can be made to a seven-course block schedule, depending on the number of lunch periods required. Figure 2.16 ( shows a one-lunch-period schedule for a school day which begins at 8:00 a.m. Double-period classes meet on alternate days for 102 minutes; singleton courses meet for 59 minutes; 7 minutes are added to Block I for homeroom activities; and 6 minutes are allocated for each transition.

If school were to start later, for example, at approximately 9:00 a.m., the third period could become the singleton, with lunch following it. Periods four and five would be blocked together, as would six and seven.

FIG. 2.16. ALTERNATE DAY BLOCK SCHEDULE BUILT FOR
7 COURSES (1 LUNCH PERIOD)

|   | Blocks and Times | M<br>Day 1<br>A | T<br>Day 2<br>B | W<br>Day 1<br>A | R<br>Day 2<br>B |
|---|---|---|---|---|---|
| P | Block I & HR<br>8:00–9:49 am | 1 | 2 | 1 | 2 |
|   |  | 1 | 2 | 1 | 2 |
| E | Block II<br>9:55–11:37 am | 3 | 4 | 3 | 4 |
| R |  | 3 | 4 | 3 | 4 |
| I | 11:43 am–12:07 pm | L U N C H | | | |
| O | 12:13–1:12 pm | 5 | 5 | 5 | 5 |
| D | Block III<br>1:18–3:00 pm | 7 | 6 | 7 | 6 |
|   |  | 7 | 6 | 7 | 6 |

Some schools, where students must travel long distances for athletic events or practice during school time (e.g., Texas, Oklahoma, New Mexico, etc.), often reserve the last period of the day for these activities. In such schools, it is possible to keep period seven as a singleton, as shown in Figure 2.17.

FIG. 2.17. ALTERNATE DAY BLOCK SCHEDULE BUILT FOR 7 COURSES (1 LUNCH PERIOD; 7TH PERIOD RELEASE FOR ATHLETICS IF NECESSARY)

| | Blocks and Times | M Day 1 A | T Day 2 B | W Day 1 A | R Day 2 B |
|---|---|---|---|---|---|
| **P** | Block I & HR 8:00–9:49 am | 1 | 2 | 1 | 2 |
| | | 1 | 2 | 1 | 2 |
| **E** | Block II 9:55–11:37 am | 3 | 4 | 3 | 4 |
| **R** | | 3 | 4 | 3 | 4 |
| **I** | 11:43 am–12:07 pm | L U N C H | | | |
| **O** | Block III 12:13–1:55 pm | 5 | 6 | 5 | 6 |
| **D** | | 5 | 6 | 5 | 6 |
| | 2:01–3:00 pm | 7 | 7 | 7 | 7 |

An additional option eliminates the singleton period entirely by adding an eighth activity or seminar period on an every-other-day basis. This option ameliorates the problem of deciding what courses to schedule during the singleton period; this adaptation also avoids the inconsistency created when a course must be offered in both singleton and block formats (see Figure 2.18). Assemblies and club meetings are often conducted during this time. This extra period also provides time to schedule intramurals, which might be a useful adaptation for middle schools. Some schools have utilized this "sponge" period as a time for teachers to provide extra help and/or permit students to retake failed or missed exams—**to provide extended learning time for those who need it!** In addition, because not all faculty are needed to "cover" this block each time it occurs, it can be allocated for departmental meetings or other professional development activities on a rotating basis. The major drawback to the seminar/activity period is the planning required to ensure all students are productively engaged.

FIG. 2.18. ALTERNATE DAY BLOCK SCHEDULE BUILT FOR 7 COURSES (1 LUNCH PERIOD; 8 BLOCKS; ACTIVITY/SEMINAR PERIOD)

| | Blocks and Times | M<br>Day 1<br>A | T<br>Day 2<br>B | W<br>Day 1<br>A | R<br>Day 2<br>B |
|---|---|---|---|---|---|
| **P** | Block I & HR<br>8:00–9:36 am | 1 | 2 | 1 | 2 |
| | | 1 | 2 | 1 | 2 |
| **E** | Block II<br>9:41–11:11 am | 3 | 4 | 3 | 4 |
| **R** | | 3 | 4 | 3 | 4 |
| **I** | 11:16 am–11:50 pm | L U N C H | | | |
| **O** | Block III<br>11:55–1:25 pm | 5 | 6 | 5 | 6 |
| | | 5 | 6 | 5 | 6 |
| **D** | Block IV<br>1:30–3:00 pm | 7 | Activity/<br>Seminar | 7 | Activity/<br>Seminar |
| | | 7 | | 7 | |

As previously mentioned, most schools must serve lunch during more than one block; this is accomplished easily in the seven-course, alternate day block schedule by sandwiching lunch periods around a singleton period placed strategically near an appropriate lunch time (see Figure 2.19).

| Fig. 2.19. Alternate Day Block Schedule Built for 7 Courses (2 Lunch Periods) | | | | |
|---|---|---|---|---|
| | Blocks and Times | M Day 1 A | T Day 2 B | M Day 1 A | T Day 2 B |
| | | ½ of School Follows This Schedule | | ½ of School Follows This Schedule | |
| P E R I O D | Block I & HR 8:00–9:49 am | 1 | 2 | 1 | 2 |
| | | 1 | 2 | 1 | 2 |
| | Block II 9:55–11:37 pm | 3 | 4 | 3 | 4 |
| | | 3 | 4 | 3 | 4 |
| | Lunch and Period 5 11:43–1:12 pm | Lunch 11:43–12:07 pm | | Period 5 11:43–12:42 pm | |
| | | Period 5 12:13–1:12 pm | | Lunch 12:48–1:12 pm | |
| | Block III 1:18–3:00 pm | 7 | 6 | 7 | 6 |
| | | 7 | 6 | 7 | 6 |

Two lunch periods could be provided through several additional strategies. If school begins closer to 9:00 a.m., lunch periods could be placed around a singleton period 3. Another plan could include an activity period meeting opposite lunch similar to the six-course schedule shown in Figure 2.11. This adaptation would reduce each instructional block by several minutes to provide time for the activity period.

Many schools require three lunch periods. It is necessary to break one of the long instructional blocks to provide the necessary slots to fulfill this need. Two basic approaches can be taken. Figure 2.20 (p. 57) illustrates one possibility in which students in one third of the school begin one of their classes (course 3) for 50 minutes, eat lunch, and return to that class for an additional 50 minutes. On the alternate day, course 4 is split.

Figure 2.21 (p. 58) offers a second adaptation. The number of singleton courses is increased to three; courses 3, 4, and 5 are now offered in 55-minute periods daily. Courses 1, 2, 6, and 7 alternate in 100-minute blocks every other day; five minutes are allocated for each transition; and six minutes are added to Block I for homeroom. Lunch is scheduled similarly to the schedule in Figure 2.20.

Various adaptations of these basic formats can be constructed depending on the size of a school, the number of courses in which each student enrolls per year, and the number of lunch periods required daily.

Schedules designed for schools that offer students eight courses annually are very similar in construction to those designed for six-course schools. Such models are the basis for the 4/4 Semester plan, to be discussed in Chapter 3. Lunch schedules and modifications will be addressed at that time.

Before moving to semester plans, however, several interesting modifications of the aforementioned alternate day schedules will be developed.

## MODIFICATIONS

Endless possibilities exist for the adaptation of the basic alternate day models. It is not necessary to alternate every day; selected days of the week can be scheduled differently. It is not necessary to alternate all periods; any number may be held as singletons and meet every day. In this section we do not address lunch or homeroom unless either presents a problem in the adaptation suggested; readers are encouraged to revisit previous sections in this chapter or in later chapters for ideas as to how to schedule lunch efficiently.

*(Text continues on page 59)*

FIG. 2.20. ALTERNATE DAY BLOCK SCHEDULE BUILT FOR 7 COURSES (3 LUNCH PERIODS; BROKEN BLOCK)

| Blocks and Times | M Day 1 A | T Day 2 B | M Day 1 A | T Day 2 B | M Day 1 A | T Day 2 B |
|---|---|---|---|---|---|---|
| | 1/3 of School Follows This Schedule | | 1/3 of School Follows This Schedule | | 1/3 of School Follows This Schedule | |
| Block I & HR 8:00–9:49 am | 1 | 2 | 1 | 2 | 1 | 2 |
| | 1 | 2 | 1 | 2 | 1 | 2 |
| Block II 9:55–11:37 pm | 3 | 4 | 3 | 4 | 3 | 4 |
| | 3 | 4 | 3 | 4 | 3 | 4 |
| Lunch and Period 5 11:43–1:12 pm | Lunch 11:43–12:07 pm | | Period 5 11:43–12:42 pm | | Lunch 10:45–11:09 am | |
| | Period 5 12:13–1:12 pm | | Lunch 12:48–1:12 pm | | Period 5 12:13–1:12 pm | |
| Block III 1:18–3:00 pm | 7 | 6 | 7 | 6 | 7 | 6 |
| | 7 | 6 | 7 | 6 | 7 | 6 |

P E R I O D

FIG. 2.21. ALTERNATE DAY BLOCK SCHEDULE BUILT FOR 7 COURSES (3 LUNCH PERIODS; 3 SINGLETONS)

| Blocks and Times | 1/3 of School Follows This Schedule | | 1/3 of School Follows This Schedule | | 1/3 of School Follows This Schedule | |
|---|---|---|---|---|---|---|
| | M Day 1 A | T Day 2 B | M Day 1 A | T Day 2 B | M Day 1 A | T Day 2 B |
| Block I & HR 8:00–9:46 am | 1 | 2 | 1 | 2 | 1 | 2 |
| | 1 | 2 | 1 | 2 | 1 | 2 |
| Period 3 9:51–10:46 a.m | 3 | | 3 | | 3 | |
| Period 4 10:51–11:46 am | 4 | | 4 | | | |
| Lunch and Period 5 | Lunch: 11:51–12:15 pm — Period 5: 12:20–1:15 pm | | Period 5: 11:51–12:46 pm — Lunch: 12:51–1:15 pm | | Lunch: 10:51–11:15 a.m. — Period 4: 11:20–12:15 pm — Period 5: 12:20–1:15 pm | |
| Block III 1:20–3:00 pm | 7 | 6 | 7 | 6 | 7 | 6 |
| | 7 | 6 | 7 | 6 | 7 | 6 |

## ALTERNATE DAY: MODIFICATION 1

While our basic plans suggest an every-day alternation of periods, it is technically feasible to schedule an infinite number of variations on this theme. We could double-block only two days a week, four days a week, two of every four days, and so on. Figure 2.22 illustrates a model in which all classes are held in single periods on Monday, Tuesday, and Friday. Periods 1, 3, and 5 meet in double periods on Wednesday and periods 2, 4, and 6 on Thursday. If it is decided not to alternate every day, we have found it best to leave Mondays and Fridays as normal or regular as possible; therefore, double periods are scheduled for either Tuesday and Wednesday or Wednesday and Thursday. Teachers often prefer to meet classes for two consecutive days at the beginning of the week before meeting the double-period classes on Wednesday or Thursday. Science teachers, for example, introduce concepts during the first two single-period classes which can then be explored during double-period labs. It is important in this adaptation to put the two double periods on consecutive days of the week to facilitate the use of equipment that is difficult to set up and take down, such as laboratory apparatus, and vocational and physical education equipment.

| FIG. 2.22. BASIC PLAN: 6 COURSES; ONE DOUBLE PERIOD WEEKLY | | | | | |
|---|---|---|---|---|---|
| Days | M Day 1 | T Day 2 | W Day 3 | R Day 4 | F Day 5 |
| P | 1 | 1 | 1 | 2 | 1 |
| E | 2 | 2 | 1 | 2 | 2 |
| R | 3 | 3 | 3 | 4 | 3 |
| I | 4 | 4 | 3 | 4 | 4 |
| O | 5 | 5 | 5 | 6 | 5 |
| D | 6 | 6 | 5 | 6 | 6 |

Half-day vocational programs that involve significant travel time, however, do not interface easily with this plan. It is also a problem for itinerant teachers who are shared by schools not following a similar schedule. Double periods that fall in the middle of the day prohibit an equal division of school time. One accommodation could be to alternate 1 with 2 and 5 with 6, but keep courses 3 and 4 as singletons (see Figure 2.23). Placing lunch between periods three and four also facilitates the exchange of students with the vocational-technical school, providing some time for both travel and lunch for students.

| FIG. 2.23. BASIC PLAN: 6 COURSES; ONE DOUBLE PERIOD WEEKLY; 2 SINGLETONS | | | | | |
|---|---|---|---|---|---|
| Days | M Day 1 | T Day 2 | W Day 3 | R Day 4 | F Day 5 |
| P | 1 | 1 | 1 | 2 | 1 |
| | 2 | 2 | 1 | 2 | 2 |
| E | 3 | 3 | 3 | 3 | 3 |
| R | L U N C H | | | | |
| I | 4 | 4 | 4 | 4 | 4 |
| O | 5 | 5 | 5 | 6 | 5 |
| D | 6 | 6 | 5 | 6 | 6 |

It also is possible to discard the weekly schedule and simply operate a schedule in which teachers meet with students for two days in single periods and then for two alternate days in double periods. This pattern is repeated throughout the school year. In Figure 2.24, we illustrate using a seven-course plan.

FIG. 2.24. TWO DAY SINGLE PERIOD–TWO DAY DOUBLE PERIOD
SCHEDULE: BUILT FOR 7 COURSES

| | Days | M Day 1 | T Day 2 | W Day 3 | R Day 4 |
|---|---|---|---|---|---|
| P | Block I | 1 | 1 | 1 | 2 |
| | | 2 | 2 | 1 | 2 |
| E | Block II | 3 | 3 | 3 | 4 |
| R | | 4 | 4 | 3 | 4 |
| I | Period 5 | 5 | 5 | 5 | 5 |
| O | Block III | 6 | 6 | 7 | 6 |
| D | | 7 | 7 | 7 | 6 |

Teachers would meet with students three days out of every four—twice in single periods and once in a double period. Lunch easily could be positioned around period 5.

As stated previously, this plan does not work well with half-day vocational program schedules unless there is an uneven division of that time. For example, the plan would be appropriate if some students were involved in four-period vocational programs and others in three-period programs. Four-period students could attend the vocational school during the morning (four single periods or two double blocks back at the home school, depending on the day) and return to the home school for lunch and periods 5 through 7. Conversely, students involved in the equivalent of three periods of vocational programming would remain at the home school for periods 1 through 4 and then travel to the vocational center for periods 5 through 7.

## ALTERNATE DAY: MODIFICATION 2

Another version of the alternate day schedule keeps selected periods as single periods and schedules the remainder of the day as double periods. Figure 2.25 illustrates a seven-course plan in which courses 1 and 2 alternate every other day in double periods, courses 3 through 5 are held as single periods daily, and courses 6 and 7 alternate every other day in double periods. This model also provides a flexible interface with vocational programs that require travel time.

| | | M<br>Day 1<br>A | T<br>Day 2<br>B | W<br>Day 1<br>A | R<br>Day 2<br>B |
|---|---|---|---|---|---|
| | Days | | | | |
| P | Block I | 1 | 2 | 1 | 2 |
| | | 1 | 2 | 1 | 2 |
| E | | | | | |
| | | 3 | 3 | 3 | 3 |
| R | Singletons | 4 | 4 | 4 | 4 |
| I | | 5 | 5 | 5 | 5 |
| O | | | | | |
| | Block II | 7 | 6 | 7 | 6 |
| D | | 7 | 6 | 7 | 6 |

FIG. 2.25. ALTERNATE DAY BLOCK SCHEDULE
(7 COURSES; 3 SINGLETONS)

This schedule allows students involved with vocational-technical programs the flexibility to mix and match academic and vocational programs of varying lengths. For example, a student might attend class at the home school for periods 1 to 3; periods 1 and 2 would be doubled and alternated; course 3 would meet for a single period every day. Period 4 could be used for travel and lunch, and the student could attend a three-period vocational program in another facility during periods 5 through 7. Conversely, a student could attend the vocational school for periods 1 to 4, travel and eat during period 5, and pick up two academic courses which are blocked and alternated every other day back at the home school.

## ALTERNATE DAY: MODIFICATION 3

In one school division in which we have worked, it was necessary to hold the first period constant daily immediately prior to an activity period (see Figure 2.26). All other periods were doubled and alternated; lunch was positioned around Block III (periods 4 and 5).

| | FIG. 2.26. ALTERNATE DAY BLOCK SCHEDULE BUILT FOR 7 COURSES (2 LUNCH PERIODS; SINGLETON PERIOD 1) | | | |
|---|---|---|---|---|
| Days | M Day 1 A | T Day 2 B | M Day 1 A | T Day 2 B |
| | ½ of School Follows This Schedule | | ½ of School Follows This Schedule | |
| Block I | 1 | | 1 | |
| | Activity Period-Channel 1 | | Activity Period-Channel 1 | |
| Block II | 2 | 3 | 2 | 3 |
| | 2 | 3 | 2 | 3 |
| Block III & Lunch | 4 | 5 | Lunch | |
| | 4 | 5 | 4 | 5 |
| | Lunch | | 4 | 5 |
| Block IV | 6 | 7 | 6 | 7 |
| | 6 | 7 | 6 | 7 |

P E R I O D

This particular alteration was made to accommodate designated vocational classes which had to meet daily because the vocational school was following a single-period schedule with all periods meeting daily. By scheduling all vocational classes during the first period and using the activity period for travel time, students could begin school at the vocational center and avoid having to be transported to their vocational classes. Period 1 need not be 50 minutes in length; it could be 60 or 70 minutes long, if desired. This plan prevented period 2 from being fragmented for vocational students. As shown, periods 2 through 7 meet every other day for 90 minutes. Lunch is placed before the 4–5 block for half of the school and after the 4–5 block for the other half.

If a third lunch period had to be scheduled, Block III, including courses 4 and 5, would need to be broken for approximately one-third of the classes. When this change is necessary, we suggest that two single-period classes be scheduled in those slots where meeting every day would not be considered as much of a negative factor. For example, classes such as band or first-year languages might be scheduled during the two single periods with lunch scheduled between. We suggest that classes such as science labs, physical education, art, and technology meet for double periods during this block with about one-third of the students having lunch early in the block and another one-third having lunch at the end of the block.

Modifications to the basic alternate day plan are endless; we end this chapter with a few practical pointers.

♦   It is important that students not be scheduled for a large number of classes requiring heavy homework duties on the same day. In fact, teachers in schools moving from the single-period schedule should indicate those classes having heavy and low homework assignments so a mixture of classes can be distributed on both days. Computer codes can be utilized to simplify and monitor this process.

♦   Care also must be taken in determining teacher planning periods. For example, in Figure 2.3, if planning is assigned during periods 1 and 3, a teacher would be off four periods on Day 1 and have no planning periods on Day 2. Another problem occurs in schools offering six courses. If teachers instruct five of six classes, as is almost always the case, in an alternate day plan teachers will have only one double planning period every other day. We have found this schedule to be problematic in schools with short lunch periods. Twenty-five minutes off during the day is probably not enough. We suggest that in such schools an hour be scheduled for either one long lunch period or two lunch periods and two activity periods. Care should be taken to schedule any activity assignments on the day when the teacher has a planning period and not during the no-planning-period day. Such a schedule would give the teacher at least an hour break on days when he or she did not have planning.

♦ Whenever both double-period, alternate day classes and singleton classes are used as part of a schedule, care should be taken to assign courses to the format in which they most appropriately fit. For example, an attempt should be made to assign all laboratory science courses, which involve considerable equipment set-up and clean-up, to double-block periods. Conversely, keyboarding, which involves the tiring repetition of a mechanical skill, may be more appropriate as a singleton course. Again, computer codes can assist in simplifying the prioritization of specific courses to specific scheduling formats.

♦ Some schools have been tempted to let the alternate day schedule "float," so that if an "odd" day is missed because of inclement weather, the schedule resumes on an "odd" day when school opens again. This causes a potential problem when teachers make long-range plans for field trips and guest speakers. If a day is missed prior to the scheduled event, the class for which the speaker or trip has been planned may not be scheduled to meet. Therefore, most schools implementing the alternate day plan have established a calendar of "Day 1's" and "Day 2's" for the entire semester. Given such a calendar, however, it is possible to have an inequitable distribution of days to courses because of weather or other interruptions. One possible remedy to this problem is to fix the majority of the days in a semester's calendar and "float" several days during the last week. Thus, missed days could be made up as needed to equalize instructional time prior to exams. If snow days are made up by attending school on a Saturday, substituting a school day for a teacher work day, or extending the semester or school year, schools should make up the missed odd or even days accordingly.

♦ We suggest that schools not ring bells for transitions unless the entire school moves at that time. As an alternative, some schools have used the intercom and a musical tone as a less distracting means of synchronizing movements throughout the day.

♦ Unless a separate homeroom period is maintained or first period is held constant, students begin the school day in different classes on Day 1 and Day 2. Therefore, two sets of attendance cards are necessary if attendance is to be taken during the first class. If early morning attendance-taking is not necessary and a single period (e.g., fifth period) occurs every day, attendance could be taken during this class, and only one set of cards would be required. The practice of reporting "period attendance" for the purpose of deterring class cutting is simplified in alternate day schedules because only three or four reports are required daily, rather than six, seven, or eight.

## CONCLUSION

Alternate-day schedules provide several benefits for students, teachers, and administrators. In addition, these plans are relatively easy to implement, with fewer concerns brought forth from teachers and parents than several of the plans to be presented in future chapters. However, relative simplicity has a trade-off; in comparison to Day 1, Day 2 plans, we believe the scheduling models to be described in coming chapters offer many more advantages and stand a greater chance of effecting the changes some high schools so desperately need.

# 3

# THE 4/4
# SEMESTER PLAN

A variety of issues are unaddressed by the alternate day schedules which were presented in Chapter 2:

- Teachers still must work with 100 to 180 different students the entire school year.
- As many as five or six different preparations may still be assigned to teachers.
- Grades and records must be kept for 100 to 180 students all year.
- Students continue to be responsible for six to seven different subjects all year and the homework and tests connected with those subjects.
- Students failing a course must continue attending class the entire year, and they have no opportunity to retake a course until summer school.
- Students have no additional opportunities for acceleration compared to single-period daily schedules.
- Some critics argue that alternate day plans disrupt the continuity of instruction, especially in such subjects as foreign languages, selected music classes, and mathematics.

The 4/4 semester plan, or what some refer to as the accelerated schedule, begins to deal with many of the above issues. This model of scheduling, which is being adopted by an increasing number of schools across the country, has been operating in selected high schools in Canada for more than 10 years.

This chapter begins with an introduction to the basic features of and rationale behind the semester plan. We also address several instructional and curricular concerns raised by the 4/4 plan. Second, we develop the model more fully by detailing bell schedules and adding lunch and activity periods. Finally, we offer specific advice on a variety of aspects of the plan to school personnel who may be considering its implementation.

## THE BASIC PLAN

In the 4/4 semester plan the school day is divided into four instructional blocks of approximately 90 minutes each, and the school year is divided into two semesters. During the first semester, students are enrolled in four courses which meet daily. Instruction, which previously had been stretched over the course of an entire 180-day school year, is now compressed into one semester of double-block periods. At the end of the fall semester, students receive credit for each course successfully completed and enroll in four additional courses for the spring semester. Generally, most teachers instruct three of the 90-minute blocks and use the fourth block for planning. The basic model is illustrated in Figure 3.1.

### DISCUSSION

The semester plan offers many of the advantages of alternate day plans. First, we revisit and update the list of these benefits, which was developed in Chapter 2. Second, we discuss additional benefits and issues that arise from the semester plan.

♦   **All teachers benefit from increased "quality" instructional time.** Gains in minutes of "quality" instructional time are similar to those in alternate day plans. One aspect of the 4/4 plan may, however, actually increase the amount of useable teaching time. Teachers working in schools that have implemented alternate day plans report that they must spend considerable time reviewing material which was presented two days previously, or in some cases four days because of the weekend. Because

| | | Semester 1 | Semester 2 |
|---|---|---|---|
| FIG. 3.1. BASIC 4/4 SEMESTER BLOCK SCHEDULE (8 COURSES) | | | |
| P | 1 | Course 1 | Course 5 |
| E | 2 | | |
| R | 3 | Course 2 | Course 6 |
| I | 4 | | |
| O | 5 | Course 3 | Course 7 |
| D | 6 | | |
| S | 7 | Course 4 | Course 8 |
| | 8 | | |

classes meet every day in the semester plan, there is a reduced need for daily review, and therefore more time for new instruction.

♦ **Teachers are able to plan extended lessons.** Class periods are similar in length to alternate day plans; therefore, extended single lessons still are possible. In addition, because classes meet daily, it is possible to provide greater continuity of lessons.

♦ **The number of class changes is reduced.** Just as they are in alternate day plans, school discipline and climate are improved in semester plans. The number of daily class changes is the same as in alternate day plans; however, students' class schedules are simplified because they travel to the same four classes every day for the entire semester.

♦ **Teaching with a variety of instructional models is encouraged.** Similar benefits accrue to teaching in the semester plan.

♦ **Compared to every-day (all-year) models, students have fewer classes, quizzes, tests, and homework assignments on any one day.** This benefit is much greater for students in the semester plan because, in addition to attending fewer classes daily, they attend fewer classes for the entire semester; thus, they juggle the requirements for fewer classes.

♦ **Work missed because of a student absence is easier to gather and monitor.** Again, this is also true for semester plans. Students are enrolled in just four courses; thus, only four teachers must be conferred with to gather make-up work. Because of the concentrated nature of courses in the semester plan, the importance of making up missed work is increased. Students could fall far behind in their courses simply by missing school for two or three consecutive days.

♦ **Itinerant teacher schedules can be simplified.** If it is possible to schedule itinerant teachers on a semester basis, travel can be reduced, or even eliminated, and these personnel are better able to develop relationships with teachers and students in the schools to which they are assigned. Of course, such arrangements are possible only if the other schools in which the teachers work are operating under similar schedules. Schools operating semester plans, who share itinerant teachers with non-semesterized schools, must continue to allow for travel time between blocks or periods.

In addition, the implementation of the semester or 4/4 plan provides the following benefits not offered by alternate day schedules:

♦ **Teachers work with fewer students during any one semester.** We believe that one of the impossible demands placed on high school teachers is that they "get to know" and address the "individual differences" of between 100 and 180 students every day, all year long. It is no wonder that high school teachers are seen as being "subject-centered" rather than "student-centered." To attempt to be "student-centered" and address the needs and individual personalities of so many students is to attempt the impossible. In the 4/4 plan teachers work with only 60 to 90 students during any one semester; chances are improved that relationships can be developed and student needs addressed. Teachers in schools having implemented the 4/4 plan report becoming more attached to, and more accountable for, their students.

♦ **Teachers prepare for fewer courses each day.** Although teachers generally instruct three classes daily in semester schools, we recommend that one, or at most two, different preparations be assigned for the semester. In addition, we recommend that one (or both) of these preparations be repeated in the second semester. Semester plans require a reorganization of the curriculum and a redesign of the traditional lesson format. It is best to limit the number of preparations as much as possible to allow for the increased planning necessary to complete this task.

♦ **Teachers must keep records and grades for only 50 to 90 students per semester.** Grade books may be organized for fewer students, and teachers must complete fewer report cards, attendance sheets, and other forms of record-keeping, for any single reporting period.

♦ **Students who have failed a course have an early opportunity to retake it; thus, they can regain the graduation pace of their peers.** At the beginning of the second semester in high schools across the country, teachers are confronted with students who have failed their courses for the first semester and who are smart enough to realize that the possibility of passing the course by year's end is slim. These students rarely respond to teachers' suggestions to work hard now, in preparation for repeating the course during summer school or next fall; they often become discipline and attendance problems. The 4/4 plan offers students an opportunity to repeat a failed class during the school year. Because students can attain 32 year-long course credits (64 semester half-credits) over a four-year high school career under this plan, and fewer than 32 credits are required for graduation, there is room in students' schedules to repeat six or more failed courses during the four years of high school and still graduate with their class. Thus, summer school, which often requires tuition payment and individual transportation arrangements beyond the ability of lower-income students, may be less necessary.

Similarly, with the increasing trend toward the long-term suspension of students for disciplinary problems related to drug use and violent behavior in schools, the 4/4 Semester plan may offer some new flexibility for administrators. Most expulsions result in a total loss of credits for classes in which the offending student was enrolled. The suspended student, therefore, falls another year behind his or her peers, a situation from which it is very difficult to recover. If a student were suspended in the second semester, he or she could possibly have earned four credits prior to the suspension. If the student were suspended in the first semester, it may be possible, depending upon the nature and severity of the offense, to limit the removal to the first semester, thereby maintaining the possibility for the student to earn some credit during the year. We do not suggest "soft" treatment of violent or incorrigible high school students; however, we are aware that administrators desire a variety of disciplinary options and often wish there were a less severe alternative to a full year's expulsion.

♦ **Students have greater opportunities for acceleration.** In a typical high school career, there are several decision points that determine whether or not a child accelerates in a particular subject. The most celebrated of these decisions occurs near the end of seventh grade when students may or may not be recommended to enroll in algebra. If students do not take algebra in eighth grade, it is almost impossible to accelerate to or beyond the calculus track during high school. Thus, many students are denied the opportunity to take this college course, and many other students are forced to attempt algebra when they are not quite ready for it. In the semester plan there is much greater flexibility with regard to acceleration. A student who takes algebra during the first semester of ninth grade and excels can move on to geometry in the second semester, thereby "catching up" to the calculus track. This same opportunity is available to students who have fallen behind their age group because of retention during the elementary or middle school years. Such a student could "catch up" by taking required core courses in consecutive semesters.

♦ **Students may enroll in a greater number and variety of elective courses in comparison to traditional six- or seven-period schedules.** The 4/4 model offers students the possibility of amassing 32 credits by the end of their high school years. Given the increasing graduation requirements brought on by the reform movements of the 1980s, enrollments in elective courses have been reduced, and, as some have argued, this may have resulted in students receiving a less well-rounded high school education [Association for Supervision and Curriculum Development, 1985]. Schools changing to the 4/4 plan from six- or seven-period schedules should experience a reduction in student scheduling conflicts because there are now eight slots in which to place singleton courses. In addition, because students must select one or two additional courses, low-enrollment electives in small schools, which are often in danger of being discontinued, should experience an increase in registrations.

♦ **Fewer textbooks are required.** For example, because half of the students scheduled to take English 9 do so in the fall, those students scheduled for the course in the spring may use the same sets of books. This savings could be applied to the purchase of additional instructional materials needed to provide a variety of activities within longer blocks of time.

## DEVELOPING THE MODEL

The major purpose of this section is to develop more fully the basic 4/4 semester model described briefly in the previous section. Accordingly, we now begin to add details, including a bell schedule with a homeroom time and several options for lunch. Each plan, unless it is an example which has been implemented by an actual school, is developed based upon a seven-hour (420-minute) school day.

Our first detailed bell schedule (see Figure 3.2, p. 74) includes four 90-minute instructional blocks, five additional minutes for homeroom added to the first block, a single lunch period of 35 minutes (effectively 45 minutes because it is sandwiched between two class changes), and 5 minutes of passing time at each class change.

Some school administrators express disbelief when we suggest the possibility of allowing all students in a school to eat lunch at the same time. Typical concerns include the lack of sufficient seating in the cafeteria, the inability of the cafeteria personnel to serve a large number of students in a short amount of time, and worries regarding discipline. Each of these concerns is valid; however, we

| | | |
|---|---|---|
| **FIG. 3.2. 4/4 SEMESTER BLOCK SCHEDULE**<br>(4 BLOCKS DAILY; 8 COURSES ANNUALLY; ONE LUNCH PERIOD) | | |
| Blocks | Fall Semester | Spring Semester |
| Block I<br>8:00–9:35 am | Course 1 | Course 5 |
| Block II<br>9:40–11:10 am | Course 2 | Course 6 |
| 11:15 am–11:50 pm | Lunch | |
| Block III<br>11:55 am–1:25 pm | Course 3 | Course 7 |
| Block IV<br>1:30–3:00 pm | Course 4 | Course 8 |

are aware of schools with more than 1000 students who have moved to this format and are pleased with the arrangement.

In general, students are permitted to eat their lunches in unrestricted areas throughout the entire school. They are allowed to congregate outside, in the hallways, in common areas, and in teachers' classrooms. Very often this time is also used to schedule club meetings, teachers' office hours, and tutorial sessions. The library, computer labs, and gymnasiums are open and supervised for students' use. Serving areas are not restricted to the standard cafeteria lines; satellite serving stations and food bars are arranged so that students and teachers may purchase food quickly. Schools operating under such a system often allow 40 to 60 minutes for lunch. Students are informed of and realize that this "open" lunch is a privilege and that it may be withdrawn if abused. Lunch time detention hall is conducted and abhorred by students, who, if so assigned, miss the freedom of socializing with their peers.

As before, we realize that many schools must operate more than one lunch period. Figure 3.3 illustrates the bell schedule used during the 1992–93 school year at Governor Thomas Johnson High School in Frederick, Maryland. It includes four 90-minute instructional blocks, two lunch periods of 40 minutes scheduled before and after the third block, and five minutes of passing time between blocks.

| FIG. 3.3. GOVERNOR THOMAS JOHNSON H.S., FREDERICK COUNTY, MD, BELL SCHEDULE (4/4 SEMESTER BLOCK SCHEDULE; 4 BLOCKS DAILY; 8 COURSES ANNUALLY) | | |
|---|---|---|
| 8:00–9:30 am | Block I<br>Fall-Course 1<br>Spring-Course 5 | |
| 9:35–11:05 am | Block II<br>Fall-Course 2<br>Spring-Course 6 | |
| 11:10 am–1:25 pm | Lunch A<br>11:10–11:50 am | Block IIIB<br>Fall-Course 3<br>Spring-Course 7<br>11:10 am–12:40 pm |
|  | Block IIIA<br>Fall-Course 3<br>Spring-Course 7<br>11:55 am–1:25 pm | Lunch B<br>12:45–1:25 pm |
| 1:30–3:00 pm | Block IV<br>Fall-Course 4<br>Spring-Course 8 | |

Orange County High School in Orange, Virginia, implemented the schedule illustrated in Figure 3.4 during the 1993-94 school year. In this variation, blocks continue to be 90 minutes long; however, a 60-minute block of time between the second and third classes is divided equally between lunch and a study/activity period. Five minutes continue to separate classes. Notice that this adaptation is based upon a longer 440- (vs. 420-) minute school day.

| FIG. 3.4. ORANGE COUNTY H.S., ORANGE COUNTY, VA 4/4 SEMESTER BLOCK SCHEDULE (4 BLOCKS DAILY; 8 COURSES ANNUALLY; 2 LUNCH/STUDY PERIODS) | | |
|---|---|---|
| 8:00–9:30 am | Block I | |
| 9:35–11:05 am | Block II | |
| 11:10–11:40 am | Lunch A | Study/Activity B |
| 11:40 am–12:10 pm | Study/Activity A | Lunch B |
| 12:15–1:45 pm | Block III | |
| 1:50–3:20 pm | Block IV | |

Accomplishing a similar plan within the confines of a 420- minute day would require that a combination of instructional blocks and/or lunch/activity periods be shortened. Figure 3.5 illustrates a schedule with instructional blocks of 86 minutes, 26-minute lunch periods, 26-minute activity periods, 4 minutes added to the first block for homeroom, and 4 class changes of 4 minutes each.

Allowing for three lunches in the semester plan is a bit more difficult. There are two basic choices, one of which involves splitting a block and the other that creates a very early or very late lunch period. Splitting a block can be accomplished in two different ways: a block can be divided by lunch into two singleton courses that meet every day, all year long (Figures 3.6 and 3.7), or a semester course can be divided by lunch with students attending half of the class prior to lunch and the second half after lunch (Figure 3.8). Regardless, it is only necessary for one-third of the school to operate on this broken-block lunch schedule.

| FIG. 3.5. 4/4 SEMESTER BLOCK SCHEDULE (4 BLOCKS DAILY; 8 COURSES ANNUALLY; 2 LUNCH/STUDY PERIODS; 420 MINUTES) | | |
|---|---|---|
| 8:00–9:30 am | Block I | |
| 9:34–11:00 am | Block II | |
| 11:04–11:30 am | Lunch A | Study/Activity B |
| 11:34–12:00 pm | Study/Activity A | Lunch B |
| 12:04–1:30 pm | Block III | |
| 1:34–3:00 pm | Block IV | |

Figure 3.6 (p. 78) illustrates a case in which two singleton courses have been created, but for only one-third of the school.

FIG. 3.6. 4/4 SEMESTER BLOCK SCHEDULE BUILT FOR 8 COURSES
(3 LUNCH PERIODS; TWO SINGLETONS FOR 1/3 OF SCHOOL)

| Blocks and Times | Fall | Spring | Fall | Spring | Fall | Spring |
|---|---|---|---|---|---|---|
| | 1/3 of School Follows This Schedule | | 1/3 of School Follows This Schedule | | 1/3 of School Follows This Schedule | |
| Block I & HR 8:00–9:35 am | Course 1 | Course 5 | Course 1 | Course 5 | Course 1 | Course 5 |
| Block II 9:40–11:10 am | Course 2 | Course 6 | Course 2 | Course 6 | Course 2 | Course 6 |
| Lunch and Block III 11:15–1:25 pm | Lunch 11:15–11:50 / Course 3 11:55–1:25 | Lunch 11:15–11:50 / Course 7 11:55–1:25 | Course 3 11:15–12:00 / Lunch 12:05–12:35 / Course 7 12:40–1:25 | Course 3 11:15–12:00 / Lunch 12:05–12:35 / Course 7 12:40–1:25 | Course 3 11:15–12:45 / Lunch 12:50–1:25 | Course 7 11:15–12:45 / Lunch 12:50–1:25 |
| Block IV 1:30–3:00 pm | Course 4 | Course 8 | Course 4 | Course 8 | Course 4 | Course 8 |

In Figure 3.7 (p. 80), two singletons are created for all students and staff. The problem caused by adding singletons is similar to a problem that arises in the seven-period alternate day schedule when singletons are added: some courses must be taught in both block and single-period formats, which means they become very different courses requiring different preparation for teachers.

In Figure 3.8 (p. 81), one-third of the school must break Block III to allow for a third lunch period. Students have class for 45 minutes, go to lunch, and then return to the same class for an additional 45 minutes. Some teachers in certain subjects, such as foreign languages and keyboarding, may prefer this split-block format. Where this arrangement is desired, complete the master schedule first and then assign teachers and/or classes to the appropriate lunch schedule. If desired, this plan could be rotated on a six- or twelve-week cycle for all groups, so no one group of classes has the split block year-long.

Figure 3.9 (p. 82) illustrates the addition of a third early lunch period which follows Block I.

We add a third lunch period in Figure 3.10 (p. 83) by pairing lunch with activity periods.

Finally, four lunch periods are accomplished in Figure 3.11 (p. 84) by adding activity/lunch periods before and after Block III.

*(Text continues on page 85)*

FIG. 3.7. 4/4 SEMESTER BLOCK SCHEDULE BUILT FOR 8 COURSES
(3 LUNCH PERIODS; TWO SINGLETONS FOR ENTIRE SCHOOL)

| Blocks and Times | Fall | Spring | Fall | Spring | Fall | Spring |
|---|---|---|---|---|---|---|
| | 1/3 of School Follows This Schedule | | 1/3 of School Follows This Schedule | | 1/3 of School Follows This Schedule | |
| Block I & HR 8:00–9:35 am | Course 1 | Course 5 | Course 1 | Course 5 | Course 1 | Course 5 |
| Block II 9:40–11:10 am | Course 2 | Course 6 | Course 2 | Course 6 | Course 2 | Course 6 |
| Lunch and Block III 11:15–1:25 pm | Lunch 11:15–11:45<br>Course 3 11:50–12:35<br>Course 7 12:40–1:25 | | Course 3 11:15–12:00<br>Lunch 12:05–12:35<br>Course 7 12:40–1:25 | | Course 3 11:15–12:00<br>Course 7 12:05–12:50<br>Lunch 12:55–1:25 | |
| Block IV 1:30–3:00 pm | Course 4 | Course 8 | Course 4 | Course 8 | Course 4 | Course 8 |

**FIG. 3.8. 4/4 SEMESTER BLOCK SCHEDULE BUILT FOR 8 COURSES (3 LUNCH PERIODS; BROKEN BLOCK)**

| Blocks and Times | Fall | Spring | Fall | Spring | Fall | Spring |
| --- | --- | --- | --- | --- | --- | --- |
| | 1/3 of School Follows This Schedule | | 1/3 of School Follows This Schedule | | 1/3 of School Follows This Schedule | |
| Block I & HR 8:00–9:35 am | Course 1 | Course 5 | Course 1 | Course 5 | Course 1 | Course 5 |
| Block II 9:40–11:10 am | Course 2 | Course 6 | Course 2 | Course 6 | Course 2 | Course 6 |
| Lunch and Block III 11:15–1:25 pm | Lunch 11:15–11:50 / Course 3 11:55–1:25 | Course 7 11:55–1:25 | Course 3 / Lunch 12:05–12:40 / Course 3 con't | Course 7 / Course 7 con't | Course 3 11:15–12:45 / Lunch 12:50–1:25 | Course 7 11:15–12:45 / Lunch 12:50–1:25 |
| Block IV 1:30–3:00 pm | Course 4 | Course 8 | Course 4 | Course 8 | Course 4 | Course 8 |

FIG. 3.9. 4/4 SEMESTER BLOCK SCHEDULE BUILT FOR 8 COURSES (3 LUNCH PERIODS; EARLY LUNCH)

| Blocks and Times | ⅓ of School Follows This Schedule | | ⅓ of School Follows This Schedule | | ⅓ of School Follows This Schedule | |
|---|---|---|---|---|---|---|
| | Fall | Spring | Fall | Spring | Fall | Spring |
| Block I & HR 9:00–10:35 am | Course 1 | Course 5 | Course 1 | Course 5 | Course 1 | Course 5 |
| Block II 10:40–12:10 am | Course 2 | Course 6 | Lunch 10:40–11:15 | | Course 2 | Course 6 |
| | | | Course 2 11:20–12:50 | Course 6 11:20–12:50 | | |
| Lunch and Block III 12:15–2:25 pm | Lunch 12:15–12:50 | | Course 3 12:55–2:25 | Course 7 12:55–2:25 | Course 3 12:15–1:45 | Course 7 12:15–1:45 |
| | Course 3 12:55–2:25 | Course 7 12:55–2:25 | | | Lunch 1:50–2:25 | |
| Block IV 2:30–4:00 pm | Course 4 | Course 8 | Course 4 | Course 8 | Course 4 | Course 8 |

| FIG. 3.10. 4/4 SEMESTER BLOCK SCHEDULE BUILT FOR 8 COURSES (3 LUNCH/STUDY PERIODS) | | |
|---|---|---|
| Blocks and Times | ⅓ of School Follows This Schedule | ⅓ of School Follows This Schedule | ⅓ of School Follows This Schedule |
| Block I & HR 8:00–9:30 am | Course 1 (5) | Course 1 (5) | Course 1 (5) |
| Block II 9:34–11:04 am | Course 2 (6) | Course 2 (6) | Course 2 (6) |
| Lunch, Study/Activity, and Block III 11:08–1:26 pm | **Lunch A** **11:08–11:28 am** / **Study/Activity** **11:32–11:52 am** / Course 3 (7) 11:56–1:26 pm | **Study/Activity** **11:08–11:28 am** / **Lunch B** **11:32–11:52 pm** / Course 3 (7) 11:56–1:26 pm | Course 3 (7) 11:08–12:38 pm / **Lunch C** **12:42–1:02 pm** / **Study/Activity** **1:06–1:26 pm** |
| Block IV 1:30–3:00 pm | Course 4 (8) | Course 4 (8) | Course 4 (8) |

FIG. 3.11. 4/4 SEMESTER BLOCK SCHEDULE BUILT FOR 8 COURSES (4 LUNCH/STUDY PERIODS)

| Blocks and Times | ¼ of School Follows This Schedule | ¼ of School Follows This Schedule | ¼ of School Follows This Schedule | ¼ of School Follows This Schedule |
|---|---|---|---|---|
| Block I & HR 8:00–9:30 am | Course 1 (5) | Course 1 (5) | Course 1 (5) | Course 1 (5) |
| Block II 9:34–11:04 am | Course 2 (6) | Course 2 (6) | Course 2 (6) | Course 2 (6) |
| Lunch, Study/Activity, and Block III 11:08–1:26 pm | **Lunch A** 11:08–11:28 am<br>**Study/Act.** 11:32–11:52 am<br>Course 3 (7) 11:56–1:26 pm | **Study/Act.** 11:08–11:28 am<br>**Lunch B** 11:32–11:52 pm<br>Course 3 (7) 11:56–1:26 pm | Course 3 (7) 11:08–12:38 pm<br>**Lunch C** 12:42–1:02 pm<br>**Study/Act.** 1:06–1:26 pm | Course 3 (7) 11:08–12:38 pm<br>**Study/Act.** 12:42–1:02 pm<br>**Lunch D** 1:06–1:26 pm |
| Block IV 1:30–3:00 pm | Course 4 (8) | Course 4 (8) | Course 4 (8) | Course 4 (8) |

In Figure 3.12, an interesting variation of the 4/4 Semester plan is designed by "sliding" blocks through the day on a four-day cycle. The slide prevents any one class from attaining the label of "my last-period class."

| FIG. 3.12. 4/4 SEMESTER BLOCK SCHEDULE WITH A SLIDE (4 BLOCKS DAILY; 8 COURSES ANNUALLY; 1 LUNCH PERIOD) | | | | |
|---|---|---|---|---|
| | Fall Semester | | | |
| Blocks | Day 1 | Day 2 | Day 3 | Day 4 |
| Block I 8:00–9:35 am | Course 1 | Course 2 | Course 3 | Course 4 |
| Block II 9:40–11:10 am | Course 2 | Course 3 | Course 4 | Course 1 |
| Lunch 11:15 am–11:50 pm | Lunch | | | |
| Block III 11:55 am–1:25 pm | Course 3 | Course 4 | Course 1 | Course 2 |
| Block IV 1:30–3:00 pm | Course 4 | Course 1 | Course 2 | Course 3 |

## CRITICAL ISSUES REGARDING THE 4/4 SEMESTER PLAN

The following are matters to be addressed when implementing the 4/4 Semester plan. The care with which these points are dealt with will determine if they become benefits of, or drawbacks to, this model. We generally classify these matters as instructional issues, student issues, and teacher issues. We conclude with a detailed discussion regarding the most critical administrative issue—cost.

## INSTRUCTIONAL ISSUES

### *RETENTION OF LEARNING*

Perhaps the thorniest question that arises regarding the 4/4 semester plan is the following: "Does this plan mean that a student could complete Algebra I during the first semester of 9th grade, not enroll in math second semester, not take math over the summer, and conceivably not have math again until the second semester of 10th grade?" The answer to this question is "Yes, it is possible." We would, however, recommend that the next math course be taken first semester of 10th grade. Still, that leaves the likelihood that a full semester and summer would pass between sequential courses. Many teachers fear a great loss of learning in this circumstance and an unreasonable requirement for review. They also foresee a problem when students who have recently finished a prerequisite course are mixed with those who completed the prerequisite a year ago.

The experience of schools with the 4/4 plan over the last several years may assuage concern regarding this issue. Teachers from Governor Thomas Johnson High School in Frederick, Maryland, reported that they could discern very little difference between the retention of students who had just recently completed a prerequisite and other students with greater time lapses between courses. Another point that teachers make is that there has always been a need for some review after the summer at the beginning of the school year. An additional semester away from a course, when added to the three months of summer, did not increase the need for review.

Several studies from the field of cognitive psychology may be applied to this issue. One study dealt with the retention of learning for college students over time [Semb, Ellis, and Araujo, 1993]. We believe this research can be appropriately applied to the issue of retention over time in the 4/4 semester plan because of its similarity to college schedules. The researchers in the study compared the learning of students at the end of a course, four months later, and again after eleven months. They discovered that students retained 85 percent of what they had originally learned after four months and 80 percent of what they had originally learned after eleven months [p. 309]. One would expect, therefore, that high school students would retain slightly more than 85 percent of their original learning after a three-month summer vacation, somewhat more than 80 percent of their original learning after a semester and summer (seven months), and slightly less than 80 percent of their original learning if an entire year came between enrollment in two sequential courses. Yes, students do forget more over time; however, the slight decline in retention from three months to either seven months or twelve months may be worth other benefits of the 4/4 semester plan.

Not surprisingly, the researchers discovered that retention over time was greatly affected by the degree of original learning; that is to say, the better students learn material in the first place, the more likely they are to retain it [p. 308]. Students in the study were given different learning experiences; the more effective method resulted in 90 percent retention of original learning after four months and 87.4 percent retention of original learning after eleven months. The rate of decline in retention for both methods, however, was similar. Early results from several schools implementing the 4/4 semester plans suggest that teachers believe more learning to be occurring, as measured by increased student grades. For example, after one year of implementation, students in Pulaski County High School in Virginia earned 20 percent more A's and B's and 20 percent fewer D's and F's.

Another interesting finding of the study related to the retention rates for different kinds of knowledge is that retention of recall facts (fill-in responses) was significantly lower than for recognition, comprehension, and mental skills (application of knowledge and skills to new situations) [Semb et al., 1993]. An earlier study suggested that recall and recognition of facts decline more quickly than retention of concepts [Conway, Cohen, and Stanhope, 1991]. A third experiment reported a decrease in retention of knowledge items but not for comprehension items [Glasnap, Poggio, and Ory, 1978]. These results provide evidence that learning at higher cognitive levels (comprehension and application) on Bloom's [1956] taxonomy may be lost less rapidly than learning at the lowest level (knowledge). Therefore, it may be more critical for teachers to review basic knowledge-level information (i.e., specific terminology) at the beginning of a new course than to worry about whether or not students have retained the basic concepts taught in previous sequentially related courses. Not surprisingly, studies suggest that knowledge-level learning occurs more rapidly than comprehension or application [Lyon and Gettinger, 1985]. Thus, the knowledge that is lost more quickly over time also can be regained more quickly with review.

Finally, in a recent evaluation of several Copernican Plan schools (see Chapter 4 for a description of the "Copernican Plan"), results indicate that longer gaps between sequential courses were not significant in terms of their effect upon retention. A team of Harvard evaluators administered "gap" tests to students after the first year of the program at Masconomet High School in Boxford, Massachusetts. These tests, which were administered in September, December, and March, from three to fifteen months after the completion of the courses, revealed "no consistent significant differences" between the retention of Copernican students and traditional students [Carroll, 1994, p. 109]. In addition, Copernican students completed 13 percent more courses than did those within the traditional schedule.

### MINUTES PER COURSE

Another problematic issue to address involves the number of actual classroom minutes spent per credit. When a school currently operating a six- or seven-period schedule changes to the 4/4 Semester plan, the number of instructional minutes allocated per course may be reduced unless the school day is lengthened. For example, in a seven-period school with a 420-minute day, classes could be 50 minutes with seven five-minute class changes and 35 minutes for lunch. A 4/4 school could have four 90-minute classes (with the addition of five minutes to one class for homeroom activities), four five-minute class changes, and a 30-minute lunch period. In comparison, schools operating 50-minute periods provide 9000 minutes of instruction (50 minutes x 180 days) per course, while schools in the 4/4 semester plan with 90 minutes per class session provide instructional time of 8100 minutes (90 minutes x 90 days). We have argued in Chapter 2 that 8100 minutes in a block schedule is more useful instructional time than 8100 minutes in an every-day period schedule, but is it the equivalent of 9000 minutes?[1]

In Virginia the accreditation standard for the allocation of a credit is 9000 minutes (150 hours), including transitions between classes; however, the accreditation standards also permit local school boards to certify courses that meet the content standards based upon the achievement of instructional objectives, but provide fewer than 9000 minutes. Other districts have lengthened their school day. To achieve 9000 minutes according to Virginia standards requires class periods of 95 minutes with 5 minutes allocated for passing time, for a minimum school day of 430 minutes or 7 hours and 10 minutes. A lunch period longer than 30 minutes or the addition of a homeroom or advisory period would extend the day even more.

When six- or seven-period schools change to class periods of 90 minutes or less in the 4/4 plan, some teachers have found it necessary to re-examine their curricula, reduce review, and eliminate less important objectives. Curriculum integrity with the 4/4 semester plan is a major issue to be addressed. We argue that even if teachers reduce their curriculum somewhat, the quality of curriculum and instruction will improve for reasons we have discussed earlier. However, if schools are able to lengthen the school day to achieve the same number of course minutes as traditional plans, such rationalization becomes unnecessary. Schools already operating eight-period days actually gain instructional minutes for each course when changing to the 4/4 plan.

It should be noted, however, that while the nominal instructional minutes *per course* may be reduced when changing from a six- or seven-period every-day schedule to the 4/4 plan, *overall instructional time increases*. Seven 50-minute classes that meet for 180 days provide 63,000 minutes of annual instruction (7 classes x 50 minutes x 180 days). Eight 90-minute blocks that meet for 90 days provide 64,800 minutes of instruction (8 classes x 90 minutes x 90 days).

In addition, students in the 4/4 plan will have completed more credits prior to the administration of state or national assessments. For example, in Virginia a state-wide achievement test is given during the second semester of the 11th grade. In schools operating six-

---

[1] The number of minutes that constitute a "credit" varies greatly depending upon the state. Some states require as little as 120 hours (7200 minutes) or as many as 165 hours (9900 minutes).

period, every-day or alternate day schedules, students could have completed 12 courses and should be in the middle of their 13th through 18th classes; students in seven-period, every-day or alternate day schedules could have acquired 14 credits and should be involved with their 15th through 21st classes; in 4/4 schools, however, students could have completed 20 courses and be enrolled in their 21st through 24th classes.

## CURRICULUM ORGANIZATION

For teachers who have worked in short periods for their entire careers, it is possible for a false sense of "I have plenty of time" to develop when beginning any block schedule. Several teachers from 4/4 schools have reported that during the first semester of their program, a sense of panic arose when the Thanksgiving holiday arrived, and with that the realization that the "year" was more than half over!

A crucial part of the planning process is the inclusion of time for the development of course-pacing guides. Schools implementing the 4/4 semester plan often allocate a week or more of summer work for teachers to collaboratively plan timetables for units and concepts to be taught during the semester. This blueprint reduces the possibility of succumbing to the "I have plenty of time" fallacy.

The jury is still out on curriculum coverage. In our work we have heard numerous reports, from "I covered less, but they learned it better" to "I never taught so much in my life." A thorough large-scale evaluation of student achievement within the 4/4 semester plan is necessary to compare the extent of student learning with more traditional scheduling systems.

## COURSE SEQUENCING AND FOREIGN LANGUAGE

Because of the concern regarding retention of learning (discussed previously), some schools have altered the sequence of course offerings in particular disciplines. This issue arises frequently when discussing foreign language sequences, because foreign language teachers are one of the most vocal groups expressing concern with regard to the retention issue. They fear that students will require extensive review when beginning new courses because they do not take foreign language all year long. It is possible to alter the sequence of language courses to ameliorate this concern. Students could complete Spanish I during the first semester of an academic year, Spanish II during the spring semester, Spanish III during the first semester of the next year, and Spanish IV during the second semester of that year. Four years of language instruction would have been attained during two years. If this sequence began in 9th grade (or earlier), students who desire more language instruction could begin and complete an additional four-year language sequence during high school.

An issue that must be addressed regarding the ordering of foreign language is the appropriate years in which to begin and end the sequence. If students arrive from middle school having completed a credit of language instruction, it would be possible for them to fulfill a four-year language sequence by the middle of the 10th grade. Some would argue that if students intended to continue their language instruction at the college level, a two-and-a-half-year lay-off would not be advisable. A variety of possibilities exist; they include the following:

♦ Students could enroll in only one level of foreign language annually. Our experience and research suggest that student performance would not be affected adversely if students enrolled in foreign language every other semester.

♦ Students could begin the foreign language sequence in their junior year; thus, the four-year sequence would be completed at the end of the senior year. Although foreign language specialists recommend an early beginning to second-language acquisition, they generally suggest instruction begin during the elementary years or before. We suggest that there is little difference between the ability of freshmen and juniors to form sounds and acquire a new language.

♦ Schools could add additional levels of high school foreign language to the curriculum; the equivalent of eight years would be possible.

♦ Students desiring additional foreign language instruction could participate in dual-enrollment college courses.

An interesting possibility for intensified language instruction exists within the parameters of the 4/4 semester plan. Perhaps every two or four years a school could offer a full-semester schedule of a language participation. For example, students might complete French I and be aware that during their junior year the schedule offered in Figure 3.13 would be available.

| FIG. 3.13. 4/4 SEMESTER BLOCK SCHEDULE FOR INTENSE FOREIGN LANGUAGE ACQUISITION (4 BLOCKS DAILY; 8 COURSES ANNUALLY; 1 LUNCH PERIOD) | | |
|---|---|---|
| Blocks | Fall Semester | Spring Semester |
| Block I 8:00–9:35 am | Course 1 | French II–V |
| Block II 9:40–11:10 am | Course 2 | French II–V |
| Lunch 11:15 am–11:50 pm | Lunch | Lunch |
| Block III 11:55 am–1:25 pm | Course 3 | French II–V |
| Block IV 1:30–3:00 pm | Course 4 | French II–V |

In this possibility, the student would spend the complete semester studying French. To maintain one block for teacher planning time, two teachers would be necessary to provide this experience (3 blocks plus 1 block or an even 2–2 split), although it would be possible for the student to enroll in only three blocks of French and an additional fourth course; then one teacher's load could accomplish the three blocks of French instruction. It also would be possible to conduct part or all of this semester in a French-speaking country. Because students are able to earn 32 credits in high school, completing other requirements would not be a problem.

Course sequences also could be changed in other disciplines. For example, students desiring to accelerate (or catch up) in mathematics could enroll in Algebra I during the fall and, if they successfully complete the course, enroll in geometry for the spring term. It would be possible to alter sequences for all math courses.

## MUSIC PROGRAMS

One of the most problematic issues confronting schools considering the adoption of the semester plan is the issue of scheduling music programs. Many fine music programs exist across the country, and these programs are very often supported by avid boosters' clubs with formidable political clout. It is typical for schools to offer two or three different levels of band (concert band, symphonic band, wind ensemble, etc.), each of which becomes a multi-grade-level singleton in the school schedule. Persons familiar with school scheduling realize that schools are often scheduled around the band, chorus, or orchestra. In addition, school music programs are involved in activities throughout the entire school year—marching band in the fall, concerts during the December holidays, and contests and parades during the winter and spring. All of which brings us to the question of accommodating and facilitating music programs within the 4/4 Semester plan. If we were to treat music programs as any other course, students would enroll for *either* the fall or spring semester and would be involved in a different course during the alternate semester. Virtually all music supporters see this as an untenable situation. We see basically four approaches to addressing this problem:

♦ *Require students to enroll in music both semesters.* If we opt for this policy, students would earn two credits of music yearly. For many schools and students this would not be a problem, especially if the school were changing from a six- or seven-course schedule. In a six-course schedule, students have five other courses in addition to band; in a seven-course schedule, they have six other options in addition to band. Each semester of the year in the 4/4 plan, students would take three courses in addition to their music selection, for a total of six other selections annually. In other words, if students opt for two semesters of music, they would still have the same number (or more) choices as they do in traditional schedules. The central question regarding this policy, however, is the following: Should 25 percent of a student's high school education be devoted to music? Lively debate among parents, teachers, and administrators is spurred by this question.

♦ *Require enrollment one semester; make a second semester of participation elective.* Some schools have decided that if students are to participate in a music program, they *must* enroll in the class during one semester. For example, big football schools may require fall participation in marching band. The second semester of participation becomes a choice for the student. At Pulaski County High School in Dublin, Virginia, where this policy was implemented, approximately 90 percent of first-semester participants opted for a second semester of band. Several key members of the band chose not to take band second semester; they did, however, agree to practice on their own, meet for after-school rehearsals, and participate in spring band performances and contests. What many had feared would be a major problem turned out to be a minor technical difficulty. Some schools have decided to give band classes offered each semester different names, for example, Marching Band in the fall and Symphonic Band in the spring.

♦ *Offer music programs as year-long single-period classes paired with another single-period class.* Another possibility is to offer the music program as a single daily period within the first or second half of a block. For example, orchestra, choir, and band might be offered during the first half of a 90-minute block all year long. The pool of students enrolled in these three courses would be offered a limited selection of other courses during the second half of the block. These courses would also be year-long. Many possibilities exist. Additional sections of band, orchestra, and chorus could be offered during the second half of the block, thus permitting students to take two different music classes. Other likely pairings would include AP courses, the performing arts, yearbook, school newspaper, athletics,[2] and foreign language classes. While these courses could run every day for half of the block, we believe that a better alternative would be to operate these year-long single-period classes every other day in 90-minute blocks. Such a plan would allow courses to extend throughout the year and would also take advantage of the benefits of extended teaching periods.

♦ *Offer six semester-long courses and two year-long courses for all students.* Another option would be to offer only six semester-long courses annually during three blocks and require all students to select two year-long single-period courses, one of which could be a music course. It is likely, however, that this option would force courses into operating within a single-period format which we would prefer to teach in a block. Again, as mentioned above, these two courses could be offered every other day in block format. Another option would be to require students to enroll in one year-long single-period course which would be paired with a seminar/activity period.[3] Again, this could be scheduled to occur every other day in blocks.

## SPECIAL EDUCATION

We see the 4/4 Semester plan as having many benefits for special education resource students and teachers. When students must focus on only four subjects for the semester, their chances for success may be greater. Some schools may wish to allow such students to enroll in just three courses per semester and reserve the fourth block for resource assistance. In schools where "inclusion" has begun, a block schedule provides several possibilities. One of the problems facing inclusion schools is the ratio of special education teachers to students. Often, a number of special education students must be "clustered" into a limited number of regular education classrooms

---

[2] Many schools in Oklahoma, Texas, and New Mexico must begin their athletic program during the school day. Offering band during the first half of the last block and athletics during the second half of the block solves two problems.

[3] We discuss the seminar activity period in great detail in Chapter 2.

because there isn't sufficient staff to co-teach in multiple classrooms during any one period. This sometimes causes difficulty in the regular education classroom. In a block-scheduled school, it is possible for the special education resource teacher to travel to two or three different classes during a block, thereby reducing the need for clustering. We also suggest that students mainstreamed into core classes such as English and mathematics be given priority for in-class assistance.

## COOPERATIVE WORK PROGRAMS

Work programs and internships are not affected adversely by the 4/4 plan; in fact, they may be facilitated. The main concern arises when the in-class aspect of the co-op program is a one-credit course with a required minimum number of work hours on the job site for which one or two additional credits are granted. What do we do then? Offer the course in the first semester and compress the work experience into a semester? Personnel running co-op programs would see this as an undesirable situation. It would also be technically possible to complete the class sessions during the first semester and extend the work experience throughout the year. Again, most personnel supervising programs suggest that the in-class experience should parallel the field work.

We offer three other options, two of which are purely scheduling twists, the third of which may enhance the connections between vocational and academic programs. Our first scheduling twist is relatively simple: offer the in-class work (for example, Marketing) during a single period all year long at the end of the students' in-school time (see Figure 3.14).

FIG. 3.14. 4/4 SEMESTER BLOCK SCHEDULE FOR COOPERATIVE
EDUCATION PROGRAMS (2 BLOCKS DAILY; 1 YEAR-LONG
COURSE; FIELD EXPERIENCE; 1 LUNCH PERIOD)

| Blocks | Fall Semester | Spring Semester |
|--------|---------------|-----------------|
| Block I<br>8:00–9:35 am | Course 1 | Course 3 |
| Block II<br>9:40–11:10 am | Course 2 | Course 4 |
| Lunch<br>11:15 am–11:50 pm | Lunch | |
| Period 5<br>11:55 am–12:40 pm | Course 5<br>(i.e., Marketing) | |
| Periods 6–8<br>12:40 pm–3:00 pm | Field Experience | |

Depending on the number of credits allocated for the field experience component (two or three), students would be able to attain seven or eight credits during the year. Our second variation, illustrated in Figure 3.15 (p. 98), offers Marketing in an alternating-day format opposite extended days of field experience. On Day 1, a student would attend Marketing class for a double period and then travel to the job-site for the remainder of the day. On Day 2, the student would leave for the field experience immediately following lunch or Block II.

FIG. 3.15. 4/4 SEMESTER BLOCK SCHEDULE FOR COOPERATIVE EDUCATION PROGRAMS (2 BLOCKS DAILY; MARKETING IN ALTERNATING BLOCKS; CO-OP SHORT DAY–LONG DAY SCHEDULE; 1 LUNCH PERIOD)

| Blocks | Fall Semester | Spring Semester |
|---|---|---|
| Block I 8:00–9:35 am | Course 1 | Course 3 |
| Block II 9:40–11:10 am | Course 2 | Course 4 |
| Lunch 11:15 am–11:50 pm | Lunch | |
| Block III 11:55 am–1:25 pm | Day 1 Marketing / Day 2 Field Experience | Day 1 Marketing / Day 2 Field Experience |
| Block IV 1:30–3:00 pm | Field Experience | |

Our third variation marries the vocational class to an academic class. For example, during Block III students could enroll in both Marketing and English 12 as year-long courses. They could be offered every day for half of a block, or preferably on alternate days for the full block (see Figure 3.16).

| FIG. 3.16. 4/4 SEMESTER BLOCK SCHEDULE FOR COOPERATIVE EDUCATION (3 BLOCKS DAILY; MARKETING AND ENGLISH 12 YEAR-LONG ON ALTERNATE DAYS; 1 LUNCH PERIOD) | | |
|---|---|---|
| Blocks | Fall Semester | Spring Semester |
| Block I 8:00–9:35 am | Course 1 | Course 5 |
| Block II 9:40–11:10 am | Course 2 | Course 6 |
| Lunch 11:15 am–11:50 pm | Lunch | |
| Block III 11:55 am–1:25 pm | Day 1 Marketing / Day 2 English 12 | Day 1 Marketing / Day 2 English 12 |
| Block IV 1:30–3:00 pm | Field Experience | |

An approach to the schedule suggested in Figure 3.16, which would enhance "tech-prep" vocational-academic connections, would be for the Marketing teacher and the English 12 teacher to team-teach a two-credit class. This could occur with two groups of students in Block III. The teachers could divide the time from 11:55 a.m. until 1:25 p.m. flexibly; all students would leave for the co-op experiences at 1:30 p.m. The English course could include technical writing and reading, as well as presentation skills directly related to the field of marketing. It also might be desirable to pair a mathematics course or science course with the vocational offering in a similar fashion such as geometry with drafting, horticulture with biology, or food services with chemistry. Because these pairings occupy a full block, they could occur during either Block I, II, or III; however, the preferred time slot would be Block III, immediately prior to the co-op experience.

## ADVANCED PLACEMENT COURSES

When schools consider the implementation of the 4/4 semester plan, one issue that must be addressed is Advanced Placement (AP) courses. Specifically, instructors, parents, and students are concerned about the schedule's potential effect on AP testing success. AP exams traditionally have been given in May; thus, if AP courses are scheduled for the fall and completed in January, how will students remember what they need to know to pass the test in May? Conversely, will students who begin taking the course in January have covered sufficient material by May to be successful? Schools implementing the 4/4 plan have addressed the issue in several different fashions. Some schools schedule AP courses for both semesters and allocate two credits, often giving the course a different name in the spring. Other schools provide review sessions in the spring in preparation for the exam for students who have completed AP courses in the fall. A third tact is to continue the course year-long in a single period or an alternate day block, offering a credit for research or independent study in the second half of the block. Because many students enroll in more than one AP course, several schools have offered two matched courses in single periods (or double periods on alternate days) all year long, similar to the approach discussed previously regarding music. Finally, several other schools have allowed students to enroll in a nine-week elective in a block followed by 27 weeks of instruction in an AP course, so that students have ample time to cover course content, yet are still enrolled in the class when the exam is administered. We believe that it may be more beneficial to enroll in the AP class for the first 27 weeks of the school year followed by nine weeks of an elective or AP review class, whichever is more appropriate for the individual student.

Given the large number of schools across the country who have adopted the 4/4 semester plan, we believe that AP exams should be administered at least twice annually, in both January and June.

(May administration always has been a problem!) We highly recommend that school systems and professional organizations lobby for this service; after all, the schools and their students are the customers!

### COMMUNITY COLLEGE DUAL-ENROLLMENT

The 4/4 semester plan, because it allows students to acquire 32 year-long credits in high school, should be a boon to dual-enrollment courses. In fact, many students would have the possibility of completing nearly a year of college credit courses if so desired. Providing these courses would be facilitated by an alteration in the school calendar. If school could begin early enough in August to allow for 90 days of instruction before the winter holidays, high school and college semesters would be more closely aligned. Much has been discussed regarding the creation of a seamless K-16 curriculum that better integrates secondary and post-secondary education. Many possibilities exist which would be facilitated by the 4/4 plan [Edwards, 1994]. One of the 4/4 plan's selling points is that it is more like a college schedule and, thus, prepares students for this transition.

## STUDENT ISSUES

### TRANSFER

One of the major issues with the implementation of the 4/4 semester plan is the question of how to accommodate transfer students. Students arriving mid-year to a 4/4 school from a six- or seven-period school must somehow be placed in the schedule. This particular issue has sometimes caused schools considering this model of scheduling to eliminate it as one of the possibilities. A discussion of the difficulties caused by transfer and several possible means for dealing with the issue follow.

All schools considering the 4/4 plan need to answer the following question: "Is the level of transfer within the school year likely to cause educational problems for students and teachers?" The main concern of school personnel is that students will be arriving throughout the year from traditionally scheduled schools and will need to be inserted into courses which have already covered twice as much content—in short, they will be behind and at a disadvantage.

In addition, these same students will have been enrolled in other classes, which, because they can only enroll in four courses, must be dropped. Also, students leaving the 4/4 school will have some difficulty merging into a more traditionally scheduled school. The following points are worth considering:

- We believe that for most schools transfer should not be a deal breaker. Transfers from high school to high school during the school year are made throughout the United States already. It is not unusual for students to arrive in a school where one or more of the courses in which they were enrolled is not offered, or where there are requirements that differ from those of their previous school. Guidance personnel already address the problems of transfer on an almost daily basis. One teacher once commented: "This schedule will work for 90 percent of our students; transfer is a guidance problem. It really doesn't affect me."

- We agree that if a school has a transience rate of 30 percent during the school year, as many urban schools do, the constant coming and going of students within this plan would be a major problem. But at what level do we scrap the idea as being unworkable? Schools with less than 5 percent movement during the year are able to deal with the issue on an individual student basis. When the rate approaches 10 percent or higher, an institutional response is necessary. Amherst County High School in Amherst, VA, created a system called the Advancement Center to deal with the problem. As part of their three-course load, each semester a teacher from each of the disciplines of science, mathematics, English, and the social sciences is assigned to the Advancement Center for one of the four blocks every day. New students arriving at the school are assigned to the Advancement Center for assessment and appropriate placement into the schedule. The Advancement Center also is used to provide extra help to currently enrolled students. Staff assignment to the Advancement Center may be appropriate for the department head as part of a reduced load, especially if traffic through the center is generally light.

+ Parents have some choice regarding whether or not they move during the school year and as to where they move if they must. We already know that mid-year transfers put students at an educational disadvantage. If moving into or out of a 4/4 semester plan exacerbates the problem, an additional disincentive to moving may dissuade parents from changing schools during the year.

+ The problems caused by transferring students differ depending on when the change occurs. Students arriving during the first semester are generally behind in courses. One strategy is to have these students drop the core classes in which they are behind, complete elective classes, and then restart core classes during the second semester. Courses with a developmental, sequential curriculum, such as mathematics and some sciences, are likely to be dropped. During the second semester, the reverse is likely true: students transferring in are ahead of those who have just begun the course. These students can easily fit into any of the classes in which they had been enrolled. Depending upon the time of enrollment, guidance personnel may decide to grant credit for some courses (based on end-of-course tests, if available), while placing students in the schedule to finish others.

+ Larger schools may be able to operate a single-period daily schedule or an alternate day block schedule parallel to the semesterized plan. Because courses within these schedules run the entire year, transfer students could be accommodated easily.

+ Finally, the question arises: "For whom should we plan the educational program of the school? The 90 percent who remain all year or the 10 percent who come and go?"

## CREDITS REQUIRED FOR GRADUATION

As is readily apparent from some simple calculations, it is technically possible for students to graduate early under this plan. The potential exists for the student to earn 8 credits per year for a total of 32 credits in a high school career.[4] With many states requiring fewer than 24 credits for graduation, it would be possible for some students to graduate in three years. In general, this is not something that we recommend; however, for specific students with clear goals, early graduation could be an option.

Because early graduation was not their objective, most schools implementing the 4/4 plan have adopted strategies to keep students productively engaged for four years of high school. One strategy has been to increase local graduation requirements. Most states permit localities to add on to minimum state graduation standards. Additional local requirements in the arts, foreign language, and business and vocational education can be added to complete student schedules. A second strategy has been to require that certain core courses be taken each year. For example, some districts have required that English 12 and Government be taken during the senior year. A third strategy is simply to use the guidance advisement process to chart appropriate sequences for students that preclude graduating early. A fourth strategy has been to encourage students to participate in dual-enrollment and/or Advanced Placement courses. This has the potential benefit of reducing the necessary semesters required for graduation from college. Orange County High School in Orange, Virginia reported a dramatic increase in students participating in dual-enrollment courses after the implementation of the 4/4 semester plan.

The early graduation option may have advantages in certain situations. Overcrowding in schools may be ameliorated to a certain degree by allowing students to graduate early. Students in co-op programs with post-graduation jobs in hand may find it advantageous. Highly academic students may wish to begin college a semester or a year early. Students with an interest in technical school training may be able to begin this track earlier. Over-aged students, who may have been retained in elementary or middle school and

---

[4] Obviously, this possibility already exists for eight-course schools.

who finally become motivated, may see the opportunity to complete high school requirements more quickly and "catch up" to their age-peers. We must be realistic in stating that there is a potential down side financially to early graduation; early graduation means reduced membership and, therefore, reduced funding in some states. Regardless, the early graduation possibility exists more in the 4/4 plan than in six- or seven-course models.

## STUDENT CHOICE

An obvious benefit of this program to students is increased course choice. Students from schools previously operating six- or seven-period schedules would now be able to complete eight courses annually.

## SCHEDULE BALANCE

One issue that must be addressed in the 4/4 semester plan is work load for students each semester. It would be unwise to schedule four core classes which require significant homework, projects, and frequent tests during the same semester. It is best to balance the two semesters evenly with regard to electives and academics: for example, two core subjects and two electives each term. Figure 3.17 (p. 106) illustrates one example of a well-balanced student schedule, which also provides possibilities for interdisciplinary connections by scheduling mathematics, science, and computer applications one semester, and American History, English, and arts and crafts the next.

We are not aware of any computer scheduling system which will accomplish the task of automatically balancing students' load by semester, although the design of such a function should not be difficult. Instead, we know of several schools where, after computer scheduling, the guidance counselors reviewed each student's load by hand and made adjustments as needed. The natural balance achieved through random assignment made a significant number of changes unnecessary. Regardless, student loads must be balanced.

| | | Semester 1 | Semester 2 |
|---|---|---|---|
| **P** | 1 | Algebra II | English 11 |
| **E** | 2 | | |
| | 3 | Chemistry | American History |
| **R** | 4 | | |
| **I** | 5 | Computer Applications | Arts and Crafts |
| **O** | 6 | | |
| **D** | 7 | Marching Band | Concert Band |
| **S** | 8 | | |

FIG. 3.17. BASIC 4/4 SEMESTER BLOCK SCHEDULE;
SAMPLE STUDENT SCHEDULE (8 COURSES)

## ATTENDANCE POLICIES

Schools adopting the 4/4 semester plan must adapt existing attendance policies to meet the new calendar by which credit is earned. For example, although we generally do not support such policies, it is not unusual to have an attendance policy which states that if a student misses 20 or more days of class, no credit may be granted. The natural translation of this policy to the 4/4 plan is to disallow credit if a student misses 10 or more class periods.

## ATHLETIC ELIGIBILITY

Similarly, in Virginia, students are required to pass five subjects "or the equivalent" to maintain their athletic eligibility. Schools implementing the 4/4 plan have decided that "the equivalent" is for students to pass three of four courses per semester. State requirements regarding eligibility differ, and policies must be adapted to fit the new schedule.

## DISCIPLINE

Our experience, and data collected by many high schools who currently operate the 4/4 semester plan, indicate that disciplinary problems decrease. However, in extreme circumstances, when a student is expelled for an extended period of time, the 4/4 plan may offer a variety of new options. Often when a student is suspended, he/she is removed for the remainder of the academic year, a circumstance which results in the student being another year behind his/her peers. In the 4/4 plan the option exists to remove the student for the remainder of the semester. School boards could still expel for the school year, but if circumstances warranted a lesser punishment, it would be available on a semester basis, and the student would be able to earn four credits during the year.

In addition to issues related to long-term suspension, school officials may need to rethink shorter suspensions. In many states, school administrative personnel are able to exclude students from school for up to 10 days without school board action. Such a punishment becomes much more severe in the 4/4 plan, because a 10-day suspension would be the equivalent of 1/9 of a course.

## TEACHER ISSUES

### PLANNING TIME

One of the major advantages of the 4/4 semester plan is that teachers generally are provided with a full 90-minute block of planning time daily. On occasion, the desire for this extended preparation period has been a major motivation on the part of teachers to adopt the plan, especially in schools where teachers previously were required to teach five of six or six of seven periods. It can be argued that movement to the new system requires additional preparation time, specifically for the design of more active learning activities appropriate for longer instructional periods and to pace courses properly.[5] In districts where elementary school teachers receive minimal planning time, a 90-minute daily preparation period for high school teachers may become a

---

[5] In Chapter 7 we discuss innovative schedules which can provide extended blocks of time for teacher planning or professional development activities.

controversial issue.

We must note, however, that not all duties (lunchroom, hall duty, etc.) may be covered by administrators; it may not be possible to protect the entire 90 minutes of planning time every day. If teachers must provide non-instructional supervision, we hope that every attempt would be made to accomplish this as part of their three-course load. Regardless, even if this is not possible, 30 minutes of assigned duty during a 90-minute block still leaves a 60 minute planning period.

## COURSE PREPARATION

Implementation of the 4/4 semester plan automatically reduces to three the highest possible number of different courses for which a teacher is responsible at any time. Considering the fact that some teachers currently have as many as six different daily preparations, this is a decided improvement. However, our recommendation is that teachers receive a maximum of two different preparations, and that during the second semester at least one of these preparations be repeated. If we have any hope that teachers will alter their teaching strategies, we must provide adequate support. With only three classes, including a maximum of two different preparations and 90 minutes of daily planning, teachers should have adequate time to prepare; therefore, it may be reasonable to expect innovation and experimentation from teachers in the 4/4 semester schedule.

## CONTRACTUAL ISSUES

It is highly likely that aspects of the 4/4 semester plan may violate union contracts in some districts. Union contracts that are overly specific regarding the definition of periods, the number of minutes of teaching time, the number of minutes of duty time, the number of courses taught per year, and so on may be in conflict with various aspects of the 4/4 Semester plan. It has been our experience, however, that this plan is beneficial to both teachers and students. Consequently, it is very possible that contract waivers can be acquired when the faculty of a school opts for its implementation.

# COST

One of the first questions that comes to school administrators' minds regarding the 4/4 semester plan is whether or not they can afford it. If students are taking more subjects, doesn't this mean that more staff will be needed? The 4/4 plan actually can be cheaper, but the answer to this question depends on the current scheduling plan in use.

If a school is currently utilizing an eight-period schedule, no change in staff costs or class size should occur if teachers continue to instruct the same number of courses (five or six). If a school changes from either a five-of-six or six-of-seven plan, an increase in either class size or staffing is to be expected. Schools changing from a five-of-seven schedule can expect a reduction in class size or, conceivably, could reduce staff, an option we would not recommend. Regardless, the cost of the plan is either in terms of increased (or decreased) numbers of students per section or increased (or decreased) numbers of staff necessary. To understand the potential costs of such a change, we have made the following computations based on a hypothetical high school with 1000 students and 60 teachers who teach a full load daily.

Figure 3.18 illustrates our calculations of the average number of students per section in our sample school, if teachers taught 5 of 6 courses.

---

FIG. 3.18.    5 OF 6 COURSES

6 courses per student x 1000 students = 6000 student-courses

5 courses per teacher x 60 teachers = 300 course sections

$$\frac{6000 \text{ student-course}}{300 \text{ course-sections}} = 20 \text{ students per course section}$$

---

We realize this is a ballpark estimate and will vary depending upon the number of students who leave to attend vocational programs, the number of low-enrollment electives, the number of high-enrollment classes (such as band), and a variety of other factors.

Our experience, however, has shown that many of these factors cancel each other out, and the estimates computed can at times be frighteningly accurate. What would happen if we change from the above situation to the 4/4 semester plan?

As can be seen by the calculations in Figure 3.19, if the number of faculty were maintained at 60, the average class size would increase by 2.2 students per section (20 to 22.2). This change in class size would be balanced against the fact that teachers were working with only three classes daily. In the example shown in Figure 3.18, teachers work with 5 classes of 20 daily for a total of 100 student contacts. In the 4/4 semester plan (Figure 3.19), each teacher works with 3 sections of 22.2 students daily for a total of 66.6 student contacts. We would argue that the relatively minor increase in section size is a reasonable trade-off for a major decrease in daily student contacts.[6] Research on class size suggests that increased achievement is attained primarily when we are able to lower class size below 15 [Glass and Smith, 1978]; we believe an increase from 20 to 22.2 would have no significant effect on achievement. The arguments for reducing class size between 30 and 15 students generally revolve around the "stress" caused by larger classes. Again, we would argue that stress will be lowered to a greater degree by fewer student contacts and fewer course preparations than it will be exacerbated by a slight increase in section size.

FIG. 3.19.    6 OF 8 COURSES (3 OF 4 EACH SEMESTER)

8 courses per student x 1000 students = 8000 student-courses
6 courses per teacher x 60 teachers = 360 course sections

$$\frac{8000 \text{ student-course}}{360 \text{ course-sections}} = \textbf{22.2 students per course section}$$

---

[6] We realize that annual student contacts increase under this plan. We believe that 66.6 students each semester (a possible 133 annually) is better than 100 students all year long.

Each of these arguments is somewhat more important when we discuss moving from schedules in which teachers teach six of seven classes to the 4/4 semester plan.

As can be seen in comparing Figures 3.19 and 3.20, section size would increase 2.8 students from 19.4 in the 6-of-7 course plan to 22.2 in the 4/4 semester plan. Still, the number of student contacts would drop dramatically from 116.4 (19.4 x 6 classes) to 66.6 (22.2 x 3 classes).

---

FIG. 3.20.   6 OF 7 COURSES

7 courses per student x 1000 students = 7000 student-courses
6 courses per teacher x 60 teachers = 360 course sections

$$\frac{7000 \text{ student-course}}{360 \text{ course-sections}} = \textbf{19.4 students per course section}$$

---

When changing from a school schedule in which teachers instruct five of seven courses to teaching three of four, the opposite effect occurs. As is illustrated in Figure 3.21, this change would result in a decrease in section size from 23.3 to 22.2 in the 4/4 semester plan (Figure 3.19). Student contacts would drop from 116.5 to 66.6. Class size is reduced because teachers are teaching more minutes in a 6 of 8 plan (75 percent) than a 5 of 7 plan (71 percent).

---

FIG. 3.21.   5 OF 7 COURSES

7 courses per student x 1000 students = 7000 student-courses
5 courses per teacher x 60 teachers = 300 course sections

$$\frac{7000 \text{ student-course}}{300 \text{ course-sections}} = \textbf{23.3 students per course section}$$

---

It is possible to move to the 4/4 plan from 5-of-6 courses or 6-of-7 course plans without raising class size; however, such a change would involve adding staff. Figure 3.22 computes the number of additional staff required to move from a situation in which teachers instruct five of six courses to the 4/4 plan, in which teachers instruct six of eight courses, without increasing class size.

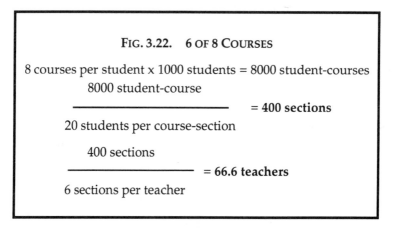

FIG. 3.22.    6 OF 8 COURSES

8 courses per student x 1000 students = 8000 student-courses

$$\frac{8000 \text{ student-course}}{20 \text{ students per course-section}} = \textbf{400 sections}$$

$$\frac{400 \text{ sections}}{6 \text{ sections per teacher}} = \textbf{66.6 teachers}$$

As can be seen, an additional 6.6 staff positions (an 11 percent increase) would be necessary to maintain class size at a constant 20. A move to the 4/4 from 6-of-7 without adding students to each section would necessitate an increase of 8.8 faculty members (14 percent) to maintain class size at the 19.4 used in the example. Conversely, 2.8 fewer staff members (a decrease of 5 percent) would be necessary when moving to the 4/4 plan from a 5-of-7 schedule.

One fiscally interesting aspect of this plan relates to the attempts many six-period schools have made to add an additional instructional period for the dual purposes of increasing student choice and teacher planning time. Often, the move to a 5-of-7 plan is rejected by school boards because of its cost. For schools moving from 5-of-6, the 6-of-8 plan is less expensive to implement than the 5-of-7 plan. To maintain 20 students per section in a 5-of-7 plan from a 5-of-6 plan requires a 16 percent increase in either staff or class size per section; to maintain 20 students per section in the 6-of-8 plan requires an 11 percent increase in either staff or class size per section.

# CONCLUSION

In this chapter we have presented a detailed description of the 4/4 semester plan, or what some refer to as an accelerated high school schedule. This model appears to be growing in popularity in high schools throughout the United States. In its basic format, the school day is divided into four instructional blocks of approximately 90 minutes each, and the school year is divided into two semesters. Students normally take four classes that in traditionally scheduled schools would continue for 180 school days, but in the 4/4 semester plan, because of the longer class periods, classes are compacted into 90 days or one semester. The plan gives the student opportunities to complete eight credits each school year for a total of 32 credits during four years of high school. As a rule, teachers teach three classes each semester for a total of six classes annually.

The 4/4 semester plan offers numerous benefits to both teachers and students. Major benefits for teachers include a reduction in the number of class preparations as well as a reduction in the number of students and class records for which a teacher must be responsible during any one semester.

Major benefits for students include the provision of opportunities for students to (1) repeat "failed" courses and still graduate on time, which may encourage some students to stay in school longer; (2) be accelerated in a subject or subjects when appropriate; and (3) focus on fewer classes at any one time.

Despite the many advantages of the 4/4 semester plan for both teachers and students, several scheduling issues are left unaddressed. For example, students in the 4/4 semester plan still must fail before they can gain extended learning time. We begin to explore this important concern and several other scheduling matters in Chapters 4 and 5.

# 4

# MORE INTENSIVE SCHEDULING: QUARTER-ON/QUARTER-OFF, TRIMESTER, AND SINGLE-COURSE PLANS

Several additional scheduling issues are left unaddressed by the alternate day and semester plans which were discussed in Chapters 2 and 3.

♦ It is a well-known educational axiom that some students need more time than others to master the knowledge and skills necessary to pass courses, yet the traditional system requires the student to experience failure before additional learning time and opportunities are granted. The only options for most students who experience failure are to attend summer school, to repeat a course during the following academic year, or, in the 4/4 plan, to repeat courses during the second or following semesters. Some teachers may choose to offer additional assistance before or after school or during planning and lunch periods, but a systematic plan is rarely implemented to address this issue. In short, historically, schools have not had an institutional plan to provide for students who demonstrate degrees of failure or degrees of success.

♦ In contrast, while some students need more time to master concepts and skills, other students need less time than we currently provide and should be able to progress at an accelerated pace. Is there a structured manner in which we might exempt such students from unnecessary repetition and provide enrichment activities to them instead? Is there a schedule which would allow some students to accelerate in certain subjects?

♦ Many districts and states are beginning to suggest community service as part of course or graduation requirements; however, students who are involved in their studies, extra-curricular activities, and after-school employment may find difficulty in meeting these new requirements.

♦ Some states and districts are considering a requirement for all seniors to produce a portfolio or demonstration product which represents their achievements in high school. When will this work be prepared and presented?

♦ Single-period, alternate day, and semester plan schedules do not offer students the possibility of concentrating for an extended length of time in a single area of interest.

♦ If "variety is the spice of life", then why do we persist in running the same schedule every day (or every other day) without a break in routine? There is a mind-numbing sameness to each day in the school year. Why not provide a break in this routine?

Arguments can be made for giving both teachers and students selected periods of concentrated time for focused study and/or activities. For example, highly academic students will participate in some vocational classes if they can attend those classes along with their peers for relatively short, concentrated periods of time such as two to six weeks. Such focused periods of time also provide teachers and students needed opportunities for field activities, job shadowing, and independent study.

In this chapter and in Chapter 5, we offer scheduling plans built around the concept that each school day represents a separate unit of time that can be grouped in various configurations and/or terms. This conceptualization enables schedulers to extend possibilities for varying the school day and school year for both students and teachers. Such thinking also makes it possible to schedule in accordance with what we know about teaching and learning. For example, we know that some students need more time to learn certain concepts or materials than do other students; we know that some instructional strategies fit some time frames better than do other strategies; and we know that in order to accomplish some tasks well, varying time periods are needed during different learning stages: for example, less time may be required for introduction or explanation and more time for application.

In Chapters 4 and 5, we discuss high school schedules which are built around the 180-day school calendar used by most districts in the United States today, but we recombine these days in configurations to form various teaching and learning blocks or instructional terms. Each of these schedules can offer possibilities and challenges.

The Quarter-On/Quarter-Off plan illustrates the potential of offering concentrated instructional time that may be spent in clusters of related classes such as English, social science, foreign language, and art or music. The model allows an interdisciplinary team to work together with one group of students for the first 45 days of a semester and with another group of students for the remaining 45 days of the semester. During the second semester, the pattern is repeated. It is possible within this plan for students who need additional learning time to spend three or even four semesters mastering the concepts and skills of a subject.

The Trimester plan (60–60–60) permits even more focused time on fewer subjects than the Quarter-On/Quarter-Off plan. Currently, the trimester plan appears to be most acceptable in high schools strongly supporting Tech-Prep programs and in high schools with alternative programs; however, modifications of the trimester plan seem to be gaining attention in schools that are attempting to build schedules that vary the amount of learning time for students.

The Intensive Single Course Schedule plan has been implemented in selected private schools throughout the country, especially preparatory schools which serve students who typically had not done well in traditionally organized high schools. One variation of this plan, the Copernican Plan, was developed and reported by Joseph M. Carroll [1990, 1994a, 1994b] and will be discussed in this chapter.

# THE QUARTER-ON/QUARTER-OFF PLAN

One adaptation of the 4/4 semester plan is illustrated in Figure 4.1. In this model, students enroll in four courses which meet in double periods for 45 days. During that time, students may complete the equivalent of the first semester of each course. During the second quarter students may enroll in four different courses and complete the first half of each of these courses. During each of these quarters it is preferred that students be assigned classes which are common to a particular cluster. For example, English, social studies, art, and music classes might form a cluster for one quarter. During the following quarter students might be enrolled in a science, mathematics, health/physical education, and technology cluster. In the third quarter students continue and/or complete classes 1 through 4, and in the fourth quarter they complete courses 5 through 8.

| | | Semester 1 | | Semester 2 | |
|---|---|---|---|---|---|
| | | **FIG. 4.1. "QUARTER-ON/QUARTER-OFF" BLOCK SCHEDULE (8 COURSES)** | | | |
| | | Quarter 1 | Quarter 2 | Quarter 3 | Quarter 4 |
| P | 1 | Course 1 | Course 5 | Course 1 | Course 5 |
| | 2 | | | | |
| E | 3 | Course 2 | Course 6 | Course 2 | Course 6 |
| R | 4 | | | | |
| I | 5 | Course 3 | Course 7 | Course 3 | Course 7 |
| O | 6 | | | | |
| D | 7 | Course 4 | Course 8 | Course 4 | Course 8 |
| | 8 | | | | |

To most readers, this plan may seem to have few advantages; however, it does address several issues. Schools considering the use of the semester plan often express concern regarding the fact that when students complete a fall course, for example, mathematics, they generally do not enroll in another mathematics course until the fall or possibly the spring of the next school year. Thus, students potentially could have a year's hiatus from mathematics instruction. Although we attempt to refute this argument in Chapter 3, it is often argued that the loss of learning from such an extended lay-off would require an enormous amount of review. By dividing semester classes into quarters, as illustrated in Figure 4.1, we spread the instruction, and thereby address this criticism to some degree.

More important, the "Quarter-On/Quarter-Off" plan creates a realistic structure to provide more time for learning for some students. In the 4/4 semester plan students have the opportunity to repeat failed courses during the school year, but they still must "fail" to be permitted more time for learning.

In the "Quarter-On/Quarter-Off" plan, students may be allowed more time to learn material without having to fail a course. For example, a student might enroll in Algebra I as Course 1 (Figure 4.1) during the first quarter. If the student were progressing well, during the second quarter he or she would begin a new class, Course 5. During the third quarter the student would complete the Algebra class and, in the fourth quarter, Course 5 would be finished. However, if, at the end of the first quarter, our hypothetical student were having difficulty in Algebra, rather than beginning Course 5, during the second quarter the student could be scheduled for either specific remedial assistance or to repeat the first quarter of Algebra I. The instructor of this repeated course would solidify the concepts already taught in the first quarter and perhaps give the student a head start on the second half of the course. This student then would rejoin his or her peers during the third quarter and, hopefully, complete Algebra I with the same group with whom he or she began the course.

Other students may need more than three quarters to complete Algebra I successfully. For example, if at the end of the third quarter concepts had not yet been mastered, the fourth quarter could be used to provide additional time. Thus, most students would complete the course in the standard amount of time—two quarters of double-period blocks; some students, however, might require three quarters for completion, and a few might need four quarters or more of double-period blocks to master the objectives of the course. The goal would be to provide extended learning time for those students needing it without requiring them to FAIL, and at the same time allow those students not needing additional time to continue on to other instructional opportunities.

Several issues arise regarding the "Quarter-On/Quarter-Off" plan:

◆ Because students have the possibility of attaining eight credits annually, for a total of 32 credits during the high school years, extra time can be provided for several courses without forcing students to spend extra years in high school.

◆ If students complete the requirements of a course in three quarters, a half-credit elective or study period would need to be provided for the fourth quarter. Scheduled time in the Resource or Advancement Center working in an individually selected software package for these students would be one possibility (See Chapter 3 for more details regarding the Advancement Center.).

◆ It might be possible for a few students to complete courses in one quarter of double-period blocks. If these students were scheduled into fairly heterogeneous sections of the class, much of their work and learning would need to be completed independently because some students in the class would be progressing at a slower rate. Again, these accelerated students might be assigned time in the Advancement Center or Computer Lab to assist them in completing their goals. Another possibility would be to "track" special sections of a class and allocate only one quarter for the completion of the course. Allowing students to complete courses in fewer hours than their classmates dovetails well with the notion of "compacting" curriculum espoused by educators of gifted education (Reis & Renzulli, 1992), but flies in the face of current seat-time course hour requirements mandated in many states. Also, a waiver may be required from state accrediting agencies to allow the granting of credit to students who complete requirements in fewer hours than required. Credit allocation could be based upon the successful completion of end-of-course examinations.

♦ Significant consideration must be given to the redesign of curriculum in the Quarter-On/Quarter-Off system. How should half of a course be designed? What topics should be grouped together? How much review is necessary prior to beginning the second half of a course? Are there specific sequences which must be avoided or followed?

♦ Such a system may be supportive of the concepts espoused by the accelerated schools movement [Levin and Hopfenberg, 1991]. Exposing children to the entire curriculum and then returning with additional time during the academic year to re-teach specific deficits could help some students maintain grade-level progress.

## TRIMESTER MODEL

The trimester model, as illustrated in Figure 4.2, offers students the opportunity to focus on two related core classes for an intensive period of instruction. In this model, students enroll in two classes every 60 days. One class meets in the morning, and then, after a lunch period, the second class meets in the afternoon.

| FIG. 4.2. TRIMESTER PLAN (6 COURSES) | | | |
|---|---|---|---|
| | Trimester 1 60 Days | Trimester 2 60 Days | Trimester 3 60 Days |
| Morning Trimester Course | Course 1 | Course 3 | Course 5 |
| Lunch | Lunch | | |
| Afternoon Trimester Course | Course 2 | Course 4 | Course 6 |

Murray High, an alternative public school in Albermarle County, Virginia, employs a trimester schedule similar to the one shown in Figure 4.2. This school serves a population of approximately 100 students with a staff of one principal, a guidance counselor, seven teachers, and a secretary. Students judged to be "at risk" are recommended for application to the school, but they may not be forced to attend. Many of the courses offered are multidisciplinary. For example, during a trimester, students might enroll in a two-credit class entitled "Ready, Set, Go!"—a combination of English and vocational studies. The two teachers instructing the course plan and work together; students might attend the English component of the class in the morning, which relates communication skills to the workplace, and then spend the afternoon developing vocational skills. Students become involved in "job-shadowing" and other outside activities as part of these courses. One day a week is usually allocated for these out-of-school-building activities, and teachers use some of this day for planning their instructional units. Another creative multidisciplinary course offered at the school is "Investigations in Mathematics and Science." Students from all grade levels may enroll in this course for two credits at a time. Thus, a ninth grade student might be taking Earth Science and Algebra while an eleventh grade student is enrolled for Chemistry and Algebra II. A focus for discussions and activities across disciplines is assisted by organizing the classes around designated themes. For example, the theme of "Motion" could be applied to any of the sciences. Projects and consultations and tutoring sessions with the teachers are also a part of the course.

Seventh or eighth courses can be added easily to this schedule as singletons that run all year long; such a plan could be beneficial for such courses as band, chorus, or orchestra, where teachers may prefer to meet throughout the entire school year (see Figure 4.3). These courses could be placed after lunch, prior to the morning trimester course, or at the end of the day.

| FIG. 4.3. TRIMESTER PLAN (7 COURSES) | | | |
|---|---|---|---|
| | Trimester 1 60 Days | Trimester 2 60 Days | Trimester 3 60 Days |
| Morning Trimester Course | Course 1 | Course 3 | Course 5 |
| Year-long Course | Course 7 | | |
| Lunch | Lunch | | |
| Afternoon Trimester Course | Course 2 | Course 4 | Course 6 |

Some schools have considered the trimester schedule as a means to facilitate the implementation of academic-technical programs [Bottoms, Presson, and Johnson, 1992]. In the trimester schedule, students focus on two full-credit, related academic and technical courses during each 60-day period. These core courses would be supported by reduced-credit exploratory courses which reinforce and enrich the concepts developed in the core classes. For example, during one trimester a student might enroll in electronics and applied physics for the academic-technical core. Many aspects of the supporting exploratory music class, such as wave theory and electronic music, would be practical and/or artistic applications of the core classes of both applied physics and electronics. Other related core and exploratory courses that could be taken concurrently include the following: drafting and geometry with architectural history as an exploratory, biology and health sciences with physical fitness as an exploratory, and chemistry and food services with marketing as the exploratory (see Figure 4.4, p. 124).

| Fig. 4.4. Tech-Prep Trimester Plan (7 Courses) | | | |
|---|---|---|---|
| | Trimester 1 60 Days | Trimester 2 60 Days | Trimester 3 60 Days |
| Morning Trimester Course | Course 1 Electronics 150 Minutes | Course 3 English/ Communications 150 Minutes | Course 5 Financial Studies 150 Minutes |
| | Break 10 Minutes | | |
| Year-long Courses | Music 80 Minutes | Art 80 Minutes | Cultures 80 Minutes |
| Lunch | Lunch 30 Minutes | | |
| Afternoon Trimester Course | Course 2 Applied Physics 150 Minutes | Course 4 Graphics 150 Minutes | Course 6 Languages 150 Minutes |

Many of the concerns expressed regarding the 4/4 Semester plan are similar for Trimester plans. The trimester schedules previously presented have been adapted for specialized schools (i.e., an alternative school and a vocational technical school). In a more traditional setting, however, how could one accommodate a course such as band, which must continue year-long? One school we have worked with has created a mix of year-long courses and trimester block courses. Basic core courses such as English, mathematics, science, and social science are taken in the trimester format; many electives continue in shorter daily periods for the entire year. It would be advisable to pair the two year-long courses together with lunch periods, as shown in Figure 4.5.

| FIG. 4.5. TRIMESTER PLAN (8 COURSES) | | | |
|---|---|---|---|
| | Trimester 1 60 Days | Trimester 2 60 Days | Trimester 3 60 Days |
| Trimester Course 140 Minutes | Course 1 | Course 3 | Course 5 |
| 5 Minutes | Class Change | | |
| Lunch 25 Minutes | Lunch | | |
| Year-long Course 50 Minutes | Course 7 | | |
| 5 Minutes | Class Change | | |
| Year-long Course 50 Minutes | Course 8 | | |
| 5 Minutes | Class Change | | |
| Trimester Course 140 Minutes | Course 2 | Course 4 | Course 6 |

## TRIMESTER SCHEDULE WITH TWO EXTENDED LEARNING TIME (ELT) PERIODS[1]

In Figure 4.6, another modification of the Trimester Plan is shown. Here, students take two classes for 120 minutes each day for 60 days, then another two classes for 60 days, and then end the year with two classes, for a total of six core and elective classes.

---

[1] Parry McCluer High School in Buena Vista, Virginia.

| | 60 Days | 60 Days | 60 Days |
|---|---|---|---|
| FIG. 4.6. TRIMESTER PLAN EXTENDED CLASSES FOR ENHANCED LEARNING | | | |
| Block I 8:17–10:17 | Course 1 | Course 3 | Course 5 |
| 10:17–10:27 | Break | | |
| Block II 10:27–12:27 | Course 2 | Course 4 | Course 6 |
| 12:27–12:53 | Lunch | | |
| Block II ELT 12:53–1:38 | Course 2 Extended Learning Time | Course 4 Extended Learning Time | Course 6 Extended Learning Time |
| Block I ELT 1:41–2:26 | Course 1 Extended Learning Time | Course 3 Extended Learning Time | Course 5 Extended Learning Time |
| 2:26–3:15 | Professional Planning and Student Activities | | |

After lunch, two 45-minute extended learning periods are provided. It is with the extended learning periods that this Virginia public school attempts to address the dicey problem of allowing more or less time for students to learn. At the beginning of each trimester, all students are scheduled for both morning and afternoon sessions of the two courses; thus, a total of two hours and 45 minutes is available for instruction in each class. As the trimester progresses and it becomes obvious to the teacher that certain students do not need the additional learning time, these students are permitted to stop attending the extended learning sessions and to contract with other instructors to complete independent study work for credit. Extended learning time periods also are used to provide year-long rehearsal time for performing groups on a weekly basis.

If a plan allows more time for some students, it may be necessary to rethink the grading system. Students not completing courses in the standard time frame cannot summarily be given the grade of "F." For students who have been unable to master course objectives before the end of the instructional term, it may be more appropriate to award the grade of "Incomplete" ("I")[2] or a new grade we suggest, "Exposed" ("E").

We would advocate awarding the grade of "I" under the following conditions:

♦ The student has completed at least 50 to 75 percent of course requirements.

♦ The student for some reason, such as excessive absences, missing assignments, and/or insufficient mastery of course content, has not yet earned a passing grade,

♦ The student has demonstrated a level of achievement to suggest that unmastered course objectives or assignments could be completed in a reasonable amount of time, for example, two weeks of daily assistance in an "extended learning period."

Students receiving the "I" grade would be scheduled to remove it during the next available instructional term. Students may be able to complete sufficient additional study in the Advancement Center (Chapter 3) to be able to meet course requirements and earn a passing grade and credit. Credit would not be granted until the "I" was removed and a passing grade attained.

The "Exposed" grade might be awarded to students under somewhat different circumstances:

♦ The student attended classes on a regular basis, put forth effort, attempted at least 75 percent of the work assigned, participated in class activities, and, in various ways, demonstrated that he/she gained *some knowledge*, and thereby was not deserving of the grade "F."

♦ The student for various reasons was unable to achieve a passing letter grade.

---

[2] We sometimes refer to this grade as "NY", "Not Yet"!

♦ The student's deficits were beyond the level that one could reasonably expect to be remediated in a continuation section offered during an extended learning period, through the Advancement Center, or during a short instructional term (see Chapter 5); thus, the "I" or "NY" grade would be inappropriate.

Students receiving a grade of "E" would not be permitted to enroll in the next sequential course until they had successfully completed the course in which the "E" was received. In addition, the "E" would not be computed into the student's grade point average. The student, however, would be granted "credit" for the course, and the course would apply toward graduation requirements. Students who later decided to progress to the next sequential course would be required to remove the "E." This could be accomplished by repeating the course during summer school, the next academic year, or short instructional term. Upon completion, a regular grade would be earned, the "E" would be removed from the transcript, and the student would be permitted to enroll in the next sequential course.

By awarding the grades of "I" or "E" we attempt to give students and teachers a greater range of grading and credit-granting options. We have found teachers more likely to make allowances for differences in student learning if a system is in place to assist them; however, if each individual teacher is expected to provide for those differences, fewer individual accommodations will be made. We believe that we should make students responsible for performance as long as possible; occasionally, this practice may require delaying the awarding of a final grade, which says to the student: "The door is closed; you had your chance!" **Punitive grading will quickly erase the benefits that might accrue from a scheduling system designed to provide more time to learn for those who need it!**

A second possible variation for some students would be to substitute a limited set of one-third-credit electives for each of the 45-minute extended learning periods. Students, counselors, and parents could decide whether students should spend the full two hours and 45 minutes in each core course or spend the minimum two hours and enroll in electives.

## INTENSIVE SCHEDULING

Finally, we know a preparatory school in Virginia at which students enroll in only one core course every 45 days. (See Figure 4.7 for a similar schedule.)

| FIG. 4.7. SINGLE COURSE PLAN (4 CORE COURSES) | | | | |
|---|---|---|---|---|
| | Quarter 1 45 Days | Quarter 2 45 Days | Quarter 3 45 Days | Quarter 4 45 Days |
| Morning Core Session | English | History | Science | Mathematics |
| Year-long Course | Foreign Language, Arts. or Music | | | |
| Lunch | Lunch | | | |
| Year-long Course | Foreign Language, Arts, or Music | | | |
| Afternoon Core Session | English | History | Science | Mathematics |

Foreign language, the arts, and music courses are year-long courses. This form of schedule, known as "intensive scheduling," provides concentrated study in one core course at a time.

Similarly, a middle school in Colorado created a block schedule for their Intensive Core Program (ICP). In this plan, students only participated in one core subject every 4-1/2 weeks; thus, students attended English, social science, science, and mathematics on a rotating 4-1/2-week schedule each semester. Operating in an eight-period schedule (one period was lunch), students spent two morning blocked periods in core, two afternoon blocked periods in core, and three periods in electives. Teachers, students, and parents were enthusiastic about the program. Student grades were reported as being significantly higher within a tighter range, and although some detractors had predicted a fall in achievement testing because some core subjects were completed far in advance of the testing date, no significant differences were found between ICP and non-ICP students [Alam & Seick, 1994].

Intensive scheduling was also a prime component in the "Copernican Plan" developed by Joseph Carroll [1990, 1994a, 1994b].

## THE COPERNICAN PLAN

Carroll [1994a] reports that the Copernican Plan has fundamentally altered the way high schools utilize time. All versions of the plan utilize the concept of "macroscheduling" [Carroll, 1990], the functional equivalent to the term "intensive scheduling" mentioned above. For example, classes may be taught in varying periods of time but almost always longer than the traditional 40-to-60-minute class periods. Typically, classes in the Copernican Plan are scheduled in blocks of time of 90 minutes, two or four hours per day, and for only part of the school year, such as 30, 45, 60, or 90 days per class. Students in the plan are "enrolled in significantly fewer classes each day, and teachers deal with significantly fewer classes and students each day" [Carroll, 1994a, p. 106]. Schedules reviewed in *The Copernican Plan Evaluated: Evolution of a Revolution* [Carroll, 1994b] included many of those discussed in this book: trimester plans, semester plans, a quarter-plan, single-core course plans, and an alternate day plan. Carroll contends that the Copernican Plan creates a classroom environment which fosters improved relationships between teachers and students and more manageable workloads for both teachers and students. "In theory," Carroll states, "the outcome should be schools that are more successful" [1994a, p. 106]. According to Carroll, the Copernican Plan projects the following specific advantages:

> Virtually every high school in this nation can decrease its average class size by 20 percent; increase its course offerings or number of sections by 20 percent; reduce the total number of students with whom a teacher works each day by 60 to 80 percent; provide students with regularly scheduled seminars dealing with complex issues; establish a flexible, productive instructional environment that allows

effective mastery learning as well as other practices recommended by research; get students to master 25 to 30 percent more information in addition to what they learn in the seminars; and do all of this within approximately present levels of funding. [Carroll, 1994a, p. 106]

Carroll's original idea envisioned a variety of learning situations during the school day—macro-classes, which meet two hours daily for 60 days or four hours daily for 30 days; and year-long courses such as music, physical education, study/help sessions, and seminars, which would meet on alternate days throughout the year for approximately 70 minutes in two blocks [Carroll, 1990]. In Figure 4.8 (p. 132) we have adapted one version of the Copernican Plan to fit a 420-minute school day. Students enroll in two macroclasses which meet for two hours daily each trimester. In addition, students participate in two other instructional blocks. During one of these blocks, physical education and an issues-related seminar alternate every other day for 60 minutes. The second 60-minute block includes a music class, perhaps, and a help/study session, also alternating every other day.

In 1994 Carroll reported extensively on the results of eight high schools operating varying versions of the Copernican Plan. The following are several of the findings of these evaluations:

- ◆ Six of eight schools reported improved student attendance.
- ◆ Four of six schools reported that student suspension data experienced a decrease.
- ◆ Seven of eight schools reported reductions in the dropout rate.
- ◆ Seven of eight schools reported greater content mastery as measured by student grades.
- ◆ All eight schools reported greater mastery of content as measured by the number of credits earned per student.
- ◆ In the 33 comparisons made between traditional and Copernican programs, 27 favored Copernican Plans, five favored traditional plans, and one showed no change [Carroll, 1994b].

| FIG. 4.8. COPERNICAN PLAN (ADAPTED FROM CARROLL, 1990, P. 361) | | |
|---|---|---|
| | 60 Days | 60 Days | 60 Days |
| Block I 7:30–9:30 | Course 1 | Course 3 | Course 5 |
| 9:30–9:40 | Break | | |
| Block II 9:40–11:40 | Course 2 | Course 4 | Course 6 |
| 11:46–12:46 | Seminar/Music/PE | Lunch 1 |
| | | Seminar/Music/PE |
| 12:52–1:24 | Lunch 2 | |
| 1:30–2:30 | Help/Study/PE/Music | |

## CONCLUSION

In Chapters 2 through 4, schedules were presented that divide the 180-day school year into large blocks of time such as semesters, quarters, and trimesters. In general, students enroll in fewer courses per day or per term in each of these models. While we believe, and a growing body of research reveals, that these models offer improved possibilities for teaching and learning, we could not logically state that they constitute "flexible" schedules. Chapter 5 begins to examine new possibilities for flexibility as we move beyond the narrow conceptualization of an instructional term as only semesters, trimesters, or quarters. In Chapter 5 we explore the concept of the short (less than 30 days) instructional term, and we mix and match school terms of differing lengths to create a new breed of school calendar.

# 5

# INSTRUCTIONAL TERMS WITHIN THE 180-DAY SCHOOL YEAR

The purpose of this chapter is to discuss the application of the concept of the short instructional term, which may occur either as a break in the schedule in the *middle* of courses, *or* as a break in the schedule *after the completion* of a series of courses—for example, a "May Term" at the end of the year or a "Winter Term" inserted between the two semesters of a 4/4 semester plan. For the duration of these short terms the daily course schedule is suspended, yet students still attend school and participate in a variety of activities. In this chapter, special instructional terms can be as short as one day or as long as 30.[1] Such breaks have long been part of college schedules and are often part of the schedule of independent preparatory schools and military academies.

Short terms designed for specific instructional purposes can be utilized regardless of the basic scheduling plan adopted by a high school. A short term can be created for schools operating standard 6-, 7-, or 8-period daily schedules. The routine of an alternate day format may be broken by offering a short term for specialized needs. Even within the 4/4 semester plan it is possible

---

[1] Certainly, this break could be longer than 30 days, but we could hardly call it a "short instructional term" if it were.

to consider the use of an instructional term between semesters or, perhaps more appropriately, as a term within a semester. It is also possible to place a short term at the end of the academic year, such as the 75–75–(30) schedule discussed by us previously and more fully developed in this chapter [Canady and Rettig, 1993].

What are the best uses of short terms in a high school schedule? How does such scheduling help both students and teachers? What differing purposes do terms scheduled during the middle of courses and terms scheduled at the end of courses serve? What are the problems and challenges caused by these terms? How long should instructional terms be? Are they worth the scheduling effort? In each section we shall discuss the purpose of the proposed instructional term, the logic behind its placement within an overall school schedule and calendar, and the benefits we believe can be achieved by utilizing this particular scheduling concept.

## SHORT TERMS SCHEDULED IN THE MIDDLE OF COURSES

We see three main purposes for scheduling short instructional terms *prior* to the completion of courses:

+ The term(s) can provide an educational and psychological break in the mind-numbing sameness of the school routine.

+ The term(s) can provide more time for instruction and learning **for those students who need it** *before* courses have been completed.

+ The term can provide enrichment activities for *all* students, especially those who need less time to learn core instructional material.

As previously mentioned, such terms can be inserted into any schedule; we begin with an illustration utilizing a seven-period alternate day block schedule as a basis.

### ALTERNATE DAY BLOCK SCHEDULE WITH A 30-DAY MIDDLE TERM

In the schedule illustrated in Figure 5.1, we insert a 30-day middle term half-way into the school year within an alternate day block schedule. This schedule would be nearly identical if we positioned

| | | Term I 75 Days | | Middle Term 30 Days | Term II 75 Days | |
|---|---|---|---|---|---|---|
| | Blocks and Times | Day 1 A | Day 2 B | Full or Half Day Schedules* | Day 1 A | Day 2 B |
| **P E R I O D** | Block I & HR 8:00– 9:52 am | 1 | 2 | Remedial and enrichment activities, field trips, | 1 | 2 |
| | | 1 | 2 | | 1 | 2 |
| | Block II 9:58– 11:42 am | 3 | 4 | community service, full and half-credit electives. | 3 | 4 |
| | | 3 | 4 | | 3 | 4 |
| | Lunch 11:48 am– 12:18 pm | LUNCH | | | | |
| | Period 5 12:18– 1:10 pm | 5 | 5 | Remedial and enrichment activities, field trips, | 5 | 5 |
| | Block III 1:16– 3:00 pm | 7 | 6 | community service, full and half-credit electives. | 7 | 6 |
| | | 7 | 6 | | 7 | 6 |

**FIG. 5.1. ALTERNATE DAY BLOCK SCHEDULE BUILT FOR 7 COURSES WITH 30-DAY MIDDLE TERM**

*Of the 420 minutes available during each day of the middle term we allocate 30 for lunch, 60 for a study and activity period, and 330 minutes for instruction.

the middle term in a seven-period, every day plan.

Students in this schedule, built on a school day having 420 minutes, would be enrolled in seven courses. Six of the seven courses would meet every other day in double periods for approximately 104 minutes. The seventh course, scheduled into period 5, would meet daily for 52 minutes. We allow 30 minutes for lunch and six minutes for class changes. After 75 days students would take mid-term examinations, and students and faculty, in most school districts, would break for the December holidays. One obvious benefit of this plan would be the completion of mid-term examinations and the first semester prior to the traditional holiday vacation. Upon the return of the students in January, the regular schedule would be suspended and the 30-day term would be conducted. We foresee a variety of exciting activities occurring during this specially designed instructional mid-term block of time. At the end of the 30-day middle term, students would resume their full load of courses and complete the regular school year on the alternate day plan.

## DISCUSSION

Educators have long been aware of the axiom that time is a major variable in the learning process [Carroll, 1963]. Little has been done, however, to create a flexible system to provide students with either more or less time to learn as is indicated by their individual needs. We briefly discussed this issue in Chapter 4 in relation to the possible uses of the Quarter-On/Quarter-Off plan and the Trimester plan to allow variable learning time. We see the use of short instructional terms as providing even more flexible possibilities for meeting this goal. First, we provide some background.

The allocation of credit by Carnegie Units, based upon a fixed amount of seat-time per credit hour, is a prime example of how we have largely ignored the issue of individual needs for learning time. Although the Carnegie Unit has come under attack in recent years, and states and schools have begun to struggle with the possibilities of "achievement-based" graduation standards, the structures available to students who need more or less time to learn remain largely unchanged. The only structured means for gaining more time for instruction and learning is to **FAIL** a course and retake it in the summer or during the next academic year or term. We find it ironic that students must fail to get more time to learn. Even then, in most schools today the **schedule** requires that students retake an entire course, not just master previously unaccomplished objectives.

The problem in providing additional time for learning is mostly a scheduling concern. How is it possible to provide extra time and instruction for some students and not others without failing students? We could go beyond the bounds of the standard school day and year and offer students extra assistance before and after school, during vacations, or at the end of the school year; however, most students would see these "opportunities" as being punitive. We believe that a mechanism must be devised to permit differential amounts of time for learning during the current school year and day. We also recognize that students having difficulty learning are not a homogeneous group. Some need more additional time than others; however, designing a flexible scheduling system to meet *individualized* needs regarding the time required for learning is nearly impossible.[2]

We believe that a reasonable step toward a fluid system designed to meet instructional needs is the institution of specially designated terms of instruction built into the school schedule. After a fixed period of regular course instruction, we suggest that schools regroup students based upon their progress within individual courses. Those who are struggling would be provided additional time and instruction during a special school term. Students who have mastered concepts would be allowed to participate in a variety of enrichment activities, or they may be accelerated by taking other courses which have been altered or designed to be taught within the new concentrated time blocks. We recommend that all students, to some extent, would spend time during the special terms involved in enrichment. We would not want to fill any student's special term exclusively with remedial activities. What we basically are suggesting is that high school schedules **be designed around students' instructional needs and that the schedules developed accommodate**

---

[2] Although, through the use of technology, it is certainly possible to tailor learning plans for individual students, most schools still do not have the required hardware and software to implement such systems.

**differing degrees of success and failure.**

Carnegie Unit supporters might argue that the creation of special terms within the school schedule would reduce the minutes available to instruct the core material required for any one course below an acceptable level. On a mathematical level this is obviously true. For example, if we were to insert a 30-day term into the alternate day block schedule illustrated in Figure 5.1, the number of minutes allocated to a block course is reduced from 9360 to 7800 (104 minutes x 90 days vs. 104 minutes x 75 days). However, it is our contention throughout this chapter that not all students need the full 9360 minutes to master course material. We also argue that some students need more than 9360 minutes. During the mid-year term, an additional 9900 minutes (330 minutes x 30 days) would be available for additional instruction in a course for students needing more time. It is therefore conceptually possible that a student might receive 17,700 minutes of instruction (7800 minutes + 9900 minutes) in the course in question. Thus, the maximum and minimum amount of instructional time provided students would be 17,700 minutes and 7800 minutes, respectively. We find it highly unlikely that a large number of students would require the upper limit in terms of instructional minutes. We find it more probable that students might receive assistance in several subjects during 10-, 15-, or 30-day instructional terms as well as participate in several enrichment courses or activities. Again, we point out the need to build schedules based on the instructional needs of students!

For students not requiring any remedial assistance the possibilities for using the instructional terms are virtually endless. A block of time consisting of 9900 minutes is more than enough time to allow for a full-credit course or two half-credit electives, which would allow students in this schedule to accrue eight credits per year. A small sample of the many possibilities follows:

♦   Students in need of additional work in any one of their courses could be scheduled for remedial sessions.

♦   Students desiring more in-depth work in any one of their subjects could enroll in a special projects course.

♦   Depending upon the length of the term, students could complete either one full-credit course or two half-credit courses.

- Students could complete community service requirements or projects without interrupting their academic programs.

- Field trips of extended duration would be possible; in Virginia, for example, biology teachers could spend a number of days with students studying marine life in the Chesapeake Bay.

- Limited English Proficiency students could be given intense English language immersion.

- Resource special education students could be provided intense tutorial assistance during the short term, which might make an increased level of mainstreaming possible during the regular school sessions. Conversely, students could be mainstreamed into certain short-term courses that match their abilities and interests. Because they would be able to concentrate on only one course during the term, successful completion of the course might be more possible.

- Students interested in working on the yearbook, literary magazine, or drama production would have a concentrated amount of time to devote exclusively to these activities.

- A team consisting of, for example, drama, art, and music teachers could work all day with a group of 60 to 80 students and produce a musical.

- Students could participate in a long research project related to one or more of their regular courses.

- Certain courses could be offered for students who need to be accelerated. For example, an entire history course could be offered during the 30-day term.

- AP-prep or SAT-prep courses could be offered.

- In some states a minimum number of attendance days is required for course credit to be earned, even if a student has achieved mastery of course content. If students were absent because of illness or other reasons during the regular term, part of the short term could be utilized to attain this minimum attendance requirement.

♦   Instructional terms built into the 180-day school calendar provide excellent opportunities for internships, especially work experiences associated with many of the Tech Prep programs. If a student wants a concentrated work experience with an auto mechanic or carpenter, he/she could be scheduled full time with such a person for the specific instructional term. With such a schedule the student does not have to have his/her work experience fragmented with other school activities, a situation that typically occurs in most schedules today.

## THE 4/4 SEMESTER PLAN WITH FIVE-DAY MIDDLE TERMS

It is equally possible to place a modified instructional term within a semester of the 4/4 plan. In this model students would attend four classes for 90 minutes daily for 42 or 43 days. At this point the regular daily schedule would be suspended, and a five-day instructional term would be conducted. Similar kinds of activities, **both enrichment and remedial,** could be offered as previously described. At the close of the five-day term, students and teachers would return to the regular schedule for 42 or 43 days until the end of the semester.

One common criticism of the 4/4 semester plan is that too few minutes are allocated per course. The schedule presented in Figure 5.2 further reduces the instructional minutes available per course (8100 minutes without the short term; 7650 minutes with the five-day short term). In Figure 5.3 (p. 142) we adapt the schedule in Figure 5.2 to include only six long-term courses, which could be scheduled for longer blocks, resulting in 10,200 minutes per course (85 days x 120 minutes). Given this increased amount of instructional time, it would be possible and perhaps advisable to either lengthen the short terms to 10 days or to provide additional short terms at the end of each semester, which will be discussed later in this chapter.

| FIG. 5.2. ALTERNATE SEMESTER BLOCK SCHEDULE (4 BLOCKS DAILY; 8 COURSES ANNUALLY; 1 LUNCH PERIOD; 5 DAY MIDDLE TERMS) | | | | | | |
|---|---|---|---|---|---|---|
| Blocks | Fall Semester | | | Spring Semester | | |
| | 42 Days | 5 Days | 43 Days | 42 Days | 5 Days | 43 Days |
| Block I and HR 8:00– 9:35 am | Course 1 | M i d d l e | Course 1 con't | Course 5 | M i d d l e | Course 5 con't |
| Block II 9:40– 11:10 am | Course 2 | T e r m | Course 2 con't | Course 6 | T e r m | Course 6 con't |
| Lunch 11:15 am– 11:50 pm | Lunch | | | | | |
| Block III 11:55 am– 1:25 pm | Course 3 | M i d d l e | Course 3 con't | Course 7 | M i d d l e | Course 7 con't |
| Block IV 1:30– 3:00 pm | Course 4 | T e r m | Course 4 con't | Course 8 | T e r m | Course 8 con't |

| Blocks | Fall Semester | | | Spring Semester | | |
|---|---|---|---|---|---|---|
| | 42 Days | 5 Days | 43 Days | 42 Days | 5 Days | 43 Days |
| Block I 8:00– 10:05 am | Course 1 | M i d d l e | Course 1 con't | Course 4 | M i d d l e | Course 4 con't |
| Block II 10:10 am– 12:10 pm | Course 2 | | Course 2 con't | Course 5 | | Course 5 con't |
| Lunch 12:15– 12:50 pm | Lunch | | | | | |
| Block III 12:55– 3:00 pm | Course 3 | T e r m | Course 3 con't | Course 6 | T e r m | Course 6 con't |

FIG. 5.3. ALTERNATE SEMESTER BLOCK SCHEDULE
(3 BLOCKS DAILY; 6 COURSES ANNUALLY; 1 LUNCH PERIOD; 5 DAY MIDDLE TERMS)

# SHORT TERMS SCHEDULED AFTER THE COMPLETION OF COURSES

When short instructional terms are placed *after* courses have been completed, they can serve slightly different purposes. Such terms still provide an educational and psychological break in the school routine as well as offer the possibility for enrichment activities for all students. They differ from short terms placed in the middle of a course because *most* students have now completed courses. Two points need to be made regarding such instructional terms.

First, because courses are finished, we believe students who have not completed the objectives of the course and need more time to learn should receive a grade. We suggest, as we have previously in Chapter 4, that students who did little or no work and demonstrated little or no mastery of content receive the traditional "F" or "NC"—no credit; that those students who exerted effort, demonstrated limited mastery of material, but who are so far behind as to require repetition of the course to be eligible for the next sequential class be given an "E" for "Exposed"; and that students whose mastery of objectives can be completed during the short term be awarded an "I" for "Incomplete" or an "NY" for "Not Yet." In very short terms of five or ten days, only students receiving an "I" or "NY" would be able to finish their unmastered objectives and thereby complete a course. Students earning "F"s or "NC"s would be required to retake the entire course. Students receiving an "E", who desired to take the next sequential course in the subject, would also be required to repeat the class. Course repetition could be accomplished in a second semester of the 4/4 semester plan, during summer school, or during a short term of 30 days.

Second, because courses are completed, it is now possible to use short terms for acceleration in sequential subjects. In a 15-day term, a half-credit elective could be completed; similarly, a 30-day term would provide enough time for a full-credit course. In the example illustrated in Figure 5.1, the 30-day middle term comes at the mid-point of courses. A student enrolled in French I would be halfway through the course when the middle term began; it would be unwise to enroll in French II for the middle term, prior to the completion of French I. However, in the 75–75–(30) plan shown in Figure 5.4 (pp. 144–145), if the student had completed French I in either of the 75-day terms, it would be possible to enroll for French II during the 30-day Spring Term at the end of the school year.

FIG. 5.4. THE 75–75–(30) PLAN

| Grade 9 | Fall Term—75 Days | | | | | | | Winter Term—75 Days | | | | | | | Spring Term—30 Days |
|---|---|---|---|---|---|---|---|---|---|---|---|---|---|---|---|
| **Periods** | 1 | 2 | 3 | 4 | 5/L | 6 | 7 | 1 | 2 | 3 | 4 | 5/L | 6 | 7 | Course possibilities during Spring Term: |
| Eng. A | 1 | 1 | 2 | 2 | X | A | P | 6 | 6 | 7 | 7 | X | A | P | Accelerate in a discipline such as mathematics, repeat a failed course, enroll in two half-credit electives, enroll in one full-credit elective, do internships, or provide community service. |
| Eng. B | 3 | 3 | 4 | 4 | X | 5 | P | 9 | 9 | 8 | 8 | X | 5 | P | |
| M/Alg C | 2 | 2 | P | A | X | 1 | 1 | 7 | 7 | A | P | X | 6 | 6 | |
| M/Alg D | 4 | 4 | P | 5 | X | 3 | 3 | 8 | 8 | 5 | P | X | 9 | 9 | |
| PE | P | A | 1 | 1 | X | 2 | 2 | P | A | 9 | 9 | X | 7 | 7 | |
| PE | P | 5 | 3 | 3 | X | 4 | 4 | P | 5 | 6 | 6 | X | 8 | 8 | |
| Elective | | | | | X | | | 1 | 3 | | | X | | | |
| Elective | | | | | X | | 5 | 3 | 1 | | | X | | 5 | |

FIG. 5.4. THE 75–75–(30) PLAN (CONT'D)

| Periods | 1 | 2 | 3 | 4 | 5/L | 6 | 7 | 1 | 2 | 3 | 4 | 5/L | 6 | 7 |
|---|---|---|---|---|---|---|---|---|---|---|---|---|---|---|
| Sc E | A | 6 | 6 | 7 | X | 7 | P | A | P | 1 | 1 | X | 2 | 2 |
| Sc F | 5 | 8 | 8 | 9 | X | 9 | P | 5 | P | 3 | 3 | X | 4 | 4 |
| SS G | 7 | 7 | A | P | X | 6 | 6 | 2 | 2 | | A | X | 1 | 1 |
| SS H | 9 | 9 | 5 | P | X | 8 | 8 | 4 | 4 | 5 | 5 | X | 3 | 3 |
| Elective | 6 | | 7 | 6 | X | | 7 | | | 2 | 2 | X | | |
| Elective | 8 | | 9 | 8 | X | | 9 | | | 4 | 4 | X | | |

**Key**

P   Plan time for teachers.

A   The teacher assists students who need help with homework, test make-up, etc. This duty can be rotated among teachers.

*Notes:*   The schedule includes three 112-minute blocks of time, a 48-minute singleton, a 24-minute lunch, and 12 minutes passing time for a total of 420 minutes.

5/L—This 76-minute block includes a 48-minute period for cross-grade, year-long classes or activities, such as: band, chorus, keyboarding, clubs, school newspaper, and yearbook; a 24-minute lunch period, and 4 minutes passing time. The lunch period can occur either before or after the singleton. The 5/L block could be placed after second period if the day begins late.

230 ninth grade students were divided into two groups of 115 with an average of 25–26 in each group. Group 5 continues classes year-long; it accommodates transfer students and should enroll no likely repeaters.

## THE 75–75–(30) PLAN[3]

Many students have difficulty making the transition from middle school to high school. Districts report high rates of failure for ninth grade students [Bradley, 1992; Austin Independent Schools, 1987]. We have observed that many ninth grade students have trouble preparing for six or seven different classes each day. Such problems prompted the invention of the following schedule, which addresses the particular needs of adolescents entering high school, but the plan could be adapted for students at other grade levels as well. It provides an example of a schedule in which a short term is placed at the end of the school year.

The school year is divided into three blocks of time—two 75-day terms (Fall and Winter) and a 30-day Spring Term. During each 75-day term the school day includes three 112-minute block classes, one 48-minute period (which remains constant for 180 days), 24 minutes for lunch, and 12 minutes for class changes, for a total of 420 minutes (see Figure 5.4). During each of the 75-day terms, students enroll in two academic subjects and one of the following: physical education, one full-credit elective, or two half-credit electives. Each academic class is offered in double periods daily. In addition, students may enroll in one singleton class which meets for 48 minutes daily the entire school year (see the 5/L period in Figure 5.4). For schools not having the resources to fund what is the equivalent of a seven-period schedule, this singleton could be eliminated. To facilitate the offering of classes that are more appropriately scheduled year-long, one of the three 112-minute block courses could be divided into two 54-minute year-long singletons with 4 minutes passing time between. If the school day must be shorter, block classes could be reduced in length.

For example, in the fall a student assigned to instructional Group 1 attends English for periods 1 and 2, physical education for periods 3 and 4, lunch and a singleton class such as band during the 5/L

---

[3] This section of Chapter 5 is based upon our recent *Phi Delta Kappan* article [Canady and Rettig, 1993].

period, and M/Algebra for periods 6 and 7.[4] During the Winter Term, the same Group 1 student participates in two 75-day electives for periods 1 and 2, science for periods 3 and 4, lunch and the year-long singleton in the 5/L period, and social science for periods 6 and 7.

During the 5/L period, three 25-minute lunch periods can be scheduled as well as two overlapping 48-minute single periods which meet daily all year. For example, some students could have lunch and then attend a year-long 48-minute class, such as band, chorus, yearbook, newspaper, or leadership seminar. Another group of students could meet for a 48-minute class and have lunch at the end of the 78-minute block. If necessary, a third lunch could be scheduled in the middle of period 5/L.

Students not enrolled in a singleton class during the 5/L period may be involved in seminars, clubs, service activities, or independent study assignments. This flex time could be designed to provide individual students an opportunity to return to designated teachers for additional work, based on identified student needs for remediation, acceleration, or enrichment. For example, on a rotating basis certain teachers from the various departments or instructional clusters—such as mathematics, English, science, music, performing arts, and social sciences—would be assigned to work with students during one of the 48-minute single periods. To give this block the structure needed for disciplinary purposes in most high schools today, we suggest that these individual assignments for both students and teachers be rotated on specific time cycles. A cycle could be based on weeks, months, or a designated number of days. We recommend a 10-day cycle or multiple 10-day cycles be used in scheduling these assignments.

For other students not enrolled in a class during this midday block and who do not need extended learning time, a set of seminars could be planned around current topics. In some cases members of the community might be seminar leaders—for example, an oncologist or a team of doctors in town might conduct a 10-day seminar on the relationship between smoking and lung cancer. The

---

[4] It is not necessary for instructional Group 1 to remain together for the entire school day, as is implied by our system of notation; they may be regrouped with other students in each block and each term.

medical team might show x-rays of cancerous lung tissue and/or offer the latest research on genetic engineering and how such study may lead to a cure for certain types of cancer. Other seminars might be led by teachers or guidance personnel on such topics as "Divorce and the American Home," "Jobs of the Future that Require a Strong Knowledge Base in Electronics" (or Mathematics, Science, Spanish, or English), "Getting into the College We Want," and "Obtaining a Job After High School Graduation."

Still other sessions might be planned, organized, and conducted by various students, possibly under the supervision of a teacher sponsor. We recommend that all the above seminars be planned, scheduled, and posted at least two cycles (20 days) before they are to begin. We also suggest that students register for a chosen seminar at least one cycle (10 days) in advance of starting date so proper monitoring of student activities can occur as well as adequate space and materials provided for each activity.

We understand the complexity of the scheduling suggestions presented in this model. Scheduling the 5/L block in the manner described above requires constant seminar development and schedule alterations. We recommend that all high schools adopting flexible scheduling plans employ a technical expert; this person need not be a certificated school person.

Each block class taught during the 75-day term provides 8400 minutes of instruction; 112 minutes per day for 75 days is approximately 180 46-minute class periods. A single-period elective meets for 4050 minutes (54 minutes per day for 75 days) and counts for one half of a unit.

In addition to the courses taken during the two 75-day terms, one full-credit course could be taken during the Spring Term, meeting for 8400 minutes (the equivalent of five 56-minute periods for 30 days). Two half-credit electives also could be taken during the Spring Term. In addition, students continue to participate in a sixth, year-long singleton course. The "seventh period" available during the 30-day term serves as a preparation time for teachers and allows for research, study, or early release for students; it is rotated throughout the day, occurring at different times for different groups of teachers and students.

## DISCUSSION

One way to understand the possibilities of the 75–75–(30) plan is to work through several "What ifs?"

What if a student wanted to accelerate in mathematics? The student could be assigned to instructional group 1, 2, 3, or 4 (Figure 5.4) in the fall to complete one course, and then be reassigned to either group 6, 7, or 8 in the winter to complete the next course in sequence. Students scheduled for mathematics in the Winter Term could move ahead by completing the next course during the Spring Term.

What if a student who took English in the Fall Term failed the class? This student could be assigned to repeat the subject in a new section of the course offered during the Winter Term; this class would be in lieu of an elective. The Winter Term schedule shows that four new sections of English and four new sections of M/Algebra are planned for instructional Groups 6, 7, 8, and 9. We suggest that any math or English repeaters be divided among the available sections in the Winter, so as not to create sections of all "repeaters." In addition, we recommend that fewer students be scheduled for mathematics and English in the Winter Term than in the Fall Term to accommodate additional repeaters. A conscious effort should be made during the scheduling process to assign students at risk of failing either mathematics or English to Fall Term sections. Students repeating classes could make up missed electives or a failed science or social studies course during the 30-day Spring Term.

What if a student transferred from a school that operated in a traditional six- or seven-period day? Transfer students could be assigned to instructional group 5, which follows a standard seven-period schedule. The number of sections constructed in this fashion would be adjusted based on the school's recent statistical history of incoming transfer students. A different approach to the transfer problem might be to create an Instructional Resource Center, possibly funded through Chapter I, and staffed by an English/social science teacher and a math/science teacher and supported by appropriate computer hardware and software. The center could assess incoming and departing students' strengths and weaknesses, ease transitions into and out of the school, and provide tutorial aid to all students experiencing academic difficulty (See the "Advancement Center" discussed in Chapter 3).

Additional benefits of the 75–75–(30) plan, beyond those mentioned in the alternate day and semester plans, follow:

♦ *The benefits of "Summer School" can be offered to all students at no additional cost to the students or the school district.* Many school districts require students to pay for tuition and transportation to summer school. Consequently, many low-income students, who often need to attend summer school, cannot. This plan provides the equivalent of a "summer session" as part of the regular school calendar, during which time students can accelerate in a discipline, repeat a failed class, enroll in an elective, participate in a curriculum-related field trip, or provide community service. Because the session is within the time frame of standard teachers' contracts, no major additional expenses are incurred by the district.

♦ *Increased possibilities for acceleration and continuity are provided during the regular school year.* Students conceivably can complete three consecutive courses in one calendar year; for example, three sequential math classes could be taken, one each "term."

♦ *Students have more opportunities to repeat a failed course during the regular school year.* In traditionally scheduled high schools, students must wait until summer or the beginning of the next school year to repeat a failed class. During the second term, many students who realize that it is mathematically impossible to pass a course stop working and become behavior problems. While the 4/4 semester plan allows students to repeat failed courses during the second semester, the 75–75–(30) plan permits two possibilities for repeating courses during the regular school calendar: during the Winter Term and during the end-of-the-year Spring Term.

We are convinced that the grading and promotional practices employed by many teachers and schools constitute an impediment to the progress of some students; however, these practices persist. The 75–75–(30) model offers opportunities for the timely progress of students who have failed a class. We are concerned, however, that "built-in" opportunities for students to repeat courses during the school year may result in teachers feeling that less harm will come to the failing student, thus producing more course failures. We urge administrators and teachers to use the flexibility of these schedules to give students opportunities to strengthen their skills and knowledge base so that, ultimately, they may attain a higher degree of academic success in high school, and not as a conscience-easing excuse to fail more students [Canady and Hotchkiss, 1989].

♦ Students would have the opportunity to complete community service projects during the Spring Term without interrupting their regular academic and extracurricular schedules.

♦ Students could immerse themselves totally in a course for a 30-day period. Many intense foreign language instructional programs designed for executives operate in this fashion. A student might enroll in a geology course and spend much of the instructional time in the field learning from first-hand observation. A student in the academic track could enroll in a 30-day auto mechanics course and learn how to maintain his/her car, as well as how its operation is related to a companion physics course. Limited English Proficiency (LEP) students could be given an intense period of English instruction. The possibilities for instructional use of this "end term" are endless.

♦ The Spring Term would provide a break in the routine of school. It provides a fresh start at a time of the year when it is often difficult to get students to concentrate on subjects they have been taking all year long.

♦ Because all teachers would not be needed to teach during the 30-day Spring Term, it would be possible to free groups of faculty for staff development, curriculum development, or research activities. This could be accomplished on a rotating basis over several years, with departments or interdisciplinary teams taking turns instructing or being free for other activities during the

Spring Term (see Chapter 7 for a detailed discussion of this possibility).

### ADAPTATIONS

The 75–75–(30) model was designed for an actual high school in which many ninth grade students were failing English and/or mathematics. To provide greater opportunities for at-risk students to complete these courses, the English and mathematics classes were paired together to make it possible to offer three opportunities during the regular school year for students to complete a course. Consequently, all students scheduled within this model take English and mathematics together in one term, and social science and science together in the other term. Our preference, however, is to pair mathematics with science in one term and English with the social sciences in another.

Another option, which may be advantageous to schools that offer traditional summer school opportunities for remediation and acceleration, is to place the Spring Term between the two terms, forming a 75–(30)–75 calendar. Such an arrangement offers the advantage of providing students with an earlier opportunity to retake a failed course and regain the pace of their classmates. It also offers a mid-year change of pace, which may be more advantageous than placing the term at the end of the school year.

The 4/4 semester plan schedule also can be adapted to include a short instructional term at the end of each semester. The plan illustrated in Figure 5.5 illustrates a semester schedule operating on a 75–(15)–75–(15) calendar. In this model, students may complete three courses in the first 75 days, participate in remedial activities, enrichment activities, and/or partial courses during the first 15-day short term, complete three additional courses during the second 75-day term, and participate in a second 15-day short term to end the school year.

One-credit courses could be completed if they included both of the two separate 15-day end terms. We recommend that a course, such as journalism, be divided into two concentrated, curriculum-distinct terms. The focus of the first 15-day term of a journalism class could be on editorial and feature writing, and the second term of the course could deal with basic reporting. Students during this time could go to a police station, court room, or hospital and write reports based on "live" actions and observations. Such a plan will undoubtedly prove more practical for courses with less sequential parts.

| | | | | |
|---|---|---|---|---|
| **FIG. 5.5. SEMESTER BLOCK 75–(15)–75–(15) SCHEDULE** **(3 BLOCKS DAILY; 6 OR 7 COURSES ANNUALLY; 1 LUNCH PERIOD;** **15-DAY END TERMS)** | | | | |
| Blocks | Fall Semester | | Spring Semester | |
| | 75 Days | 15 Days | 75 Days | 15 Days |
| Block I and HR 8:00– 10:05 am | Course 1 | End Term | Course 4 | End Term |
| Block II 10:10 am– 12:10 pm | Course 2 | | Course 5 | |
| Lunch 12:15– 12:55 pm | Lunch | | | |
| Block III 1:00– 3:00 pm | Course 3 | | Course 6 | |

# SCHEDULES THAT PROVIDE SHORT TERMS BOTH DURING AND AFTER THE COMPLETION OF COURSES

One weakness of plans that provide short terms *after* courses have been completed is that the instructional time comes too late to be used for mid-course assistance. Conversely, only offering middle terms, which occur *before* courses have been finished and graded, does not help students who may receive incompletes and the plan also removes the possibility of utilizing the short term of instruction for the purpose of acceleration. We suggest that it may be advisable to design a schedule that offers both types of short terms.

## SEMESTER BLOCK SCHEDULE WITH MIDDLE TERMS AND END TERMS

To accomplish this goal, we include a 30-day summer school for some teachers and students to create a semester-style [35–(5)–35]–(30)–[35–(5)–35]–(30) calendar in Figure 5.6, which includes two five-day middle terms for mid-course remediation and enrichment, and two 30-day end terms that offer possibilities for acceleration, the erasure of incompletes, and course repeating.

The middle terms scheduled during each 70-day semester would be used for mid-course assistance and enrichment activities. Courses would end after the 75 days, and acceleration would be possible during the 30-day Winter Term. Students also could be given opportunities to erase incompletes and participate in many of the other activities we have suggested previously. The 30-day Summer Term offers the same options for those who choose to attend. This schedule makes summer school an integral part of the school year.

Semester-block courses would meet for 70 two-hour sessions or a minimum of 8400 minutes; students needing additional time could attend for the full five-day middle term (5 days x 330 minutes) for an additional 1650 minutes, bringing the upper limit of minutes per course to 10,050 minutes per credit. Again, we would not recommend that any student spend an entire middle term involved in remedial work for one class. Winter and Summer Term courses would provide 9900 minutes (30 days x 330 minutes). Schools unable to offer the 30-day Summer Term could adapt this scheduling idea by shortening both the Winter and Summer Terms to 15 days each, creating a [35–(5)–35]–(15)–[35–(5)–35]–(15) plan, and thereby completing the schedule within the traditional 180-day school year.

FIG. 5.6. SEMESTER BLOCK SCHEDULE [35–(5)–35]–(30)–[35–(5)–35]–(30) PLAN
(3 BLOCKS DAILY; 6, 7, OR 8 COURSES ANNUALLY; 1 LUNCH PERIOD;
TWO 5-DAY MIDDLE TERMS; ONE 30-DAY END TERM; ONE 30-DAY SUMMER SCHOOL)

| Blocks | Fall Semester | | | Winter Term | Spring Semester | | | Summer Term |
|---|---|---|---|---|---|---|---|---|
| | 35 Days | 5 Days | 35 Days | 30 Days | 35 Days | 5 Days | 35 Days | 30 Days |
| Block I and HR 8:00–10:05 am | Course 1 | M i d d l e | Course 1 con't | W i n t e r | Course 4 | M i d d l e | Course 4 con't | S u m m e r |
| Block II 10:10 am–12:10 pm | Course 2 | | Course 2 con't | | Course 5 | | Course 5 con't | |
| Lunch 12:15–12:55 pm | Lunch | | | | | | | |
| Block III 1:00–3:00 pm | Course 3 | T e r m | Course 3 con't | T e r m | Course 6 | T e r m | Course 6 con't | T e r m |

## ALTERNATE DAY BLOCK SCHEDULE WITH A MIDDLE TERM AND AN END TERM

If the primary goal of the schedule in an alternate day plan school were to provide students with variable amounts of learning time depending on individual need, a three-week block of time could be placed at the end of each 75-day term to create a 75–(15)–75–(15) schedule (see Figure 5.7). Such an arrangement would provide 15 days during courses for mid-course assistance and 15 days at the end of the year for those who had not completed a course or courses successfully. Students who received an "Incomplete" (I) or "Not Yet" (NY) would have an opportunity to receive reteaching and retesting. Enrichment activities, community service projects, and half-credit courses would be available to other students during these time periods.

In addition to its instructional advantages, the 75–(15)–75–(15) adaptation provides an opportunity to discuss teacher contracts of variable form and duration. If we were to think of the school year in this fashion, but add a 30-day Summer Term as well (i.e., 75–(15)–75–(15)-(30)), interesting possibilities come about for teachers completing the 180-day teaching year. A teacher operating on a standard contract might negotiate to teach both 75-day terms and both 15-day terms and finish the school year as usual. Another instructor, who has been dying to take a three-week, mid-winter cruise or ski trip, could teach a 75-day term, vacation during the following 15-day term, return refreshed for the second 75-day term, participate in professional study or vacation again for the second 15-day term, and complete his or her contract by teaching the summer session of 30 days. If the teacher preferred to teach only the two 75-day terms, he/she could be placed on a 5/6 contract (150 of 180 days). Another instructor might teach all terms, including the 30-day summer session, and receive a 7/6 contract (210/180 days). To stay in contact with the schools and their colleagues, retired teachers or faculty on child care leave might opt to teach only one 15-day term and receive compensation equal to 1/12 of a salary.

| FIG. 5.7. ALTERNATE DAY BLOCK SCHEDULE BUILT FOR 7, 8, OR 9 COURSES WITH A 15-DAY MIDDLE TERM AND A 15-DAY END TERM; 75–(15)–75–(15) PLAN | | | | | | |
|---|---|---|---|---|---|---|
| | | Fall Term 75 Days | | Middle Term 15 Days | Spring Term 75 Days | | End Term 15 Days |
| | Blocks and Times | Day 1 A | Day 2 B | Full or Half Day Schedules* | Day 1 A | Day 2 B | Full or Half Day Schedules |
| P E R I O D | Block I & HR 8:00– 9:52 am | 1 — 1 | 2 — 2 | Remedial and enrichment activities, field trips, community service, full and half-credit electives. | 1 — 1 | 2 — 2 | Remedial and enrichment activities, field trips, community service, full and half-credit electives. |
| | Block II 9:58– 11:42 am | 3 — 3 | 4 — 4 | | 3 — 3 | 4 — 4 | |
| | Lunch 11:45 am– 12:15 pm | L U N C H | | | | | |
| | Period 5 12:18– 1:10 pm | 5 | 5 | Remedial and enrichment activities, field trips, community service, full and half-credit electives. | 5 | 5 | Remedial and enrichment activities, field trips, community service, full and half-credit electives. |
| | Block III 1:16– 3:00 pm | 7 — 7 | 6 — 6 | | 7 — 7 | 6 — 6 | |

* Of the 420 minutes available during each day of the middle and end terms, we allocate 30 for lunch, 60 for a study and activity period, and 330 minutes for instruction.

## CONCLUSION

No high authority mandates that the 180-day school calendar be divided into 90-day semesters and that all courses be offered in a rigid daily period format. We can design schedules that offer new possibilities for meeting students' needs. The instructional implications of building short terms into the master school schedule can be significant in terms of dealing with the diversity in many schools today. There are endless variations of this idea that could be implemented by a school, or by only a cluster of teachers: for example, the ninth grade or an interdisciplinary team. The use of short instructional terms is just one of many innovations that can help schools use the schedule as a catalyst for instructional improvement. In the following chapter we discuss "hybrid" models, which combine various aspects of the different school schedules already presented into new and different, and sometimes strange, forms.

# 6

# BLENDING SCHEDULING MODELS

It is our contention that teachers, administrators, students, parents, and community members should identify critical issues in their particular school which possibly could be addressed by modifying the schedule *before considering scheduling options.*[1] Then, and only then, should changes in the school schedule be contemplated. Again, we stress that no one schedule is perfect or suitable for every school. In this chapter we mix and blend the various models of high school schedules being implemented throughout America. Our first combination plans apply the alternate day concept to the 4/4 semester plan, the trimester plan, and then to the 72–72–(36) plan to create instructional blocks of at least three hours, possibly for the purpose of facilitating interdisciplinary instruction.

## ADDING THE ALTERNATE DAY TWIST TO THE 4/4 SEMESTER PLAN AND OTHER INTENSIVE SCHEDULES

The schedule shown in Figure 6.1 creates a 4/4 semester plan in an alternate day format. Students take four courses each semester; however, classes meet every other day for approximately three hours

---

[1] We have developed a matrix of potential goals and scheduling models which may be useful as schools evaluate various scheduling formats (see Appendix A).

so that students attend only two classes daily.

| FIG. 6.1. ALTERNATE SEMESTER/ALTERNATE DAY BLOCK SCHEDULE (2 BLOCKS DAILY; 8 COURSES ANNUALLY; 1 LUNCH PERIOD) | | | | |
|---|---|---|---|---|
| Blocks | Fall Semester | | Spring Semester | |
| Day | Day 1 | Day 2 | Day 1 | Day 2 |
| Block I and HR 8:00-11:10 am | Course 1 | Course 2 | Course 5 | Course 6 |
| Lunch 11:15 am-11:55 pm | Lunch | | | |
| Block II 12:00 am-3:00 pm | Course 3 | Course 4 | Course 7 | Course 8 |

This plan might be useful if a school wanted to emphasize interdisciplinary connections. For example, students might enroll in English for Course 1 and history for Course 3; thus, every other day students would spend the entire school day engaged in interdisciplinary activities related to these two subjects. Such an arrangement would necessitate a close working relationship between the two teachers involved and would work best if the teachers shared the same students. Another scheduling possibility would be to place the English class in the Course 1 slot and the history class in the Course 2 slot. In this schedule students would spend a half-day every day participating in interdisciplinary programming related to these classes. Again, if the teachers share the same two groups of students, they could divide the students and the time as they see fit according to the needs of their program and individual students. This schedule could be used for a select group of students, such as ninth graders, while the remainder of the school operated under a different plan.

Other beneficial course pairings would be possible in this plan. We could pair a mathematics class and a science class, an arts class with an English class for a humanities approach, or we could pair various academic courses with technical subjects to support tech-prep programming. Examples include the following: English and marketing, agriculture and biology, physics with auto mechanics, chemistry and food sciences. The extended half-day or full-day blocks of time created for two teachers and two groups of students through this plan would facilitate a variety of activities, including field trips, job shadowing, extended laboratories, and work-site visits.

Teachers in this model would teach three of four classes each semester and would have a half-day of planning every other day. It would be advantageous to schedule teachers involved in interdisciplinary classes for common planning time.

Similarly, it would be possible to add the alternate day twist to the trimester schedule described in Chapter 4. Figure 6.2 illustrates this possibility. Again, interdisciplinary courses could be offered as Courses 1 and 2, Courses 3 and 4, or Courses 5 and 6. Course 7 would be reserved for classes that would benefit from a year-long schedule.

| FIG. 6.2. ALTERNATE DAY TRIMESTER PLAN (7 COURSES) | | | | | | |
|---|---|---|---|---|---|---|
| | Trimester 1 60 Days | | Trimester 2 60 Days | | Trimester 3 60 Days | |
| | Day 1 | Day 2 | Day 1 | Day 2 | Day 1 | Day 2 |
| Morning Session 8:00–10:39 am | Course 1 | Course 2 | Course 3 | Course 4 | Course 5 | Course 6 |
| Year-long Course 10:44–11:37 am | Course 7 | | | | | |
| Lunch 11:42–12:16 pm | Lunch | | | | | |
| Afternoon Session 12:21–3:00 pm | Course 1 | Course 2 | Course 3 | Course 4 | Course 5 | Course 6 |

Following the pattern established with the alternate day 4/4 Semester plan and the alternate day trimester plan, it would be possible to create an alternate day 72–72–(36) plan, as shown in Figure 6.3. In this schedule certain courses would be offered in five periods every other day for a 72-day term (Courses 1-4), or for five periods every day for a 36-day term (Course 5), or for one period every day for the entire 180-day school year (Courses 6 and 7). Lunch could be scheduled as one of the eight daily periods, shown in Figure 6.3 as either period 4, 5, or 6. Some five-period blocks must be split by lunch, as shown during the Winter and Spring Terms. It would also be necessary to offer single-period courses throughout the entire school day. Teachers who instructed the five-period blocks would teach only two classes, one every other day. Again, this may be a good idea for ninth grade teachers and students, who would see fewer of each other both daily and each term. Teachers instructing single-period classes would have five different groups.

Many of the same advantages are realized in this schedule as in the alternate day 4/4 semester plan. Different interdisciplinary possibilities exist; paired courses could be offered in the Course 1 and 2 slots or the Course 3 and 4 slots; however, this schedule offers the additional advantage of year-long courses for such subjects as band, orchestra, chorus, keyboarding, and beginning foreign languages in the Course 6 and 7 spots. Course 6 or 7 also could be utilized as a resource period for special education students or any other student having difficulty with core courses 1 through 4, thus providing extended learning time for those who need it. In any of the models we have discussed previously, single-period, year-long classes provide a convenient time for resource assistance and extra help. In addition, intense study in a single area is possible during the Spring Term, Course 5 time.

## FIG. 6.3. 72–72–(36) ALTERNATE DAY BLOCK SCHEDULE

| Periods | Fall Term (72 Days) | | Winter Term (72 Days) | | Spring Term (36 Days) |
|---|---|---|---|---|---|
| | Day 1 | Day 2 | Day 1 | Day 2 | Everyday |
| 1 8:00– 8:49 am | Course 1 | Course 2 | Course 3 | Course 4 | Course 5 |
| 2 8:53– 9:42 am | Course 1 | Course 2 | Course 3 | Course 4 | Course 5 |
| 3 9:46– 10:35 am | Course 1 | Course 2 | Course 3 | Course 4 | Course 5 |
| 4L 10:39– 11:28 am | Course 1 | Course 2 | Lunch | Lunch | Course 5 |
| 5L 11:32– 12:21 pm | Course 1 | Course 2 | Course 3 | Course 4 | Lunch |
| 6L 12:25– 1:14 pm | Lunch | Lunch | Course 3 | Course 4 | Course 5 |
| 7 1:18– 2:07 pm | Course 6 | Course 6 | Course 6 | Course 6 | Course 6 |
| 8 2:11– 3:00 pm | Course 7 | Course 7 | Course 7 | Course 7 | Course 7 |

## EXTENDING THE SCHOOL DAY

Sometimes school must be held beyond traditional school hours, either for the convenience of working students, to meet the needs of alternative education students, or because the school building would be filled beyond capacity during normal school hours. The next several schedules illustrate possibilities for extending the school day to accommodate these needs.

In Figure 6.4 we have adapted an alternate day schedule to include late afternoon and evening classes. Two additional two-hour instructional blocks have been added to the school day. Students could attend from 8:00 a.m. to 3:00 p.m. or from 1:00 to 7:30 p.m. to earn six credits. Both students and teachers could choose the shift of their choice. Such an arrangement could alleviate overcrowding and allow students who must work to continue in school. To avoid room conflicts during Block III, which overlaps both shifts, as many teachers as possible should be scheduled for their planning period during this time.

We predict that Friday classes which do not end until 7:30 p.m. may be unpopular; therefore, Figure 6.5 (p.166) illustrates a schedule which extends afternoon and evening classes to two-and-a-half hours each session. Friday late afternoon and evening classes are eliminated by conducting sessions Monday and Wednesday or Tuesday and Thursday. All day and evening courses are allocated 10 hours of meeting time every two weeks (5 days x 2 hours or 4 days x 2.5 hours).

*(Text continues on page 167)*

| FIG. 6.4. ALTERNATE DAY BLOCK SCHEDULE EXTENDED DAY | | | | |
|---|---|---|---|---|
| Blocks and Times | M Day 1 A | T Day 2 B | W Day 1 A | R Day 2 B |
| Block I & HR 8:00–10:06 am | Course 1 | Course 2 | Course 1 | Course 2 |
| Block II 10:14 am–12:14 pm | Course 3 | Course 4 | Course 3 | Course 4 |
| Lunch 12:22–12:52 pm | L U N C H | | | |
| Block III 1:00–3:00 pm | Course 5 | Course 6 | Course 5 | Course 6 |
| Block IV 3:10–5:10 pm | Course 7 | Course 8 | Course 7 | Course 8 |
| Break 5:10–5:30 pm | Break | | | |
| Block V 5:30–7:30 pm | Course 9 | Course 10 | Course 9 | Course 10 |

## FIG. 6.5. ALTERNATE DAY BLOCK SCHEDULE EXTENDED DAY
## (NO FRIDAY AFTERNOON AND EVENING CLASSES)

| Blocks and Times | M Day 1 A | T Day 2 B | W Day 1 A | R Day 2 B | F Day 1 A* |
|---|---|---|---|---|---|
| Block I & HR 8:00–10:06 am | Course 1 | Course 2 | Course 1 | Course 2 | Course 1 |
| Block II 10:14 am– 12:14 pm | Course 3 | Course 4 | Course 3 | Course 4 | Course 3 |
| Lunch 12:22–12:52 pm | L U N C H | | | | |
| Block III 1:00–3:00 pm | Course 5 | Course 6 | Course 5 | Course 6 | Course 5 |
| Block IV 3:10–5:40 pm | Course 7 | Course 8 | Course 7 | Course 8 | No Class |
| Break 5:40–6:00 pm | Break | | | | No Class |
| Block V 6:00–8:30 pm | Course 9 | Course 10 | Course 9 | Course 10 | No Class |

* Please note that Blocks I–III operate every-other-day, so that Courses 1, 3, and 5 would be on Tuesday and Thursday during the next week. Blocks IV and V are held Monday and Wednesday or Tuesday and Thursday so that Courses 7–10 meet on the same days every week.

In Figure 6.6 (p. 168), we add four 90-minute blocks to the standard 4/4 semester plan and, in effect, create two different school days. Students and faculty could work or attend on variable schedules.

Such a schedule could assist fast-growing communities, such as Dade County, Florida, in their efforts to accommodate dramatic increases in student population while holding down construction costs for new schools. If permitted, it also would be possible for students to enroll for an overload of classes (more than four), a situation which might allow a student who needed just five credits for the completion of the diploma to graduate at the end of the semester or school year.

Again, in Figure 6.7 (p. 169), we eliminate Friday classes by extending afternoon and evening classes in Blocks V, VI, and VII to 110 minutes and eliminating Block VIII. Thus, each course receives either 450 minutes per week (5 days x 90 minutes) or 440 minutes per week (4 days x 110 minutes).

Each of the extended-day schedules described also offers a convenient opportunity to include working adults and school dropouts who may wish to complete their high school program. Evening sessions also facilitate the offering of dual-enrollment classes taught by area community colleges.

*(Text continues on page 170)*

| FIG. 6.6. ALTERNATE SEMESTER BLOCK SCHEDULE EXTENDED DAY | | |
|---|---|---|
| Blocks | Fall Semester | Spring Semester |
| Block I 7:40–9:15 am | Course 1 | Course 5 |
| Block II 9:20–10:50 am | Course 2 | Course 6 |
| Block III 10:55 am–12:25 pm | Course 3 | Course 7 |
| Lunch 12:30–1:00 pm | Lunch | |
| Block IV 1:05–2:35 pm | Course 4 | Course 8 |
| Block V 2:40–4:10 pm | Course 9 | Course 13 |
| Block VI 4:15–5:45 pm | Course 10 | Course 14 |
| Dinner Break 5:50–6:20 pm | Dinner | |
| Block VII 6:25–7:55 pm | Course 11 | Course 15 |
| Block VIII 8:00–9:30 pm | Course 12 | Course 16 |

| FIG. 6.7. ALTERNATE SEMESTER BLOCK SCHEDULE EXTENDED DAY (NO FRIDAY EVENING CLASSES) | | | | | |
|---|---|---|---|---|---|
| Blocks | Fall Semester (Spring Semester) | | | | |
| | Mon. | Tues. | Weds. | Thurs. | Fri. |
| Block I 8:00–9:35 am | Course 1 (Course 5) | | | | |
| Block II 9:40–11:10 am | Course 2 (Course 6) | | | | |
| Lunch 11:15 am–11:50 pm | Lunch | | | | |
| Block III 11:55 am–1:25 pm | Course 3 (Course 7) | | | | |
| Block IV 1:30–3:00 pm | Course 4 (Course 8) | | | | |
| Break 3:00–3:20 pm | Break | | | | |
| Block V 3:25–5:15 pm | Course 9 (Course 12) | | | No Evening Classes Friday | |
| Dinner 5:15–5:45 pm | Dinner | | | | |
| Block VI 5:45–7:35 pm | Course 10 (Course 13) | | | | |
| Block VII 7:40–9:30 pm | Course 11 (Course 14) | | | | |

# SCHEDULING THE FOUR-DAY WEEK

Because of the distance to school for many students in extremely remote areas, it may be desirable to hold school only four days each week. During the past year we have discovered school districts in Wyoming, Nebraska, Texas, and Oregon that are organized on a longer work day, but for only four days, usually Monday through Thursday. Figure 6.8 illustrates a six-period every day schedule built for a 480-minute school day. Each class meets for 70 minutes daily for a total of 280 minutes of weekly instruction, the equivalent of five 56-minute periods. We slide the six periods within the day to share the best and worst teaching and learning times.

| FIG. 6.8. FOUR-DAY SCHOOL WEEK (6 COURSES; SINGLE PERIOD SCHEDULE; 8 HOUR SCHOOL DAY; SLIDE) | | | | | | |
|---|---|---|---|---|---|---|
| | Monday | Tuesday | Wednesday | Thursday | Monday | Tuesday |
| 8:00–9:10 am | Course 1 | Course 2 | Course 3 | Course 4 | Course 5 | Course 6 |
| 9:15–10:25 am | Course 2 | Course 3 | Course 4 | Course 5 | Course 6 | Course 1 |
| 10:30–11:40 am | Course 3 | Course 4 | Course 5 | Course 6 | Course 1 | Course 2 |
| 11:40 am–12:20 pm | Lunch | | | | | |
| 12:20–1:30 pm | Course 4 | Course 5 | Course 6 | Course 1 | Course 2 | Course 3 |
| 1:35–2:45 pm | Course 5 | Course 6 | Course 1 | Course 2 | Course 3 | Course 4 |
| 2:50–4:00 pm | Course 6 | Course 1 | Course 2 | Course 3 | Course 4 | Course 5 |

One such school in Butte Falls, Oregon, reported their alternate day, four-day week [Dismuke, 1994]. In Figure 6.9 we apply the alternate day twist with an eight-period adaptation of that schedule.

FIG. 6.9. FOUR-DAY SCHOOL WEEK (8 COURSES; ALTERNATE DAY BLOCK SCHEDULE; 8 HOUR SCHOOL DAY; SLIDE)

|  | Mon. | Tues. | Weds. | Thurs. | Mon. | Tues. | Weds. | Thurs. |
|---|---|---|---|---|---|---|---|---|
| 8:00–9:45 am | Course 1 | Course 5 | Course 2 | Course 6 | Course 3 | Course 7 | Course 4 | Course 8 |
| 9:55–11:40 am | Course 2 | Course 6 | Course 3 | Course 7 | Course 4 | Course 8 | Course 1 | Course 5 |
| 11:40 am–12:20 pm | | | | | Lunch | | | |
| 12:20–2:05 pm | Course 3 | Course 7 | Course 4 | Course 8 | Course 1 | Course 5 | Course 2 | Course 6 |
| 2:15–4:00 pm | Course 4 | Course 8 | Course 1 | Course 5 | Course 2 | Course 6 | Course 3 | Course 7 |

In Figure 6.10, we have adapted the four-day week using the 4/4 semester plan by utilizing blocks of 105 minutes within a slide schedule.

| Fig. 6.10. Four-Day School Week (8 Courses; 4/4 Semester Block Schedule; 8 Hour School Day; Slide) | | | | |
|---|---|---|---|---|
| | Mon. | Tues. | Weds. | Thurs. |
| 8:00–9:45 am | Course 1 (Course 5)* | Course 2 (Course 6) | Course 3 (Course 7) | Course 4 (Course 8) |
| 9:55–11:40 am | Course 2 (Course 6) | Course 3 (Course 7) | Course 4 (Course 8) | Course 1 (Course 5) |
| 11:40 am–12:20 pm | Lunch | | | |
| 12:20–2:05 pm | Course 3 (Course 7) | Course 4 (Course 8) | Course 1 (Course 5) | Course 2 (Course 6) |
| 2:15–4:00 pm | Course 4 (Course 8) | Course 1 (Course 5) | Course 2 (Course 6) | Course 3 (Course 7) |

\* Second semester courses in parentheses.

Arguments *in favor* of the four-day week include the following:

♦ Transportation costs are reduced, which is a significant factor in school districts with a population spread over a large geographic area. It also could be a factor in cities with mandatory busing plans.

♦ Costs for utilities are reduced. In school districts with heavy heating and air conditioning needs, this reduction could be significant.

♦ Costs of busing, cleaning buildings, and serving lunches are reduced.

♦ The unscheduled fifth day may be utilized on a special-needs basis, such as the entire marching band returning for half-day rehearsals on days when football games are scheduled. Figure 6.11 shows an alternate day block schedule designed for a four-day week with a flexible Friday, which could be used for a variety of different activities.

| | Mon. | Tues. | Weds. | Thurs. | Fri. |
|---|---|---|---|---|---|
| 8:00–10:00 am | Course 1 | Course 2 | Course 1 | Course 2 | Extended Learning Time, Additional Electives, Extra Band Rehearsals, Coop. Programs, Internships |
| 10:06–12:06 pm | Course 3 | Course 4 | Course 3 | Course 4 | |
| 12:10–1:00 pm | Lunch A or Course 5A | | | | |
| 1:04–1:54 pm | Course 5B or Lunch B | | | | |
| 2:00–4:00 pm | Course 6* | Course 7 | Course 6 | Course 7 | |

FIG. 6.11. FOUR-DAY SCHOOL WEEK
(7 COURSES; ALTERNATE DAY BLOCK SCHEDULE;
8 HOUR SCHOOL DAY)

*Two 60-minute single-period courses could be placed within any 2-hour block.

Figure 6.12 illustrates a schedule designed for a magnet high school in Texas which had previous experience with a four-day week semester plan with a modified flexible Friday.

### FIG. 6.12. FOUR-DAY SCHOOL WEEK (7 COURSES; ALTERNATE SEMESTER BLOCK SCHEDULE; 8 HOUR SCHOOL DAY)

|  | Fall | Spring | Fridays |
|---|---|---|---|
| 8:00–10:00 am | Course 1 | Course 4 | Extended Learning Time, Additional Electives, Extra Band Rehearsals, Coop. Programs, Internships, etc. |
| 10:06–12:06 pm | Course 2 | Course 5 | |
| 12:10–1:00 pm | Lunch A or Course 7A | | |
| 1:04–1:54 pm | Course 7B or Lunch B | | |
| 2:00–4:00 pm | Course 3* | Course 6 | |

*Two 60-minute single-period courses could be placed within any 2-hour block.

♦ The fifth day is great, for example, for once-a-month special teacher planning days, professional development, and/or interdisciplinary team planning meetings.

♦ The fifth day or partial use of this day may be utilized for students who need extra learning time. For example, algebra students having trouble with the unit on factoring could receive a half-day of added instruction on the unscheduled fifth day in schools following a four-day-week schedule. At least half of the teachers should be available to provide extended learning time for students who need it.

♦ The fifth day, added to the weekend, gives working students a long weekend for employment.

The major arguments *against* a four-day week for schools include the following:

♦ The plan upsets the expected custodial function schools traditionally serve in communities throughout the country. This may be a bigger issue in urban areas than in rural school districts.

♦ Some community members perceive teachers now as working less than a regular work week, and a modified four-day work week contributes to that negative perception.

♦ One of the instructional benefits given for the four-day week is that the plan provides students flex time in mastering material, and those students needing extended learning time must be scheduled each week throughout the year with the appropriate teachers. This practice can cause major scheduling problems; however, with current computer technology the task should be manageable, and it offers another way to schedule according to students' needs.

♦ One of the benefits of the four-day week for teachers is that teachers gain long periods of time for planning purposes and for professional growth activities. The problem is: How can we use this same day for both teacher planning and extended learning time for students? This issue can be addressed by releasing teachers for planning activities one Friday per month and scheduling them to work at least three clock hours with students in "extra help" or enrichment sessions on the remaining three or four Fridays. Because students probably would not come for extra help beyond noon on Friday, all teachers could still have three hours for planning.

Friday transportation can be a problem in some school districts; however, by scheduling on a student-need basis, parents of high school students are often willing to provide the necessary transportation. By serving students in this capacity, community perceptions of the four-day school week are more positive.

♦ Teachers in the four-day week report the school day is long—usually eight clock hours or 480 minutes compared to the typical 380- to 420-minute school day. One way to deal with the longer school day is to rotate or slide the instructional periods throughout the four-day school schedule so that all classes meet during the morning and afternoon time periods on a four-day rotating schedule (see Figures 6.8, 6.9, and 6.10).

In some school districts, in which extremely heavy population growth is out-pacing the building of new schools, it would be possible to schedule school on Monday, Wednesday, and Friday for some students and on Tuesday, Thursday, and Saturday for others. As illustrated in Figure 6.13, students attending Session I, which is held on Monday, Wednesday, and Friday, could enroll in Courses 1 through 6, which would meet twice weekly for two hours each class, the equivalent of five 48-minute class periods. Similarly, students attending Session II would enroll in Courses 7 through 12, which would meet on Tuesday, Thursday, and Saturday.

## THE FIVE-BLOCK, TEN-COURSE, SEMESTER PLAN SCHEDULE

We are aware of an adaptation of the 4/4 semester plan which is utilized by several schools in both Canada and the United States. Students participate in five courses each semester for a total of ten classes per year. Each of these classes, however, is not allocated a full Carnegie Unit; typically, eight-tenths of a credit is earned with the successful completion of each semester course. Thus, students may earn four credits per semester (.8 credit x 5 courses) for a total of eight credits per year. To fulfill a requirement of four credits (for example, in English), a student would need to complete five courses. A bell schedule for the five-block schedule is shown in Figure 6.14 (p. 178). Classes meet daily for 75 minutes; 33 minutes are allotted for lunch, and four minutes are provided for class changes.

| Fig. 6.13. Two Sessions: Three-Day School Week (6 Courses per Session; 9 Hour School Day) | | | | | | |
|---|---|---|---|---|---|---|
| Session | Session I | Session II | Session I | Session II | Session I | Session II |
| Day | Mon. | Tues. | Weds. | Thurs. | Fri. | Sat. |
| 8:00–10:00 am | Course 1 | Course 7 | Course 1 | Course 7 | Course 3 | Course 9 |
| 10:05–12:05 pm | Course 2 | Course 8 | Course 2 | Course 8 | Course 4 | Course 10 |
| 12:10–12:50 pm | | | Lunch | | | |
| 12:55–2:55 pm | Course 3 | Course 9 | Course 5 | Course 11 | Course 5 | Course 11 |
| 3:00–5:00 pm | Course 4 | Course 10 | Course 6 | Course 12 | Course 6 | Course 12 |

FIG. 6.14. SEMESTER BLOCK SCHEDULE
(5 BLOCKS DAILY; 10 COURSES ANNUALLY; 1 LUNCH PERIOD)

| Blocks | Fall Semester | Spring Semester |
|---|---|---|
| Block I<br>8:00–9:15 am | Course 1 | Course 6 |
| Block II<br>9:19–10:34 am | Course 2 | Course 7 |
| Block III<br>10:38 am–11:53 a.m | Course 3 | Course 8 |
| Lunch<br>11:53 am–12:26 pm | Lunch | |
| Block IV<br>12:26–1:41 pm | Course 4 | Course 9 |
| Block V<br>1:45–3:00 pm | Course 5 | Course 10 |

It should be noted that this schedule would require significant redesign of curriculum. For example, if four credits of English were required, it would be necessary to reorganize objectives and units into five courses.

Another adaptation combines the 4/4 semester plan with several single-period year-long classes. This plan, illustrated in Figure 6.15, allows certain classes such as AP classes, band, and foreign language to be scheduled throughout the entire school year.

FIG. 6.15. HOLSTON HIGH SCHOOL,
WASHINGTON COUNTY, VA
COMBINATION SINGLE-PERIOD AND SEMESTER BLOCK
SCHEDULE (2 SEMESTER BLOCKS; 3 SINGLE YEAR-LONG
PERIODS; 7 COURSES ANNUALLY)

| Blocks | Fall Semester | Spring Semester |
|---|---|---|
| HR & Period 1<br>8:30–9:25 am | Course 1<br>(Year-long) | |
| Block I<br>9:30–11:10 am | Course 2 | Course 3 |
| Period 4 & Lunch<br>11:15 am–12:45 pm | Course 4 and Lunch<br>(Year-long) | |
| Block II<br>12:50–2:30 pm | Course 5 | Course 6 |
| Period 7<br>2:35–3:25 pm | Course 7<br>(Year-long) | |

## CONCLUSION

The possibilities for combining various scheduling concepts into new and unusual forms are endless. The concept of meeting classes on alternate days can be applied to the 4/4 semester plan, the trimester plan, the quarter-on/quarter-off plan, and any of the schedules with short instructional terms. Similarly, the "slide" concept can be utilized as an adaptation of any of the basic plans. Finally, it may be appropriate to add one or more short instructional terms to a school schedule to provide time for extended learning and enrichment. As always, the lens through which we evaluate the utility of a particular schedule should be the following question: Can a different schedule help us to accomplish our school's mission and goals more effectively and efficiently?

A critical factor in the accomplishment of school goals is the professional development of teachers. In the two chapters that follow we turn to this issue. In Chapter 7 we create schedules which provide extended blocks of time for teachers to plan or to engage in professional development activities without sending students home, and in Chapter 8 we discuss appropriate instructional strategies that can assist teachers in being more effective during extended class periods.

# 7

# SCHEDULES THAT EXTEND TEACHER PLANNING AND PROFESSIONAL DEVELOPMENT OPPORTUNITIES

High school schedules are often adopted to facilitate the implementation of desired instructional programs. Conversely, sometimes a scheduling change becomes a catalyst for instructional innovations.[1] Regardless, the implementation of block scheduling always brings with it a need for staff development on a variety of topics. As noted by the National Commission on Time and Learning [1994], "[It] is a myth that schools can be transformed without giving teachers the time they need to re-tool themselves and reorganize their work" [p. 8]. When high schools change from a single-period daily schedule to blocks of time, a major concern for many teachers is how to design lessons that can best be delivered in the larger

---

[1] We owe a debt of gratitude to Brenda Tanner, Director of Instruction and Staff Development for the Louisa County (Virginia) Public Schools, for her research and assistance in the preparation of this chapter.

instructional time periods. Training in cooperative learning and other models of teaching is needed to assist teachers in breaking away from their reliance upon lecture and discussion. Also, sometimes adopting a new schedule is accompanied by a reduction in the number of "tracks" in a school. While Advanced Placement (AP) and Honors classes frequently remain intact, school personnel often allow any student willing to attempt those classes to enroll. Sometimes, all other students are grouped heterogeneously. Again, teachers require significant training to develop the confidence and skills necessary to work with mixed-ability groups. In addition, teachers may require new techniques for classroom management, especially for low-level classes if tracking continues. Another programmatic innovation that often accompanies block scheduling is the implementation of interdisciplinary curriculum and instruction. Teachers and administrators need in-service in the design and instruction of integrated units and lessons.

It is virtually impossible to provide the amount and quality of staff development time educators need within current school calendars. At most, a week of preparation time precedes the arrival of students in the fall; many teacher contracts require teacher attendance only one day before school begins. One, or at the most two, staff development days are planned each semester. Often, district-initiated and site-based needs conflict regarding the utilization of this time. Occasionally, districts have been able to schedule an early release day or one-half day once a month, once every other week, or rarely, one day a week. The public, however, generally is not supportive of this method of providing staff development time. In response to complaints from parents, we have observed that many districts scale back their use of early-release days for students. In the report *Prisoners of Time*, the National Commission on Time and Learning [1994], while recognizing an urgent need for professional development time, particularly cautions against providing teacher professional time by releasing students from school.

> The last thing districts should encourage is sending children home to provide time for "teacher professional days." We will never have truly effective schools while teachers' needs are met at the expense of students' learning time. [p. 36]

Even though new programs may bring with them a need for staff development, little attention has been given to the idea that scheduling changes may be used to create blocks of time for teachers to be involved in study and learning. Joyce and Showers [1988], for example, spoke of the problem of "arranging time for study groups and coaching teams" in the school "workplace."

> The workplace was organized long before anyone anticipated that lifelong study and the careful preparation of learning environments would be necessary. . . . Now we have to face the problem of arranging time for study groups and coaching teams to operate effectively. [p. 145]

Current staff development models place a greater emphasis on the teacher as an active participant than did models of the past. Terms such as collegiality, collaboration, observation, experimentation, and problem-solving reflect the dynamic, interactive nature of what are considered to be effective staff development programs [Little, 1985; Loucks-Horsley et al., 1987; Guskey, 1986; Lieberman and Miller, 1992]. Teacher commitment is encouraged by providing teachers with opportunities to become involved in the decision-making process, from goal-setting and planning to evaluation. In order to participate, teachers need time, not time added onto or squeezed into an already hectic day, but time that is devoted specifically to staff development and personal planning.

Efforts to provide time for staff development often have resulted in attempts to compact a year's worth of staff development activities into a handful of teacher workdays scheduled prior to the arrival of students. This is time when teachers are more concerned with preparations for the opening of school than they are with their own professional growth. In other cases, teachers are brought together at the end of the school day to participate in after-school workshops or to serve on curriculum committees. Tired and loaded with the day's allotment of ungraded papers, teachers' levels of receptivity are not at their highest. In fact, many teachers' participation is limited or even prevented by extracurricular duties.

Administrators, frustrated by what is perceived to be a lack of time for staff development, need to reexamine the structure and schedule of the school day and school year. If they are willing to explore new possibilities of scheduling, they may find that perhaps the real issue is not always a lack of time, but rather the distribution of time [Loucks-Horsley *et al.*, 1987].

Although relatively new to many, the concept of embedding staff development time into the regular workday is worthy of consideration. In terms of what is expected of teachers today, it becomes imperative that new models of providing professional development and planning time be explored.

Realizing that time is a limited and valuable resource, school administrators need to explore ways of reconfiguring schedules to facilitate a variety of staff development needs. Thinking of time only in terms of days, quarters, terms, semesters, or years limits flexibility in scheduling design. If the available time in a school year, however, is seen as 180 discrete units which can be grouped according to need, the possibility exists to develop a multitude of plans.

## SCHEDULING EXTENDED TEACHER PLANNING TIME DURING THE SCHOOL DAY WITHOUT SENDING STUDENTS HOME

In Chapters 2 through 6 we illustrate how a schedule can be designed to provide longer blocks of instructional time for students and teachers; the schedule also can be reconfigured to provide teachers with extended periods of planning or staff development time. By combining regular planning periods similar to the way block schedules are created, significant blocks of uninterrupted time may be created without sending students home. Our approach to this task varies, depending on the scheduling model in use.

### DAILY PERIOD MODELS

In Figure 7.1 we illustrate how Teacher Jones could receive a half-day of extended planning/in-service time on a six-day rotating cycle; a six-day cycle is used because, in our example, Teacher Jones works in a school that operates a six-period, daily, traditional schedule. As is typical, she is assigned to teach five of the six periods; Period 1 is designated for her planning period. As shown in Figure 7.1, Teacher Jones has three periods off on the first day of the six-day cycle. If Jones is teamed with colleagues who also have been assigned

Period 1 for planning, then they would all have three periods off on Day 1 to plan, for example, an integrated unit of study. On Days 2 and 3, Jones and her colleagues would not have a planning period, and on the remaining three days, one period daily is allotted for planning.

FIG. 7.1. EXTENDED TEACHER PLANNING BLOCKS TO ALLOW ONE-HALF DAY FOR INDIVIDUAL PLANNING OR STAFF DEVELOPMENT BY TEAMS OR DEPARTMENTS (BASED ON 6-PERIOD DAY): EXAMPLE 1

| Day 1 | Day 2 | Day 3 | Day 4 | Day 5 | Day 6 |
|-------|-------|-------|-------|-------|-------|
| M | T | W | R | F | M |
| 1 | 2 | 3 | 4 | 5 | 6 |
| 1 | 2 | 3 | 4 | 5 | 6 |
| 1 | 2 | 3 | 4 | 5 | 6 |
| 4 | 4 | 4 | 1 | 1 | 1 |
| 5 | 5 | 5 | 2 | 2 | 2 |
| 6 | 6 | 6 | 3 | 3 | 3 |

This schedule may be a problem in states where union contracts specify that teachers be assigned daily planning time; however, with movement toward site-based management, contract waivers are possible if requested by the teachers in a particular building. Also, we highly recommend that contracts be written to designate planning time by minutes per week, rather than periods or minutes per day. Such an arrangement provides teachers and administrators greater flexibility in designing schedules.

The schedule illustrated in Figure 7.1 is problematic because for two days during the cycle teachers do not have an extended break for planning. In schools operating 20- to 30-minute lunch periods, such days can be exhausting. The plan may be more acceptable in a school that has a long, single, open lunch period. For example, some high schools have a 50- or 60-minute lunch period when all students and teachers eat, attend and supervise club meetings, study, and socialize. In such schools we recommend that teachers not be assigned any duties during the lunch block on days with no scheduled planning period.

To provide teachers with longer, extended planning blocks of time within a designated cycle of days, it is necessary to create a cycle of days equal to the number of periods in the day. Thus, a six-period school requires a six-day cycle, a seven-period school requires a seven-day cycle, and so on. We propose, however, that this plan NOT be instituted on a regular basis but only during designated periods of time, such as once during each of the school's grading periods.

Another plan would be to operate the same cycle illustrated in Figure 7.1 on six consecutive Mondays or any other day of the week. In our example, on the first Monday teacher Jones would have half a day available for staff development; on the next two Mondays she would have no planning time; and for the last three Mondays in the six-week cycle, she would be allocated one planning period each day.

In addition to providing extended staff development time, this schedule varies the length and frequency of instructional periods. Because Teacher Jones has planning during Period 1, she is free three periods on Day 1, no periods on Days 2 and 3, and one period each of Days 4, 5, and 6. Conversely, all teachers who teach during Period 1 work with their students three consecutive periods on Day 1, not at all on Days 2 and 3, and one period on each of Days 4, 5, and 6.

Another model of the plan, shown as Figure 7.2, offers three planning periods aggregated on Day 1 of the six-day cycle and then single planning periods on Days 2, 4, and 6 of the cycle. This plan may be preferred because teachers do not have two consecutive days in the cycle without a planning period.

FIG. 7.2. EXTENDED TEACHER PLANNING BLOCKS FOR
INDIVIDUAL PLANNING OR STAFF DEVELOPMENT BY TEAMS OR
DEPARTMENTS (BASED ON 6-PERIOD DAY): EXAMPLE 2

| Day 1 | Day 2 | Day 3 | Day 4 | Day 5 | Day 6 |
|-------|-------|-------|-------|-------|-------|
| M | T | W | R | F | M |
| 1 | 2 | 3 | 4 | 5 | 6 |
| 1 | 2 | 3 | 4 | 5 | 6 |
| 1 | 2 | 3 | 4 | 5 | 6 |
| 4 | 1 | 4 | 1 | 2 | 1 |
| 5 | 3 | 5 | 2 | 4 | 2 |
| 6 | 5 | 6 | 3 | 6 | 3 |

The schedule illustrated in Figure 7.3 (p. 188) has been prepared for a school in which teachers instruct five of seven periods. If teacher Jones were assigned periods 1 and 4 for planning, she would have a four-period planning block on Day 1 of the seven-day cycle, one period on Days 2 and 3, three periods on Day 4, two periods on Days 5 and 6, and one period on Day 7 of the cycle.

FIG. 7.3. EXTENDED TEACHER PLANNING BLOCKS FOR
INDIVIDUAL PLANNING OR STAFF DEVELOPMENT BY TEAMS OR
DEPARTMENTS (BASED ON 7-PERIOD DAY)

| Day 1 | Day 2 | Day 3 | Day 4 | Day 5 | Day 6 | Day 7 |
|-------|-------|-------|-------|-------|-------|-------|
| M | T | W | R | F | M | T |
| 1 | 2 | 3 | 4 | 5 | 6 | 7 |
| 1 | 2 | 3 | 4 | 5 | 6 | 7 |
| 1 | 2 | 3 | 4 | 5 | 6 | 7 |
| 4 | 4 | 1 | 3 | 1 | 1 | 1 |
| 5 | 5 | 2 | 5 | 2 | 2 | 2 |
| 6 | 6 | 6 | 6 | 3 | 3 | 3 |
| 7 | 7 | 7 | 7 | 4 | 4 | 5 |

If the school is operating on an eight-period day (see Figure 7.4), and Teacher Jones has periods one and eight assigned for planning, she would have a planning block consisting of six periods on Day 1 of the eight-day cycle, two periods on Day 2, one period on Day 3, two periods on Day 4, no periods on Day 5, two periods on Day 6, one period on Day 7, and two periods on Day 8.

**FIG. 7.4. EXTENDED TEACHER PLANNING PERIODS TO ALLOW A MINIMUM OF A 6-PERIOD TIME BLOCK FOR INDIVIDUAL PLANNING OR STAFF DEVELOPMENT TIME BY TEAMS OR DEPARTMENTS**

| Day 1 | Day 2 | Day 3 | Day 4 | Day 5 | Day 6 | Day 7 | Day 8 |
|-------|-------|-------|-------|-------|-------|-------|-------|
| M | T | W | R | F | M | T | W |
| 1 | 1 | 2 | 1 | 3 | 1 | 4 | 1 |
| 1 | 2 | 2 | 2 | 3 | 2 | 4 | 2 |
| 1 | 3 | 2 | 3 | 3 | 3 | 4 | 3 |
| 1 | 4 | 2 | 4 | 3 | 4 | 4 | 4 |
| 8 | 5 | 7 | 5 | 6 | 5 | 5 | 5 |
| 8 | 6 | 7 | 6 | 6 | 6 | 5 | 6 |
| 5 | 7 | 6 | 7 | 5 | 7 | 6 | 7 |
| 7 | 8 | 8 | 8 | 7 | 8 | 8 | 8 |

| 1 Day | 6 Periods Off | (6 x 1) | = | 6 |
|-------|---------------|---------|---|---|
| 4 Days | 2 Periods Off | (4 x 2) | = | 8 |
| 2 Days | 1 Period Off | (2 x 1) | = | 2 |
| 1 Day | 0 Period Off | | | |
| | | Total | | 16 |

The major advantage of extending planning periods is to provide long blocks of time for teacher planning and/or staff development **during school time.** To obtain maximum use of the plans, teachers need to be assigned planning time by departments, interdisciplinary teams, houses, or clusters. In addition, it would be advisable to pair departments most likely to share students, time, and other resources, such as social studies/English or math/science. Our suggestion for assigning planning periods by departments and/or related groups is illustrated in Figure 7.5.

| FIG. 7.5. PLANNING PERIODS BY DEPARTMENT | | |
|---|---|---|
| *Teaching Areas* | *Periods* | |
| Math | 1 | 8 |
| English | 2 | 7 |
| Science | 3 | 6 |
| Social Studies | 4 | 5 |
| Art & Music | 2 | 7 |
| Tech/PE/Health | 3 | 6 |
| Special Ed. | 4 | 5 |
| Family Living (FL) and Keyboarding (KB) and all others | 1 | 8 |

We understand that it may be difficult to free an entire department during the same block because of the need to offer sections of that subject, for example, math, during each period or block in the schedule. It may be possible, however, to release half the department or an interdisciplinary team during the same blocks. This would require the alteration of Figure 7.5. We might assign half of the math department and half of the science department planning in periods one and eight, and the other half of each of these departments planning time during periods three and six. This adaptation would reduce the number of potential scheduling conflicts that might occur if either subject were not taught during all periods in the school day. Another adaptation to this plan would be to assign the periods so no teacher would ever have a day in the cycle without at least one planning period. Also, we could schedule so that one day in every cycle each teacher would have a full day for planning. The schedule illustrated by Figure 7.6 provides a full day of planning during each eight-day cycle for every teacher.

FIG. 7.6. EXTENDED TEACHER PLANNING BLOCKS TO ALLOW A MINIMUM OF ONE-FULL DAY FOR INDIVIDUAL PLANNING OR STAFF DEVELOPMENT (BASED ON 8-PERIOD DAY)

| Day 1 | Day 2 | Day 3 | Day 4 | Day 5 | Day 6 | Day 7 | Day 8 |
|-------|-------|-------|-------|-------|-------|-------|-------|
| M | T | W | R | F | M | T | W |
| 1 | 1 | 2 | 1 | 3 | 1 | 4 | 1 |
| 1 | 2 | 2 | 2 | 3 | 2 | 4 | 2 |
| 1 | 3 | 2 | 3 | 3 | 3 | 4 | 3 |
| 1 | 4 | 2 | 4 | 3 | 4 | 4 | 4 |
| 5 | 5 | 6 | 5 | 7 | 5 | 8 | 5 |
| 5 | 6 | 6 | 6 | 7 | 6 | 8 | 6 |
| 5 | 7 | 6 | 7 | 7 | 7 | 8 | 7 |
| 5 | 8 | 6 | 8 | 7 | 8 | 8 | 8 |

Note: This plan could be utilized once per grading period or 1 day per week over 8 consecutive weeks. Teachers could be assigned 2 periods of plan time by departments or teams (e.g., math/science periods 1, 5; English/social science periods 2, 6 etc.).

## ALTERNATE DAY MODELS

Alternate-day models for achieving extended staff development time are nearly identical to single-period models. The schedule of a school following an alternate day, seven-course schedule (see Chapter 2), with course 5 meeting as an every-day single period, could be changed on an occasional basis to provide teachers with one extended period of planning time every three days. For example, if one group (team or department) of teachers were assigned periods 1 and 4 for planning time, another group periods 2 and 6, and another group periods 3 and 7, a modified three-day cycle for those teachers could be designed as shown in Figure 7.7.

FIG. 7.7. EXTENDED TEACHER PLANNING BLOCKS FOR INDIVIDUAL PLANNING OR STAFF DEVELOPMENT BY TEAMS OR DEPARTMENTS (BASED ON 7 COURSE ALTERNATE DAY SCHEDULE)

| Day 1 | Day 2 | Day 3 |
|-------|-------|-------|
| 1 | 2 | 3 |
| 1 | 2 | 3 |
| 4 | 6 | 7 |
| 4 | 6 | 7 |
| 5 | 5 | 5 |
| 7 | 3 | 1 |
| 7 | 3 | 1 |

Teachers who have been scheduled periods 1 and 4 for planning would have more than half the day for staff development or personal planning on the first day of the three-day cycle, no planning time on Day 2, and a double period of planning time on Day 3. Teachers allocated periods 2 and 6 would have their extended staff development block on Day 2 of the cycle, and teachers assigned periods 3 and 7 would be free on Day 3 for four periods. Again, it may be wise, for example, to operate this cycle on three consecutive Wednesdays or Fridays rather than three straight days.

## Staff Development Time in the 4/4 Semester Plan

In the 4/4 semester plan (see Chapter 3), the idea presented in Figure 7.7 could be modified into a four-day cycle, as shown in Figure 7.8 (p. 194). We believe that teachers involved in the 4/4 semester plan may be more excited about a schedule which provides extended teacher planning time than will teachers in a single-period schedule. For teachers who have altered their instruction to fit the block, the idea of working for an entire day with a class is less of a change and can represent a win-win situation for both teachers and students.

As the shading in Figure 7.8 illustrates, any teacher with Block 4 assigned for planning has no planning block on Day 1, one 90-minute planning block on both Days 2 and 3, and would be free half the school day on Day 4.

| | | | | |
|---|---|---|---|---|
| | FIG. 7.8. EXTENDED TEACHER PLANNING BLOCKS IN THE 4/4 SEMESTER PLAN—EXAMPLE 1: ONE-HALF DAY FOR STAFF DEVELOPMENT ON A 4-DAY CYCLE | | | |
| | Day 1 | Day 2 | Day 3 | Day 4 |
| Block 1 90 min. | Course 1 | Course 2 | Course 3 | Course 4 |
| Block 2 90 min. | Course 1 | Course 2 | Course 3 | Course 4 |
| Lunch | Lunch | | | |
| Block 3 90 min. | Course 2 | Course 3 | Course 4 | Course 1 |
| Block 4 90 min. | Course 3 | Course 4 | Course 1 | Course 2 |

A full day of staff development could be arranged for each teacher every four weeks if the schedule shown in Figure 7.9 were followed. All teachers assigned planning during the Course 4 block would have a 90-minute planning session during Block 4 on Monday, Tuesday, Thursday, and Friday. On Wednesday during Week 1, all teachers assigned to teach during Block 1 would work all day with their students in Course 1 classes; on Wednesday of Week 2, teachers assigned to teach during Block 2 would work all day with their students in Course 2 classes; on Wednesday of Week 3 teachers assigned to teach during Block 3 would work all day with their students in Course 3 classes; and on Wednesday of the fourth week, all teachers with planning scheduled for Block 4 would have a full day reserved for personal planning or staff development. It must be remembered that one-fourth of the staff would be released each Wednesday in the cycle depending on which block is their assigned planning time.

Again, when considering any of the above schedules, it also must be remembered that the extended planning time for teachers translates into extended instructional periods for students on selected days within the cycle. Each class would be scheduled to meet for the same extended periods as the teachers who are off for those particular designated blocks of time. For instance, in Figure 7.9, with extended teacher planning time in the 4/4 semester plan, each class would be scheduled to meet for one full day on Wednesday every four weeks.

| | Mon. | Tues. | Wed. | | | | Thurs. | Fri. |
|---|---|---|---|---|---|---|---|---|
| | | | W1 | W2 | W3 | W4 | | |
| Block 1 | Course 1 | Course 1 | C1 | C2 | C3 | C4 | Course 1 | Course 1 |
| Block 2 | Course 2 | Course 2 | C1 | C2 | C3 | C4 | Course 2 | Course 2 |
| Lunch | Lunch | | | | | | | |
| Block 3 | Course 3 | Course 3 | C1 | C2 | C3 | C4 | Course 3 | Course 3 |
| Block 4 | Course 4 | Course 4 | C1 | C2 | C3 | C4 | Course 4 | Course 4 |

FIG. 7.9. EXTENDED TEACHER PLANNING BLOCKS IN THE 4/4 SEMESTER PLAN— EXAMPLE 2: 1 DAY FOR TEACHER PLANNING EVERY 4 WEEKS

Figure 7.10, illustrates a situation whereby all classes meet for 90 minutes on Monday, and on Tuesday Block 1 classes meet all day. Teachers assigned planning time during Block 1 would be free for the day. Periods 2 through 4 would be scheduled similarly on Wednesday through Friday. Hopefully, during these extended instructional periods of time, teachers will include a variety of instructional strategies, activities, projects, field trips, and experiences designed to promote student involvement.

**FIG. 7.10. EXTENDED TEACHER PLANNING BLOCKS IN THE 4/4 SEMESTER PLAN—EXAMPLE 3: ONE FULL DAY FOR TEACHER PLANNING AND CLASS MEETINGS IN A SELECTED 4-DAY CYCLE**

|         | Mon.       | Tues.      | Wed.       | Thurs.     | Fri.       |
|---------|------------|------------|------------|------------|------------|
| Block 1 | Course 1   | Course 1   | Course 2   | Course 3   | Course 4   |
| Block 2 | Course 2   | Course 1   | Course 2   | Course 3   | Course 4   |
| Lunch   | Lunch      |            |            |            |            |
| Block 3 | Course 3   | Course 1   | Course 2   | Course 3   | Course 4   |
| Block 4 | Course 4   | Course 1   | Course 2   | Course 3   | Course 4   |

If teachers knew at the beginning of every quarter or semester which days on the calendar they would be assigned their block classes for an entire day, long-term plans could be made. For example, the science teachers could plan to work with each class for the full day making initial or final preparations for their projects scheduled for the Science Fair. English teachers might plan the full day to help students get started on their quarterly research paper, including such activities as topic selection, initial library research, and outlining. A drama teacher might spend the entire day working with the class in making final preparations for the play to be presented the next evening for parents. And, of course, the physical education teacher could spend the full day with each class teaching the basic principles of golf at the local golf course! The possibilities are endless.

We understand that many of the plans we suggest in this chapter violate union contractual stipulations for daily planning periods. We suggest, however, that there are many creative teachers in high schools who would look forward to spending a full day each month with each of their classes, and that union contracts could and should be altered to reflect weekly or even monthly planning minutes to allow greater flexibility for teachers and administrators at the building level. Again, the primary benefit of this type of scheduling is to provide extended blocks of time for planning, teaching, and learning for **both students and teachers.**

## SCHEDULING SHORT INSTRUCTIONAL TERMS INTO THE SCHOOL CALENDAR TO PROVIDE FULL DAYS FOR TEACHER PLANNING AND STAFF DEVELOPMENT

Another way to develop blocks of time for teacher planning and staff development would be to reconfigure the 180-day school calendar. For example, one might implement one of the schedules presented in Chapter 5, either the 75–75–(30) or the 80(10)–80(10) plan, and arrange for a percentage of teachers to be off on a rotating basis, possibly every two years.

Figure 7.11 (p. 198) illustrates how the 180-day school year can be modified to provide four terms of instruction rather than two semesters. With this schedule, **teachers provide the core of instruction during the 80-day fall and spring terms**. At the end of each term, ten days are provided for a host of activities for **both students and teachers**. For example, this ten-day term allows additional remediation time for students who have not yet mastered certain concepts, while giving other students time to extend their learning through special projects, elective studies, and field activities. The plan may also help students who have done passing work, but have been absent for more days than allowed by attendance mandates in certain states. The 10-day term would permit students to make up missed days and become eligible for credit.

| | Fall Term 80 Days | Middle Term 10 Days | Spring Term 80 Days | Final Term 10 Days |
|---|---|---|---|---|
| FIG. 7.11. THE 80(10)–80(10) PLAN | | | | |
| Block I 112 minutes | Course 1 | Elective, Community Service, Remedial Work, etc. | Course 5 | Elective, Community Service, Remedial Work, etc. |
| Block II 112 minutes | Course 2 | Staff Dev. for selected teachers | Course 6 | Staff Dev. for selected teachers |
| Period 5 48 minutes + 24-minute lunch | Course 3 & Lunch | Course 3 & Lunch | Course 3 & Lunch | Course 3 & Lunch |
| Block III 112 minutes | Course 4 | Electives, Comm. Ser., Remediation, & Staff Dev. con't. | Course 7 | Electives, Comm. Ser., Remediation, & Staff Dev. con't. |

Note: Blocks I, II, and III are the equivalent of two class periods of 56 minutes each. This plan also could be used with a single period schedule for a 6-, 7-, or 8-period day.

In addition to providing extra time for student learning, the 80(10)–80(10) plan shown in Figure 7.11 can be used to develop blocks of time for teacher study and planning. Utilizing such a schedule, high schools could rotate teacher assignments during the two ten-day terms in order to provide a portion of the teachers with extended time during which they would be free of teaching responsibilities or assigned duties.

To illustrate how this plan would work, think of a 1000-student high school with a 60-teacher faculty, with each member teaching five of seven periods. For the purpose of staff development, think of the schedule in terms of a two-year cycle, with each year containing two ten-day terms that could be used for professional growth activities. Planning biennially, administrators would then have four ten-day sessions in which to provide release time for teachers to participate in non-classroom activities such as curriculum planning, observation of peers, or other opportunities. Working with universities, for example, schools could offer mini-courses on topics such as cooperative learning, Paideia seminar teaching [Adler and Van Doren, 1984], or conflict resolution. Dividing the team of 60 full-time teachers by the four time periods allows 15 teachers, or one-fourth of the staff, to be scheduled for a ten-day period of planning and/or staff development every two years.

During this ten-day term, students normally assigned to these teachers could be regrouped according to needs and interests. Activities involving a large group of students, such as the production of a musical or special sports events such as volleyball or basketball camps, could be scheduled during this period. The ten-day term also could serve as time for students to complete mini-courses, perform concentrated research, participate in community service projects, take part in a mini-practicum or internship program, or devote concentrated time to preparing for final class exhibitions [Sizer, 1992]. Extended field trips could be taken during this period without having students miss classroom instructional time. Also, students lagging behind in their studies may be allocated this time for "catch-up."

The major question to answer regarding this plan is the following: How can we cover 100 percent of the students for 10 days with 75 percent of the faculty? This is not as difficult to accomplish as it might seem. Remember, during any one period in a school in which faculty teach five of seven periods, 28.6 percent (two of seven) teachers are not working with students. To free 25 percent of the faculty for staff development, it is necessary to increase class size and/or reduce the amount of planning time for the remaining 75 percent of the teachers who instruct during the 10-day term. For example, in our hypothetical school, average section size should be approximately 23 students. If the remaining 75 percent of the teachers took no planning time for the short term, average section size actually would be reduced to 22! If teachers retained one daily planning period, class size would increase to 26; and if two preparation periods per teacher were maintained, class size would increase to 32. Thus, by teaching for three 10-day short terms with a slight increase in class size and/or a slight decrease in planning time, teachers gain 10 days of time for staff development and curriculum development every two years, without sending the students home (see Figure 7.12).

The plan described above arranges for all faculty to be freed for planning or staff development for 10 days once every four years. If we were to reduce the number of days in the short term to five, then each group could be released annually. This change would also entail a corresponding alteration in the scheduling of instructional programming for the short terms.

Another way to allow all teachers to receive an extended block of time annually for personal planning or professional development would be for teachers to share courses during a 15-day (or 10-day) short term. One possibility would be for both teachers to begin the course together, then have Teacher A teach the next 6 days, while Teacher B was engaged in other activities. The two teachers then would rejoin forces on the eighth day of class, and then Teacher B would take over through day 14; on Day 15, both teachers would complete the course (see Figure 7.13, p. 202). This effort could be within a discipline, based upon the particular teaching strengths of each partner, or across disciplines. If half of the faculty shared courses during each of the two short terms and the other instructors worked with full groups, all teachers would have six full days to devote to professional growth or personal planning activities annually. Seventy-five percent of all staff would be working with students at any one time during the short terms; 25 percent would be released for other activities.

It also may be appropriate to provide students with specific days in school without the responsibility of the "normal day's work load." These days could be used for students to complete research projects [Sizer, 1992] or for vocational students to demonstrate their

## Fig. 7.12. Section Size Calculations: Short Terms and Planning Periods

### 5 of 7 Courses with 60 Teachers: No Short Term; Two Planning Periods Daily

7 courses per student x 1000 students = 7000 student-courses

5 courses per teacher x 60 teachers = 300 course sections

$$\frac{7000 \text{ student-courses}}{300 \text{ course-sections}} = 23.3 \text{ students per course section}$$

### 7 of 7 Courses with 45 Teachers: Short Term; No Planning Periods for Teachers Instructing During the Short Term

7 courses per student x 1000 students = 7000 student-courses

7 courses per teacher x 45 teachers = 315 course sections

$$\frac{7000 \text{ student-courses}}{315 \text{ course-sections}} = 22.2 \text{ students per course section}$$

### 6 of 7 Courses with 45 Teachers: Short Term Included; One Daily Planning Period for Teachers Instructing During the Short Term

7 courses per student x 1000 students = 7000 student-courses

6 courses per teacher x 45 teachers = 270 course sections

$$\frac{7000 \text{ student-courses}}{270 \text{ course-sections}} = 25.9 \text{ students per course section}$$

### 5 of 7 Courses with 45 Teachers: Short Term Included; Two Planning Periods Daily for Teachers Instructing During the Short Term

7 courses per student x 1000 students = 7000 student-courses

5 courses per teacher x 45 teachers = 220 course sections

$$\frac{7000 \text{ student-courses}}{220 \text{ course-sections}} = 31.8 \text{ students per course section}$$

FIG. 7.13. SHARED 15-DAY COURSE WITH 6 DAYS OF PERSONAL PLANNING OR PROFESSIONAL DEVELOPMENT

|  | Teacher A | Teacher B |
|---|---|---|
| Day 1 | Teachers begin course together. ||
| Days 2–7 | Teacher A instructs alone. | Personal Planning or Staff Development for Teacher B |
| Day 8 | Teachers rejoin for 1 day at mid-term. ||
| Days 9–14 | Personal Planning or Staff Development for Teacher A | Teacher B instructs alone. |
| Day 15 | Teachers A & B end course together. ||

achievements [Bottoms, Presson, and Johnson, 1992]. For example, students at the Paul M. Hodgson Vocational-Technical High School, Newark, Delaware, must successfully complete an Exhibition of Achievement as one of their Senior Projects.

Many other variations are possible. A similar scheme could work on a 40(5)–40(5)–40(5)–40(5) plan, with 25 percent of the teachers scheduled off five days every year. In the 75–75–(30) plan discussed in Chapter 5, 25 percent of the teachers could be scheduled off for a "mini-sabbatical" every four years for 30 days. In this plan, some could even plan trips to Europe! Although such a plan would provide 30 days off without teaching responsibilities, we question the desirability of providing such long periods of time only every four years. Again, one team might work 15 days and their co-team the other 15 days, so that all staff would receive 15 days every two years.

Another plan would be to organize the instructional program within the framework of several of the schedules developed in Chapter 5, and then schedule individuals and small groups of teachers for two or three days of staff development throughout the school year. For example, a 180-day school year could be thought of as 20 days teaching and then 2 days, and then 20(3) for a quarter plan, or a 20(2), 20(3) repeated for two quarters for a semester plan or repeated for four quarters for a 4/4 semester plan. During the school year one-fourth of the teachers could be scheduled for personal development throughout the school for two or three days each semester. The groups of 15 teachers (60 divided by 4) could be assigned by their subjects taught, teams assigned, or special interests. If such a plan were followed throughout a school district, all teachers from a particular discipline could be rotated through the schedule twice each year. For example, all English teachers could be off during the first two-day mini-term of the year, then all math teachers during the next three days, then science, and so on. If one-fourth of the 60 teachers were scheduled off at one time, they could have two days scheduled for professional development one semester and three days the next semester. If this plan were to be followed throughout a school division, provisions could be made to provide common release time for all teachers by departments, thus having predetermined days that might be used for division-wide staff development or curriculum planning. Schools that incorporate peer coaching into their staff development models could schedule release time for coaching partners to observe each other. One teacher could observe his/her partner during the first two-day release period with the roles of observer/observee reversed during the next three-day release period.

## CONCLUSION

As educators in charge of scheduling begin to visualize time as a resource which can be utilized in various configurations, other plans similar to those described in this chapter can be developed, based upon the goals and objectives of the individual school. Schools that place a high priority on teacher planning time and staff development may build time within the teaching day and/or year for teachers to participate in professional growth opportunities without sacrificing instructional time for students. By conceptualizing time and scheduling as shown by the illustrations in this chapter, a signal is sent to teachers, parents, and school board members that the learning process is valued for **both teachers and students!**

# 8

# TEACHING IN THE BLOCK

Based on our experience of working with schools in over 30 states and after talking with hundreds of teachers, students, and school administrators, we are convinced that a major need which must be addressed with the implementation of block scheduling is helping teachers gain the necessary strategies and skills to teach successfully in a large block of time. We fear that if teachers do not alter techniques to utilize extended blocks of time effectively and efficiently, the promise of the block scheduling movement will die, as did the flexible modular scheduling effort of the '60s and '70s.

We believe that it is unreasonable to expect teachers to adapt to large blocks of instructional time with either enthusiasm or success if for years they have been rewarded for being "good teachers" simply because they were knowledgeable of their content, dispensed it primarily in lecture format during daily fragmented periods of 35 to 50 minutes, assigned and "graded" reasonable amounts of homework, gave quizzes or tests at least every 10 days, and did not fail more than 25 percent of their students! A critical question for persons involved with block scheduling is: Do the majority of teachers in America truly want the TIME TO TEACH? We argue that a change to block scheduling can become a catalyst for teachers to seek different teaching strategies; in fact, this need is perceived and voiced by many teachers. This window of opportunity must not be ignored.

We urge school personnel NOT to move to any form of block scheduling if teachers are not provided with a *minimum* of five, and hopefully ten days, of staff development. These workshop days must be designed to allow teachers to participate in activities with a high degree of engagement; it would be most inappropriate to just "talk to" teachers. In these workshops strategies must be modeled for teachers who later must design instruction for students in large blocks of time. Later in this chapter we shall offer specific suggestions for the content we recommend for five-day and ten-day workshops to assist teachers in **surviving and then thriving successfully in the block!** First, however, we describe a lesson-planning format designed for long instructional blocks. Second, we discuss a variety of teaching techniques which we believe could assist teachers in utilizing blocks effectively.

## THREE-PART LESSON DESIGN: EXPLANATION, APPLICATION, AND SYNTHESIS

We have observed that teachers who are most successful in block scheduling typically plan lessons in three parts. We have "borrowed" the terms explanation, application, and synthesis to describe these parts [Hunter, 1976, 1982; Bloom *et al.*, 1956].

### EXPLANATION

Depending upon the length of the block and the nature of the lesson or topic, teachers spend approximately 25 to 40 minutes in what we call explanation. To some extent during explanation, teachers do what many teachers have done for years. They are on stage, usually in front of the class. They may or may not call on students for various responses; but for the most part, they use chalkboards, overhead projectors, and various pieces of equipment to explain what students are to learn. During this instructional phase of the lesson teachers often do what some call direct instruction and may include the steps described as Hunter's lesson design [Hunter, 1976]. During explanation the focus is on what is to be learned, appreciated, constructed, dissected, prepared, developed, located, discussed, written, or performed. This step involves identifying objectives, specifying tasks to be completed, and demonstrating to students how to meet the learning expectations successfully. During the explanation phase teachers, for example, may illustrate how to solve a particular math problem, write a succinct thesis statement, construct or read a time line in history, or store and retrieve computer data.

## APPLICATION

Following 25 to 40 minutes of explanation, teachers who seem to be positive toward teaching in the block usually move into a phase we have chosen to call application, which extends for 40 to 60 or even 70 minutes in length. Here students become more active learners as they are assisted in applying what the teacher has been explaining; some call this phase of the lesson "hands on" time! We have noted that it is the application phase that seems to give teachers the most difficulty in implementing. Apparently, many teachers do not possess sufficient strategies and/or have the classroom management skills to plan and implement active learning activities to give students opportunities to use and apply what was taught during the explanation phase. We suggest that the pre-block-scheduling workshops focus primarily on helping teachers gain skills and confidence in preparing lessons that involve students and move them toward applying what they are expected to learn. Too often teaching, learning, and testing never move beyond regurgitating "what the teacher said." **As long as the application phase of a lesson is short-changed or eliminated, retention of learning will be limited.**

Some examples of what we have seen teachers do during the application phase of a lesson include the following:

♦ An English teacher engages students in the writing process or simply allows students to use computers for word processing to correct their papers based on feedback from the teacher and/or writers' workshop group. Another teacher accompanies the class to the library to assist students with some specific research to help them begin a research paper.

♦ A social studies teacher conducts a Paideia seminar; the following day students prepare position papers either individually, in pairs, or in teams based on the seminar topic discussed during the previous class meeting.

♦ The history teacher provides opportunities for students to experience how a historian goes about the task of locating, discovering, identifying, classifying, and writing history by assigning students to become historians for a period of time in their community. They might develop guides for individually interviewing selected persons in their community, or they might decide to invite guests to come to school for class or small group interviews. Students might visit a local cemetery to collect information relative to a particular period of history, such as the years 1941 to 1945. Do they know any families who had sons or daughters die during World War II? Would they want to interview any of those family members? In what theater of operations did their family member die, Europe or the Pacific? Do they know how he/she died? What was it like living in their local community during that war? What was rationing? How did it work? The goal would be to help students "make history real and alive" and not just something that occurred in the past that we now need to memorize.[1]

♦ A science teacher moves to a laboratory activity during the application phase or conducts a Paideia seminar on a topic such as the ethics of genetic engineering.

♦ A geometry teacher accompanies students to the computer laboratory for work on their current topic, or the students work in pairs in the commons area of the school applying geometric principles of measurement which were explained earlier in the block.

♦ If the school were following one of the schedules proposed in Chapter 7, whereby teachers have one full day per month with each of their classes, a journalism teacher might have students spend either a partial or a full day visiting a court room, police station, or hospital emergency room and take notes. Later, students could use the application time in the block to work at a word processor preparing a report. Another idea would be for the teacher to have the students watch a tape of court proceedings (for example, the O. J. Simpson trial) and develop a story from a segment of the trial.

---

[1] For additional application phase ideas for history teachers, please refer to (Cohen, 1995).

♦ A foreign language teacher takes the class to the language lab as part of the lesson or brings in a native speaker of the language to provide practice for students.

We have found that many teachers, especially in physical education, the vocational arts, and some of the performing arts, such as theater, dance, and drama, often welcome longer blocks of instructional time and have no difficulty designing application activities. In our experience, staff development in the design of appropriate active learning strategies is more critical for teachers of mathematics, social sciences, English, health, and foreign languages.

## SYNTHESIS

The third instructional phase in lessons designed for block teaching is similar to Bloom's [1956] concept of "synthesis," but also includes aspects of "closure." This part of the lesson usually consumes between 15 and 30 minutes, depending on the content of the lesson and the length of the block. During the synthesis phase of the lesson, the teacher involves the students in connecting the explanation part of the lesson with the application phase. It is a time for reflection, review, and sometimes re-teaching or re-explaining; and as one teacher said to us recently, "It is a critical phase when the teacher, hopefully by leading the students, helps give meaning to the lesson. Sometimes, when appropriate, it may be a time to help answer the student's question: Why are we learning this stuff? What can we ever do with it?" The relevance of the day's learning should be reaffirmed during the synthesis phase.

We do not mean to be excessively critical of teachers. Collectively we have spent over five decades teaching in classrooms in both rural and urban schools. To a large extent we are expressing and admitting our own frustrations and deficits. We also have worked in hundreds of high schools across America conducting workshops and making presentations. It is our conclusion that for years teachers were trained and expected to teach in short, fragmented, daily periods of time, and we contend they developed teaching practices that "fit the schedule" given them! If teachers must plan to teach in 40 to 55 minutes of time, do all the administrative work expected of them during each class period, see 100 to 180 students per day, and prepare two to six preparations each day, no wonder we see so much unenthusiastic lecturing as we walk through high school hallways throughout America! What else should we expect to see?

## Instructional Strategies for the Block Schedule

In the sections that follow, we discuss several teaching models which we believe can assist teachers in creating more active classrooms and thereby engaging the interest and efforts of their students. Each of the strategies discussed is appropriate for any kind of schedule, single-period or block; however, for purposes of survival of both teachers and students, variety and activity are undoubtedly more critical for instruction in extended class periods. Included in this discussion are the following techniques: cooperative learning, Paideia seminars, and other models of teaching such as synectics, concept development, concept attainment, and inquiry. Also, we briefly describe the possibilities for simulations, learning centers, and the use of technology. Finally, although we have stated consistently that the lecture is overused and cannot continue to be the only instructional strategy employed by teachers—especially in block scheduling—we do recognize the utility of this strategy; therefore, we conclude this section by revisiting the lecture format and offering tips for its improvement and inclusion as one of many instructional tools of the professional educator.

### Cooperative Learning

Cooperative learning is a model of teaching that has received considerable attention in recent years. Research suggests that it is an effective active teaching model for use with heterogeneous groups of students [Slavin, 1980, 1988, 1990]. It is important for practitioners to learn both the theoretical basis for cooperative learning and its practical application in the classroom. While discussion of sufficient detail to enable true implementation of cooperative learning is beyond the scope of this chapter, we offer an introduction and a reference list of useful resources for those who wish to pursue this topic in greater depth. The basic formula (a gross oversimplification) for the implementation of cooperative learning includes the following six steps.[2]

## CLASS BUILDING

In this step of the process it is critical for students in a class to bond together as a cohesive group, *before* they are placed into smaller cooperative learning teams. All too often we leave this step to chance—hoping that the class will develop into a "good group." A variety of proactive techniques can be utilized to facilitate a positive classroom environment and *esprit de corps*. Basically, three kinds of strategies encourage such bonding: get-to-know-you activities, service activities, and group successes (such as working on a common problem).

We frequently have been in secondary school classrooms where students barely know each other. It is unreasonable to expect students to work together cooperatively on content if no level of trust exists. Thus, activities are needed that enable students to learn each others' names, interests, likes and dislikes, to help develop a level of comfort among students which will make the success of cooperative teams more likely. Two sources of such activities are *Communitybuilding in the Classroom* [Shaw, 1992] and *Schools Without Fear: Group Activities for Building Community* [Lehr and Martin, 1994].

In addition to get-to-know-you activities, class members tend to bond together when groups provide service to others. We see evidence of this truth every day as people struggling with natural disasters work together in the selfless pursuit of community good. Providing classes with opportunities to be of service to the school, individuals, or outside groups is also an effective means of class building.

Finally, any time a group meets with success, or for that matter cohesively weathers a failure, the group members become closer. Thus, challenging groups to achieve a certain attainable level of excellence and then helping the groups meet that challenge will draw the members closer together.

---

[2] Adapted from [Kagan, 1992].

## TEAM FORMATION

Cooperative learning teams can be composed in three different manners: teacher selection, student selection, or random selection. Most often, teachers create cooperative learning teams by dividing students into groups of four or five students. We generally recommend that each team be heterogenous in composition based primarily on the most important abilities or skills in a particular subject area. Thus, teams in mathematics might be organized based on quiz scores or the results of a unit pre-test, while physical education teams could be based on speed, strength, and agility. Regardless, an effort is usually made to create teams that are also heterogeneous based on gender, racial or ethnic background, socioeconomic status, and/or a variety of other student characteristics.

Student-selected teams occasionally are used, especially when the focus of the teams' efforts will be a project requiring substantial effort outside school. We have seen one creative way in which a high school teacher in Virginia enlisted the aid of students in forming balanced cooperative learning teams. From his class of 24 students, the teacher selected six students to be the "team formation" committee. These students were challenged by the teacher to meet privately and create six balanced three-person teams from among the remaining students in the class. The teacher then assigned one member of the committee to each team, thus creating six four-member teams. This procedure encouraged the committee to form fair and equal teams. Different students composed the committee each time teams were re-formed.

Finally, teachers may create teams through random procedures such as line-ups and numbering-off [Kagan, 1990]. These groups are typically formed for the sole purpose of class building and stay together only a short time.

In general, we recommend that teams be kept together approximately four-and-a-half to six weeks: long enough for students to form a close working relationship but short enough so that social issues do not override the academic benefits. By keeping teams together for this duration, teachers can limit the amount of time students with personality conflicts are kept together and also guarantee friends that at some point during the school year they will be on the same team. Regardless, we suggest that teachers inform students in advance of the number of weeks teams will stay together; if not, students will lobby to either disband early if they are unhappy with their teams, or stay together for eternity if the opposite is true.

## TEAM BUILDING AND TEAM IDENTITY

Similar to the step of class building, which is designed to draw the entire group together, the steps of team building and team identity are utilized to bond a four- or five-person cooperative learning team together. Typically, for team building, get-to-know-you activities are employed to facilitate positive student interaction. For example, the three-step interview [Kagan, 1990, p. 12:3] is a useful cooperative learning structure which helps students get to know each other. In this simple activity students within a four-person team pair off, one in each pair becoming the interviewer and one the interviewee. A set of generic questions is created, such as the following:

What's your name?

Tell me something about your family.

Tell me about your school career.

What are your hobbies and interests?

Tell me something interesting about yourself that others might not know.

Students in both pairs interview each other with these questions, write down the responses, and then, in a round-robin format, introduce their partners to the other pair within the team.

Another simple team-building strategy attempts to have all students on the team agree on likes and dislikes. For example, they may attempt to agree on a food, a movie, an actress, a political leader, a place, and an activity that they all like, as well as ones they dislike. The teams then share these commonalities with the rest of the class. Discovering these common likes and dislikes begins to bond the team members together.

Similar to team building, allowing teams to develop an identity brings the members together. Once students become familiar with each other they are asked to create a team name, design a team sign, and develop a team handshake. Signs are posted, and handshakes are demonstrated to the other teams. Often, team pictures are taken with an instant camera. Each of these activities takes time, but theoretically the time lost to team building and the development of a team identity is recouped later because of the close and efficient working relationships that become established.

## COOPERATIVE LEARNING STRUCTURES

In the parlance of cooperative learning, "structures" are generic activities that may be utilized and adapted to any grade level and any subject matter. Cooperative learning is far more complex than simply throwing an activity at a group of students and saying "Work together on this task." We know what happens when this occurs. Certain students take over, either through force of personality or because no one else exhibits much interest in the task. Other students become "free riders", do nothing, and create animosity because of their refusal to participate. Thus, structuring activities carefully is an important aspect of the successful cooperative learning classroom. To be effective, cooperative learning structures, as a minimum, must meet the following four criteria:

♦ The structure must have a **Group Goal**. A task must be created for students that results in a group product or group evaluation of some sort. For example, in the three-step interview described previously, the group goal is for the team to get to know each other better.

♦ The group goal must be met through the **Face-to-Face Interaction** of all team members. Team members do not toil in total independence in well-designed structures. At least part of the work must be completed through discussion and interaction among members. Again, in the three-step interview students were required to interact while interviewing their partners and again when they introduced their partners to the other pair in the team.

♦ The face-to-face interaction must result in a state of **Positive Interdependence** in which all student contributions are necessary and no one contribution is sufficient. This is the idea that the participation of all team members is necessary for success. If even one member does not pull his or her weight, the team cannot be successful. We sink or swim together. During the three-step interview, if a team member decides not to cooperate it is impossible for the partner to complete his or her job, and thus the activity falls apart.

♦ Finally, and perhaps most overlooked, although students are somewhat dependent upon each other, **Individual Accountability** is emphasized and carefully orchestrated. The essence of cooperative learning is: **"We work together, we learn together, but we are held individually accountable for our own learning."** Thus, in the interview each team member is held accountable because he or she is asked to write answers to the questions and to introduce his or her partner. These activities can be checked by the teacher, and therefore provide the necessary individual accountability.

## GROUP PROCESSING AND EVALUATION

The final step of the process of implementing cooperative learning in the classroom is for team members and the teacher to debrief regarding students' contributions to group efforts. Students are encouraged to self-evaluate and peer evaluate. Often, as part of this step, group rewards and recognition are awarded, although much controversy exists regarding the appropriateness and effectiveness of extrinsic rewards in the cooperative learning classroom [Kohn, 1991].

Cooperative learning techniques can be adapted to work with students of all ages. Several experts in the field include Robert Slavin [1990], David and Roger Johnson [1987, 1990], and Spencer Kagan [1990]. Common structures include the following: Roundtable, Pairs Check, Jigsaw, Numbered Heads Together, Think-Pair-Share, Corners, Send-a-Problem, Inside-Outside Circles, Student Teams Achievement Divisions, and more. This discussion is merely a brief introduction to the potential of cooperative learning. Readers desiring more information should consult the bibliography we have provided and consider attending one of the various training sessions offered around the country each year. We believe the proper application of cooperative learning techniques to be the single most effective means of providing active learning strategies for a wide variety of teachers and students during the application stage of lessons designed for extended blocks of time. We end with a few ideas to get teachers started.

## SOME QUICK COOPERATIVE STARTERS[3]

♦ Turn to Your Neighbor: Three to five minutes. Ask the students to turn to a neighbor and ask something about the lesson: for example, to explain a concept you've just taught; to explain the assignment; to explain how to do what you've just taught; to summarize the three most important points of the discussion, or whatever fits the lesson.

♦ Reading Groups: Students read material together and answer the questions. One person is the Reader, another the Recorder, and the third the Checker (who checks to make certain everyone understands and agrees with the answers). They must come up with three possible answers to each question and circle their favorite one. When finished, they sign the paper to certify that they all understand and agree on the answers.

♦ Jigsaw: Each person reads and studies part of a selection, then teaches what he or she has learned to the other members of the group. Each then quizzes the group members until satisfied that everyone knows his or her part thoroughly.

♦ Focus Trios: Before a film, lecture, or reading, have students summarize together what they already know about the subject and come up with questions they have about it. Afterwards, the trios answer questions, discuss new information, and formulate new questions.

♦ Drill Partners: Have students drill each other on the facts they need to know until they are certain both partners know and can remember them all. This works for spelling, vocabulary, math, grammar, test review, and so on. Give bonus points on the test if all members score above a certain percentage.

---

[3] Developed from Johnson, D., Johnson, R., & Holubec, E. [1990]. *Circles of Learning: Cooperation in the Classroom.* Edina, MN: Interaction Book Company.

- Worksheet Checkmates: Have two students, each with different jobs, do one worksheet. The Reader reads, then suggests an answer; the Writer either agrees or comes up with another answer. When they both understand and agree on an answer, the Writer can write it. Then students switch roles.

- Homework Checkers: Have students compare homework answers, discuss any they have not answered similarly, then correct their papers and add the reason they changed an answer. They make certain everyone's answers agree, then staple the papers together. The teacher grades one paper from each group and gives group members that grade.

- Test Reviewers: Have students prepare each other for a test. They get bonus points if every group member scores above a preset level.

- Composition Pairs: Student A explains what s/he plans to write, while Student B takes notes or makes an outline. Together they plan the opening or thesis statement. Then Student B explains while Student A writes. They exchange outlines and use them in writing their papers.

- Problem Solvers: Give groups a problem to solve. Each student must contribute to part of the solution. Groups can decide who does what, but they must show where all members contributed. Or they can decide together, but each must be able to explain how to solve the problem.

- Computer Groups: Students work together on the computer. They must agree on the input before it is entered. One person is the Keyboard Operator, another the Monitor Reader, a third the Verifier (who collects opinions on the input from the other two and makes the final decision). Roles are rotated daily so everyone gets experience at all three jobs.

- Book Report Pairs: Students interview each other on the books they read; then they report on their partner's book.

- Writing Response Groups: Students read and respond to each other's papers three times:
  - They mark what they like with a star and put a question mark anywhere there is something they don't understand or think is weak. Then they discuss the paper as a whole

with the writer.

- They mark problems with grammar, usage, punctuation, spelling, or format and discuss them with the author.

- They proofread the final draft and point out any errors for the author to correct.

Teachers can assign questions for students to answer about their group members' papers to help them focus on certain problems or skills.

♦ Skill Teachers/Concept Clarifiers: Students work in pairs on skills (like identifying adjectives in sentences or completing a proof in geometry) and/or concepts (like "ecology" or "economics") until both can perform the operation or explain the content easily.

♦ Group Reports: Students research a topic together. Each one is responsible for checking at least one different source and writing at least three note cards of information. They write the report together; each person is responsible for seeing that his/her information is included. For oral reports, each must take a part and help each other rehearse until they are all at ease.

♦ Summary Pairs: Have students alternate reading and orally summarizing paragraphs. One reads and summarizes while the other checks the paragraph for accuracy and adds anything left out. They alternate roles with each paragraph.

♦ Elaborating and Relating Pairs: Have students elaborate on what they are reading and learning by relating it to what they already know about the subject. This can be done before and after reading a selection, listening to a lecture, or seeing a film.

## PAIDEIA SEMINAR TEACHING

The Paideia Seminar is a group discussion technique developed by Mortimer Adler (1982) and first discussed in his book *The Paideia Proposal*. This Socratic teaching method focuses on a piece of text which all participants must read prior to the seminar. Very specific rules govern the participation of both teachers and students. Figure 8.1 lists the differences between Paideia seminars and more traditional class discussions.

FIG. 8.1.

| PAIDEIA SEMINARS | TRADITIONAL GROUP DISCUSSIONS |
|---|---|
| Consists of 97% student talk. | Consists of 97% teacher talk. |
| Average student response is 8–12 seconds. | Average student response is 2-3 seconds. |
| No teacher approval or disapproval is present (affirming feedback is taboo). | Teacher affirmation of correctness is critical. |
| Thinking, backed up by textual evidence, is paramount. | Rightness is paramount; thinking ends as soon as one is right. |
| Students listen to peers. | Students listen primarily to teacher. |
| Students have ownership for "flow". | Teacher has ownership for "flow". |
| Students are held accountable for contributions based upon pre-agreed-upon criteria. | Students may see the discussion as a "frill" just for a "participation" grade; if you miss class, so what; it was just a discussion! |

Source: Pam Brewer, Assistant Principal, Person County High School, Roxboro, NC.

The Paideia Seminar is most frequently utilized in English, the social sciences, and the humanities, but it can be adapted for use in any discipline. Its use requires specific intensive instruction by skilled trainers. The following description of this strategy, sometimes referred to as a Socratic seminar, may be helpful in demonstrating how teachers might employ the seminar during the application phase of a lesson in a block schedule.

## THE SEMINAR[4]

The Socratic seminar is a strategy for creating active learners as students engage in the exploration and evaluation of ideas. In a Socratic seminar the students and teacher examine a text as partners. The effectiveness of the seminar depends primarily on the text being reviewed, the questions asked, the teacher who leads the seminar, and the students who participate. Considering each of these four components of a seminar helps explain its unique character and format.

## THE STUDENTS

In a Socratic seminar, the students share with the teacher the responsibility for the quality of the seminar. Good seminars occur when the students read the text before the seminar occurs, listen courteously and attentively, share their ideas and questions in response to the ideas and questions of others, and search for evidence in the text to support their ideas.

Students acquire these seminar behaviors in at least three ways. First, the students hear the teacher explain, before the initial seminar, its purposes and the behaviors appropriate to these purposes. Second, the students and teacher evaluate the first few seminars and identify how the seminar process could be improved. Third, when the students realize that the teacher is really not looking for right answers but is encouraging the exchange of their opinions and ideas, they discover the excitement of exploring the important questions raised in serious writing. This excitement contributes to the development of willing readers eager to discuss ideas in a courteous manner.

## THE TEACHER

In a Socratic seminar, the teacher plays the dual role of leader and participant. As the seminar leader, the teacher keeps the discussion focused on the text, asks follow-up questions, helps clarify

---

[4] The following descriptions are based upon materials provided for workshops by Patricia A. Ciabotti, Coordinator of Coalition of Essential Schools, Broward County Public Schools, Fort Lauderdale, Florida 33301.

positions when arguments become confused, and involves reluctant students while controlling their more vocal peers.

As a seminar participant, the teacher joins with the students in the examination of the seminar reading. This requires the teacher to know the text sufficiently to recognize the potential of varied interpretations, to be patient enough to allow the students' understandings to evolve, and to be willing to explore the untraditional insights that adolescent minds may produce.

A key aspect of the teacher's role during the seminar is to avoid any evaluative statements. If students perceive that the teacher is affirming a particular point of view or position, students will be less likely to support conflicting positions and the discussion will come to a grinding halt. This may be the most difficult part for the teacher, who undoubtedly has his or her own opinion.

Obviously, assuming the dual role of seminar leader and participant is easier for the teacher if the opening question is one that truly interests the teacher as well as the students.

### THE QUESTION

The discussion in a Socratic seminar begins with a question. This question may be asked by the teacher or solicited from students when the class becomes experienced with seminars. Subsequent questions in a Socratic seminar arise from discussion of the opening question. These questions also may be asked by the teacher or by a student in response to the comments of participants.

Opening questions should have no right or wrong answers; instead, the questions should require the seminar participants to evaluate, judge, speculate, or apply a definition or principle. The questions may relate to the whole text or only a selected portion of the text; however, both the initial question and those asked subsequently should lead the seminar participants into a close examination of the text. By following this format, the line of inquiry in a Socratic seminar **evolves** rather than being predetermined by the teacher. In general, a good opening question is one that inspires at least 20 minutes of discussion without it being necessary for the teacher to formulate new questions to encourage further exchange.

## THE TEXT

The reading examined in a Socratic seminar is from a primary source rather than a summary or review. It can be a complete work, an excerpt of a work, or even two or three short works. Reading from a primary source ensures that the participants are engaged in discovering the author's ideas rather than deciphering someone else's interpretation.

The main consideration when choosing a seminar reading is its ability to provoke and sustain discussion and inquiry. A stimulating seminar text will raise questions in the minds of the participants. The text also may raise questions that may never be answered satisfactorily. (Is it true that many of life's most important questions may not have absolute answers for all of us?) Successful seminars, therefore, frequently end with the participants leaving the seminar with more questions than they brought to the seminar.

To further explain how Socratic seminars may be useful teaching strategies, especially for teachers working in an extended block of time, we offer in Figure 8.2 an adapted description written by Wanda H. Ball, an English teacher at Person County High School, Roxboro, North Carolina, who currently works in a high school having the 4/4 semester block schedule and who has employed the Paideia seminars for more than six years.

As with cooperative learning, it is difficult to capture the essence and practice of Paideia seminars through reading. We suggest that training in this exciting teaching strategy is an appropriate part of any staff development effort in preparation for, or during the implementation of, block scheduling.

## THE "OTHER" MODELS OF TEACHING

Every form of instruction is in some manner a "model of teaching." Traditionally our public schools have overused the model of teaching we call "Lecture/Discussion." This model is characterized by a preponderance of "teacher-talk" accompanied by a few questions, for which students are to provide correct answers. "Direct Instruction" is another commonly used model of teaching which was popularized by Madeline Hunter during the past 15 years. It is primarily used to teach basic skills, knowledge, and facts. "Cooperative Learning", a third model of instruction, which we

## FIG. 8.2. A TEACHER'S VIEW OF PAIDEIA SEMINARS

In my classroom, I schedule seminars on a weekly basis as I encounter a selection that lends itself to the seminar approach. All seminar readings correlate with requirements of my curriculum and are not "add-ons". With the block schedule my teaching time is very valuable; therefore, I must maximize every piece of literature I teach to get the most results from my students. The seminar allows me to require independent readings of novels without the "busy work" of study questions. When the students discuss the novel in seminar and explore the possible interpretations of the work, it is then that I know how thoroughly they have read and prepared. Watching students communicate with each other in this less-structured environment is rewarding to me; it is then that I witness their inquisitive minds processing information critically and independently.

While the students view my class and seminars as being less structured, the class actually is very structured with definite rules and procedures that allow for open communication and in-depth discussion. As a teacher, I have clear objectives in mind as I formulate questions for the seminar because I must maintain the focus on the learning process while appearing to give up total control to the students. It becomes their seminar, and I take a subordinate role, yet I remain firmly in control as the facilitator. From such an experience my students have grown substantially. They now know how to disagree with one another respectfully; yet they also know how to develop and to support their own ideas without fear of reprisal. No other strategy I have used causes these dynamics to occur.

Though the seminar is a marvelous teaching tool, it does not solve all my classroom problems. I still have the responsibility to use as many other methods as I possibly can to reach my students; however, the seminars do give me a way of getting them interested and involved. Perhaps the most frequent difficulty with seminars occurs when students do not read the assignment. I must build pre-seminar tasks into my plans to insure that my students are reading. As well, I must develop post-seminar tasks which usually are writings that extend the learning.

When my students and I are in seminar, we all are being challenged to think critically, to apply information in a relevant manner, and to become better communicators. Oddly enough, I suppose my greatest skill as a communicator may be to sit and listen to active minds at work!

Wanda Ball, English Teacher
Person County High School
Roxboro, NC

have discussed previously, has gained many followers in the past 20 years.

Each of these models has its place in the professional teachers' instructional repertoire, as do a host of other "models of teaching" which have received far less exposure. Several of these "other" models of instruction have been described by Bruce Joyce [1992] in *Models of Teaching*, and Mary Alice Gunter, Thomas Estes, and Jan Schwab [1990] in *Instruction: A Models Approach*. Included are the models of "concept development," "concept attainment," "inquiry," and "synectics." A brief description of each of these models follows.[5]

## CONCEPT DEVELOPMENT

This model, which was originated by Hilda Taba, teaches students to organize data based on perceived similarities and then to categorize and label the data, producing a conceptual map. Students explore their own thinking and begin to understand how concepts are formed. This model is appropriate for use with teaching objectives related to contrasting, applying, categorizing, and analyzing data.

The first step of concept development is *listing*. In some manner a database of knowledge regarding a particular topic must be created. The teacher may ask students to compose two sentences related to a topic, for example, "democracy." Students are then encouraged to underline the most important words or phrases in their two sentences. Through student participation each of these words or phrases is listed on chart paper or the chalkboard.

In the second step of concept development, *grouping* or *categorizing*, students are asked to choose five or six of the words or phrases which seem to be connected in some manner. They are asked to suggest, without labeling, the connection among the items chosen. Again, in our example for democracy, a student might see the relationship between "speech, assembly, religion, and privacy" as having to do with "freedoms." After several examples are shared,

---

[5] Sections on concept development, concept attainment, inquiry, and synectics have evolved from our use of Gunter, Estes, and Swabb's 1990 work, *Instruction: A Models Approach*.

students then are asked to group or categorize all data on the list. This task can be accomplished in cooperative learning groups, in pairs, or individually; markers and chart paper or blank overhead transparencies and transparency pens are useful display media.

During the third step, *labeling and defining relationships*, students name their categories and suggest conceptual connections among the different groupings. Lines, arrows, boxes, diagrams, and other visual graphic organizers are useful techniques for depicting such relationships. At this point it is effective to have several individuals, pairs, or groups present their conceptual map to the class.

In the fourth step students are asked to refine their concept map by *regrouping, reanalyzing relationships, and subsuming categories* if necessary. In this manner they use ideas from the previous student presentations to assist in improving their understanding of the concept.

Finally, students are asked to *synthesize* and/or *summarize* their understanding of the concept, usually through oral presentation or written work.

Concept development is an especially effective strategy when used as an alternative assessment (i.e., pre-test) of students' knowledge and understanding as part of the introduction of a unit or to provide closure and synthesis at the end of a unit.

## CONCEPT ATTAINMENT

By providing a series of positive and negative examples, a teacher leads students to a definition of a concept and determination of its essential attributes. This model is especially effective during the explanation phase of a lesson when attempting to teach objectives related to comprehension, comparison, discrimination, and recall.

In the first step of concept attainment, the teacher must *choose a concept, carefully define it, and identify the essential attributes of the definition*. For example, a teacher might attempt to bring students to a definition of the concept of "research" defined by Webster as "careful, systematic, patient study and investigation in some field of knowledge, undertaken to discover or establish facts or principles" [Guralnik, 1974, p. 1208]. With regard to the essential attributes, the teacher might decide that the definition she or he wanted the students to arrive at must include the notions of "careful," "systematic," "investigation," "knowledge," and "purpose."

The teacher *creates or selects both positive and negative examples of the concept* as the second step of concept attainment. For example, "George Seifert, the coach of football's San Francisco 49er's, watched many game films to learn the offensive propensities of the Dallas Cowboys prior to Sunday's big game." This example contains all of the essential attributes for the definition of "research." In contrast, "Mary enjoyed reading about the Wild West; it made her yearn to live during that era," while perhaps fulfilling the requirement for "knowledge," does not contain the other necessary attributes of the definition.[6]

The third step of the process involves *carefully introducing the lesson to the students*. The concept to be defined is *not* shared with students. The teacher should explain that positive examples of an idea will be given, as will examples which do not meet the requirements of the definition. Students will be trying to both discover the concept and define it.

Next, the teacher *presents the examples*. When the first positive example is presented, all of its attributes are brainstormed by the students and listed on the board by the teacher. For example, with regard to our previous example about "research," other potential attributes of the example were "football," "George Seifert," "games," "films," "Dallas," etc. These would have been listed. When a second, and different, positive example is given, the group should eliminate those attributes which are not common to all positive examples. Negative examples are given to emphasize the necessary qualities of the definition, but they cannot be used to eliminate attributes. Through this process the definition is pared down to its essentials.

In the fourth step students are asked to *compose a definition* for the concept by using the remaining "essential attributes". Finally, *the definition is tested by using it to evaluate several new positive and negative examples*.

While the process of concept attainment is certainly more circumspect than "Here's the definition; memorize it!", it leads students to a much deeper understanding of concepts. In addition,

---

[6] The idea for this lesson came from Kathy Pierce of the Louisa County Public Schools in Mineral, Virginia.

the process by which the definition was developed offers numerous memory cues that will assist students in retaining their new knowledge.

## INQUIRY

Given a puzzling situation, students follow a scientific process to formulate hypotheses. This problem-solving model emphasizes careful and logical procedures, the tentative nature of knowledge, and the need for group cooperation in solving problems. Learners are encouraged to seek multiple answers. The inquiry model can be utilized to meet objectives related to problem solving, analyzing, hypothesizing, and evaluating.

Inquiry requires that the teacher possess thorough knowledge of the chosen topic. Thus, the first step of this process is for the teacher to *select and research the problem*. A puzzling situation or event which is related to the content of the subject is often intrinsically motivating for students to discover the answer. For example, the following situation has been presented to classes: Two men go into a bar and order drinks. An hour later one of them dies. What was the cause of death? The goal of the lesson will be for students to discover the cause of death through a systematic process of inquiry. The second step involves a careful *introduction of the process to the students*. Students are presented with the puzzling situation and given a means for recording data (chart paper, etc.).

*Students gather relevant data* during the third step of the process. The teacher is the "fount of all wisdom"; students are encouraged to pose clearly articulated "Yes-No" questions. No student discussion during the questioning is permitted. Occasionally, groups are permitted to "caucus" to discuss their ideas. The teacher records relevant data on chart paper, overhead transparencies, or the chalkboard. For example, given the puzzling situation described above, a student might ask any of the following questions:

"Was the dead man shot by the other man?" Answer: No.

"Did the dead man die of natural causes?" Answer: No.

"Do the drinks have something to do with the death?" Answer: Yes.

"Was the dead man poisoned?" Answer: Yes.

"Did the men have the same drink?" Answer: Yes.

In the fourth step of the model, when students begin to think that they have the answer to the puzzling situation, they are encouraged to *develop a theory and describe causal relationships*. This explanation is written on the board and evaluated by the class. If it is rejected, alternate theories can be posed. During the fifth step, when a theory is accepted by the class, *the theory's rules and effects are detailed and tested*. Students' questions of the teacher continue to be the primary means of verifying theories and their rules during steps four and five.

Finally, the class and the teacher *discuss the process and possible improvements*.

Inquiry is useful for exploring the mysteries of literature and social studies, as well as science. It can be used in any phase of the three-part lesson design: as a means of developing an anticipatory set during explanation and during application or synthesis to test students' understanding of principles taught and, hopefully, learned.

## SYNECTICS

This model stimulates creative thought and problem solving through the development of metaphorical analogies. Just as the outsider can sometimes "see" more clearly than the insider who is blinded by his or her closeness to a problem or situation, these analogies distance students from the commonplace reality of a topic, encouraging creative thinking and new insights. The synectics model is particularly effective for the creative exploration of topics, problem solving, and as a pre-writing activity.

In step one of the synectics model, students are asked to describe the topic, either orally or through writing. Similar to the first step of concept development, the most important words and phrases generated are listed by the teacher. For example, in using this model with a group during a workshop, one of the authors utilized the topic of "computer technology." Each participant was asked to write a short paragraph on the topic, and then to underline the most important words and phrases, which were shared with the entire group on chart paper (Figure 8.3).

---

FIG. 8.3. STEP 1. DESCRIBE THE TOPIC

What are the most important words and phrases
in your short paragraph about technology?

| | | | |
|---|---|---|---|
| efficiency | programming | necessity | time-saving |
| education | knowledge | dependent | user-friendly |
| specialist | money-saving | analysis | everyday life |
| helpless | facilitates | outdated | life-saving |
| frightening | problems | reliability | |

---

In the second step, students are asked to read over the list and
to select an item from a general category such as plants, machines,
places, appliances, and automobiles which best captures the essence
of the list. For example, using the list generated from the topic of
computer technology, the group was asked to select a "vehicle"
which came to mind after reviewing the list of words (Figure 8.3)
that had been generated. A list of vehicles was created (Figure 8.4).
One student offered a "roller coaster" because computer technology
was "frightening" and they felt "helpless" and "dependent," similar
to the way they felt on a roller coaster.

---

FIG. 8.4. STEP 2. CREATE DIRECT ANALOGIES

What vehicle does the list in Step 1 bring to mind? Why?

| | | | |
|---|---|---|---|
| cruise ship | sports car | bike | rollercoaster |
| *jet* | train | monorail | UFO |
| motorcycle | monorail | skateboard | bobsled/luge |
| rollerblades | go-cart | unicycle | elevator |

---

A class vote was held to select the vehicle which the group
thought most nearly captured the sense of the words generated
in Step 1; "jet" was chosen. Participants then were asked to close
their eyes and imagine how it would feel to be a jet. A list of these
"feelings" was created (Figure 8.5).

---

### FIG. 8.5. STEP 3. CREATE PERSONAL ANALOGIES

How does it feel to be a . . .?     (Jet)

| | | | |
|---|---|---|---|
| power | sense of unknown | cold | organized |
| weighted down | marvel | amazement | dependent on pilot |
| strong | invincible | inflexible | fast |
| protected | rusty | exhausted | intelligent |
| blinded | anticipating | shaky | superior |
| helpless | secure | ready to land | |

---

Students then were asked to identify words from among these feelings which constituted a pair of opposites, called "compressed conflicts." A second vote was taken, and the pair *invincible-helpless* was selected by the class as most closely capturing the sense of the list of feelings (Figure 8.6).

---

### FIG. 8.6. STEP 4. IDENTIFY COMPRESSED CONFLICTS

What pairs of feelings seem to be in opposition to each other?

| | |
|---|---|
| strong-rusty | strong-helpless |
| secure-helpless | superior-shaky |
| inflexible-organized | rusty-protected |
| blind-intelligent | strong-exhausted |
| invincible-rusty | *invincible-helpless* |
| power-exhausted | invincible-blinded |
| cold-protected | unknown-secure |

---

Next, participants were asked to imagine a creature that came to mind as they thought of the compressed conflict *invincible-helpless*. From the list generated (Figure 8.7), a final vote was taken and *human* was chosen as the creature that came closest to capturing the conflicts expressed by this pair.

---

### FIG. 8.7. STEP 5. CREATE NEW ANALOGIES

What creature comes to mind when you think
of the compressed conflict *invincible-helpless?*

| | | | |
|---|---|---|---|
| whale | bald eagle | elephant | dinosaur |
| cow | piranha | *human* | spore |
| yellow jacket | woman | man | jellyfish |
| tick | | | |

---

Finally, in the sixth step of the process, students were asked to re-describe the original topic of computer technology by orally stating how computer technology and being "human" were similar. Each person was asked to write a second paragraph, using either "human" or another creature from the list in Figure 8.7 as a basis for a discussion of the topic. Insights into the nature of computer technology were far more sophisticated and moving than the original paragraphs used to begin the lesson.

Synectics is a creative means for examining and re-examining topics. It is probably most useful in social studies and English, although occasionally it may be used with science, math, and health, to explore the ethical and affective aspects of these subjects.

### *SIMULATIONS*

Simulations are educational games which attempt to create the appearance or effect of a real environment or situation. They are intended to have students experience a process or event in a manner closely resembling reality, but without the dangers and risks. These games are often utilized in social science and science classrooms to simulate economic, political, and environmental situations. Advantages of simulations include the following:[7]

♦ Participants receive an experience similar to that in the real world.

♦ Participants have opportunities to solve complex problems and to observe others solving problems.

---

[7] Advantages, issues, and steps based upon Cruickshank [1980].

+ Simulations provide greater possibilities for transfer to real-life situations.

+ Simulations provide a responsive environment with immediate feedback.

+ Simulations foster an understanding of events of extended duration in compressed time.

+ Simulations are psychologically engaging and motivating.

+ Simulations are safe.

Several issues that must be addressed regarding simulations include the following:

+ Many faculty are unfamiliar with simulations and require training.

+ Simulations require extended blocks of time; thus, they fit nicely into block schedules.

+ Simulations tend to be less available than other teaching materials; few teachers know they exist.

+ Simulations can be expensive.

+ Because they require active and vocal participation, simulations can be noisy.

+ Just as any other instructional strategy, simulations can be applied only to certain teaching objectives.

Cruickshank's [1980] research in the field of educational games and simulations suggests the following steps for their use:

+ Prepare thoroughly. Choose a simulation which closely matches the instructional objectives and takes into account students' previous experience with both the content and process of the simulation.

+ Plan an introduction that motivates students' participation and includes a careful outline of the rules of play. Do not attempt to cover every detail of the game; get started as soon as possible.

+ Carefully assign students' roles. How will high-status roles be assigned for this simulation and for other games over time?

- ◆ If teams are utilized, make sure they are heterogeneous.
- ◆ Remove yourself from control of the simulation as much as possible. Facilitate and advise; avoid directing the action.
- ◆ When the simulation is completed, encourage students to reflect upon the process, its relationship to the objectives of the lesson, and improvements that could be made.

We believe that simulations can be stimulating activities which are utilized most appropriately during the application stage of lessons. Because of the length of time required to engage in such activities, they are a natural addition to a teacher's collection of instructional strategies, especially social studies and science faculty operating in block schedules. We include a short bibliography of sources for simulations in the reference section of the book.

## TECHNOLOGY

A lengthy discussion of the potential for the use of technology in instruction is beyond the scope of this book; however, longer blocks of time open up a number of possibilities for greater use of computer labs and, perhaps more important, offer innumerable opportunities for the integration of technology with classroom instructional models. We have provided a short bibliography for the field of instructional technology in the reference section of the book.

## LEARNING CENTERS OR STATIONS

For decades, learning centers have been a basic part of the elementary teacher's classroom structure; some middle school teachers include them in their classrooms, but we have found very few high school teachers who utilize learning centers on any regular basis. We believe the longer teaching block may offer an opportunity for high school teachers to consider including centers as one of their many teaching tools.

Learning centers can be designed to provide for varied interests and competencies of students; they can add interest and motivation to a topic; centers may provide for student independence, responsibility, and individualization; and centers can be a way to permit students to **apply** skills and information in a meaningful context.

Materials for high school learning centers could include some of the following, adapted to the appropriate specific subject:

+ Various media such as newspapers, audio and video tapes, magazines, selected library books, and/or computer software;

+ Task cards;

+ Activity packets;

+ Case studies to be analyzed;

+ Equipment, such as a microscope in science or jump ropes at a particular physical education station;

+ Tools, ingredients, or materials required to complete a particular task in a home economics or electronics classroom;

+ Paints, tools, and possibly directions for completing a particular art or crafts project;

+ Devices for measuring or completing various tasks in a geometry class;

+ Short science experiments at stations; and

+ Listening centers in a language class.

If teachers have prepared students to utilize various types of cooperative learning strategies, tasks requiring cooperative learning work groups can be included in various centers. Several of the cooperative learning "starters" suggested previously may be useful as center activities for students during the application phase of a lesson.

If centers are to work successfully, teachers must organize and implement them cautiously; with centers it is easy for a classroom to get out of control! In fact, for this reason they may not be appropriate for some teachers and some classrooms. Before beginning work in the centers, discuss the rules and procedures that must be followed and have such information posted at each center. As part of the organizational structure for a classroom with centers/stations, it will be helpful to have a display area in each classroom, or possibly in the hallway outside the classroom, to show work accomplished.

## *LECTURES*

In various forms, the lecture historically has been the most widely used teaching model in high school classrooms throughout the country. Although in recent years the lecture has come under attack, we take the position that the lecture, well done and under appropriate circumstances, can be effective and should be utilized. Cashin [1985] defines lecture as "teaching by the spoken word with emphasis on one-way communication; the teacher talks, and (hopefully) the students listen" [p. 2]; and we might add, hopefully the students learn! In the above definition, we accept the fact that in many lectures some two-way communication may occur, usually in a question-and-answer format, with the teacher asking most of the questions and the students trying to regurgitate the responses they think the teacher wants.

Because "lecture success" is so dependent on the person doing the lecture model, the following section, based on Henry Ellington's paper entitled "Some Hints on How to be an Effective Lecturer" [1984, pp. 1–4], focuses on ways to make the lecture model more effective.

♦ To plan for a successful lecture, we suggest that the teacher first determine the purpose of the lecture. In some cases the purpose may be fairly obvious; in other cases, the teacher will need to determine the objectives of the particular lesson. Keep in mind that the lecture is best suited to the achievement of objectives of the lower cognitive type.

♦ Next, select the content of the lecture. What is it the teacher expects the students to learn that best fits the lecture mode? Basic structures which can be adopted to the lecture format are the following:

   • Providing a simple list of topics, which, in turn, are examined and discussed

   • Showing classification hierarchies that indicate the relationship between the various topics, subgroups, and topics being examined

   • Illustrating chained structures, in which students are led through the various stages of an argument, proof, or derivation in a logical sequence

- Examining inductive structures, which begin by looking at specific cases or examples of an "as-yet-unstated" general principle or rule and then use selected processes to arrive at the principle or rule by a process of induction

- Focusing on problem-centered structures, which begin with a statement of the problem, various possible solutions presented by the teacher, and finally a possible solution which may be determined by involving the students in discussion

- Examining comparative structures, in which two or more points of view are compared under a series of headings

- Illustrating a variation of information and the relationship of the information by using a matrix structure

- Explaining linked structures to help students see linked patterns, concepts, or topics by moving from one to another along lines of association or logical relation

- Illustrating networks to show how concepts and subsystems are interrelated

Most lectures will be enhanced if the teacher includes some form of visual aid such as transparencies, printed handouts, or graphic organizers—visual charts and diagrams to help students understand the relationship of various components in a selected body of information.

Visuals are most critical when the primary purpose of the lecture is to assist students in "untangling" complicated concepts or ideas. For example, an empty diagram or flow chart would be a useful graphic organizer as a history teacher explains the branches of government and how each branch is related or the sequence of events through which a bill becomes a law in the United States. A biology teacher could use the lecture model with visual organizers during the explanation phase of the lesson to demonstrate a particular genetic pattern that students will examine later under a microscope during the application phase of the lesson.

Not only can the lecture model be enhanced with the use of visuals, but it also will be improved by including selected periods of structured talk and/or review at appropriate intervals. We have developed the review activity outlined in Figure 8.8 (p. 238), which we find useful in the lecture model. If teachers will follow the steps of "The Five Minute Pause that Refreshes the Memory" on a regular basis when lecturing, students will be more attentive, take better notes, be more alert throughout the lecture, not need to ask the teacher as many questions, and likely retain the information for a longer period of time.

## DESIGNING A STAFF DEVELOPMENT PLAN

If a school or school district can provide only five days of staff development for the purpose of developing alternative instructional strategies for teachers who will be working in one of the block schedules described in this book, we suggest the following curriculum for those five days.

### DAY ONE

If available, we recommend that teachers receive training by peers who already have demonstrated subject area excellence within a block-scheduled instructional situation. Our observation has been that, while teachers may benefit greatly from training in generic non-subject-specific instructional strategies, what they really want, and find credible, is to work with someone who is succeeding in the trenches *in their subject*. Thus, we suggest that the person in charge of planning staff development amass a group of teachers from different disciplines, preferably from different schools, to create a program similar to that shown in Figure 8.9 (p. 239).

FIG. 8.8. THE FIVE MINUTE PAUSE THAT REFRESHES THE MEMORY (AND INCREASES THE ODDS FOR RETENTION!)

Following a brief* lecture or part of a lecture:

1.  Have students review the notes from the presentation independently.

2.  Have students meet in groups of four or five:

    ♦ to review their notes as a team,

    ♦ to identify/highlight the critical points made during the presentation, and

    ♦ to discuss and clarify any misunderstandings (Students may ask the teacher for clarification, but only if members of the group disagree or can not answer.).

3.  Have students in teams accomplish one or more of the following:

    ♦ to complete a Pluses, Minuses, and Interesting Points (PMI) chart regarding the content, and/or

    ♦ similarly, to note one point you agree with, one point you disagree with, and one point your find interesting or unusual, and/or

    ♦ similarly, to list comments which support, refute, clarify, or question the material, and/or

    ♦ to formulate two good test questions regarding the content.

When students come to expect this pattern on a regular basis, they will take better notes and the entire process can occur in about five minutes. It may be advantageous to repeat the "Five Minute Pause that Refreshes Your Memory" two or three times during a block.

*We define brief as somewhere between 15 and 30 minutes depending upon the age and maturity of the students and the complexity of the content being presented.

FIG. 8.9. SURVIVING AND THRIVING IN THE BLOCK SCHEDULE

| | |
|---|---|
| 8:30–8:45 am | Welcome and Plan for the Day |
| 8:45–9:45 am | Panel Discussion: Generic Tips on Lesson Design and Teaching in the Block |
| 9:45–10:00 am | Break |
| 10:00 am–12:00 pm | Subject-Specific Sessions: Lesson Design, Instructional Strategies, Assessment, and Model Lesson |
| 12:00–1:00 pm | Lunch |
| 1:00–2:45 pm | Subject-Specific Breakout Sessions Continue |
| 2:45–3:00 pm | Break |
| 3:00–4:00 pm | Concluding Panel: Q & A |

## DAYS TWO AND THREE

After time spent with subject specialists, we recommend two days of training to provide an introduction to the process of implementing cooperative learning in the classroom.

## DAYS FOUR AND FIVE

We believe that many teachers would also benefit from two days of training in the Paideia approach to seminars.

## DAYS SIX TO TEN

If staff development preparation efforts can be extended to ten days, we suggest adding a second day with subject-specific facilitators; teachers could design units and individual lessons. Two days of training in several of the models of teaching, such as concept development, synectics, and inquiry, would also be beneficial. Because of the many possibilities that are generated through block scheduling, we suggest two days of instruction regarding the design of interdisciplinary units.

In addition to the time spent training teachers in the use of more active instructional strategies, schools that opt for scheduling models such as the 4/4 semester plan will need to allocate a minimum of two days of teacher work time to review and re-pace course timelines for content coverage. Obviously, significant funds and time will be required if more extensive curriculum review is necessary.

## CONCLUSION

We believe that the success or failure of the block scheduling movement will be determined largely by the ability of teachers and administrators to work together to improve instruction. Regardless of a school's time schedule, what happens between individual teachers and students in classrooms is still most important, and *simply altering the manner in which we schedule schools will not ensure better instruction by teachers or increased learning by students*. We strongly believe, however, that a well-designed school schedule **can be** a catalyst for critical changes needed in high schools across America. Educators must not ignore the window of opportunity that has been opened through the hope, energy, and enthusiasm of teachers, administrators, parents, and students. We must support their efforts with intelligence, patience, and resources. Then, perhaps, high schools in our country will become more humane and effective places for teaching and learning.

# REFERENCES

Adler, M. & Van Doren, C. (1984). The conduct of seminars. In M. Adler (Ed.), *The Paideia program: An educational syllabus* (pp. 15–31). New York: MacMillan.

Alam, D. & Seick, R. E., Jr. (1994, May). A block schedule with a twist. *Phi Delta Kappan*, pp. 732–733.

Association for Supervision and Curriculum Development (1985). *With consequences for all: A report from the ASCD Task Force on increased high school graduation requirements* (Stock No. 611–85418). Alexandria, VA: Author. (ERIC Document Reproduction Service No. ED 182 465)

Austin Independent Schools (1987). *Caution: Hazardous grade. Ninth graders at risk.* Austin, TX: Author. (ERIC Document Reproduction Service No. ED 290 971)

Bloom, B. S. (Ed.). (1956). *Taxonomy of educational objectives: Handbook I: Cognitive domain.* New York: David McCay Co.

Bottoms, G., Presson, A., & Johnson, M. (1992). *Making high schools work through integration of academic and vocational education.* Atlanta: Southern Regional Education Board.

Boyer, E. L. (1983a, Winter). The American high school. *American Educator*, pp. 30–33, 40–45.

Boyer, E. L. (1983b). *High school: Report of secondary education in America.* New York: Harper.

Bradley, A. (1992, November 18). Reforming Philadelphia's high schools from within. *Education Week*, pp. 1, 17–19.

Canady, R. L. (1994). High School alternative scheduling to enhance teaching and learning. *The Video Journal of Education* (videotape), 4(2).

Canady, R. L. & Hotchkiss, P. R. (1989, September). It's a good score! Just a bad grade. *Phi Delta Kappan*, pp. 68–71.

Canady, R. L. & Rettig, M. D. (1993, December). Unlocking the lockstep high school schedule. *Phi Delta Kappan*, pp. 310–314.

Carroll, J. B. (1963). A model of school learning. *Teachers' College Record*, 64, 723–733.

Carroll, J. M. (1990, January). The Copernican plan: Restructuring the American high school. *Phi Delta Kappan*, pp. 359–365.

Carroll, J. M. (1994a, October). The Copernican plan evaluated: The evolution of a revolution. *Phi Delta Kappan*, pp. 105–113.

Carroll, J. M. (1994b). *The Copernican plan evaluated: The evolution of a revolution*. Copernican Associates: Topsfield, MA.

Cashin, W. E. (1985). *Improving lectures*. (Idea paper No. 14). Manhattan, KS: Kansas State University. (ERIC Document Reproduction Service No. ED 267 721)

Cawelti, G. (1994). *High school restructuring: A national study*. Arlington, VA: Educational Research Service.

Cohen, P. (1995, Winter). Changing history: The past remains a battleground for schools. *Curriculum Update*. (Association for Supervision and Curriculum Development: Alexandria, VA)

Conway, M. A., Cohen, G., & Stanhope, N. (1991). On the very long-term retention of knowledge acquired through formal education: Twelve years of cognitive psychology. *Journal of Experimental Psychology: General, 120*, 395–409.

Cruickshank, D. R. (1980, Winter). Classroom games and simulations. *Theory into Practice*, pp. 75–80.

Cushman, K. (1989, Summer). Schedules that bind. *American Educator*, pp. 35–39.

Cusick, P. A. (1973). *Inside high school*. New York: Holt, Rinehart and Winston.

Dismuke, D. (1994, December). Students go for four. *NEA Today*, p. 19.

Doyle, W. & Ponder, G. (1977–78). The practicality ethic in teacher decision-making. *Interchange, 8*(3), 1–12.

Edwards, C. M. (1993). The four-period day: Restructuring to improve student achievement. *NASSP Bulletin, 77*, 77–88.

Ellington, H. (1984). *Some hints on how to be an effective lecturer*. Aberdeen, Scotland: Scottish Central Institutions Committee for Educational Development. (ERIC Document Reproduction Service No. ED 289 489)

Emrick, J., & Peterson, S. (1978). *A synthesis of findings across five recent studies in educational dissemination and change*. Santa Monica, CA: Rand Corporation.

Fullan, M. (1982). *The meaning of educational change*. New York: Teachers College Press.

Fullan, M. (1991). *The new meaning of educational change*. New York: Teachers College Press.

Fulong J. & Morrison, G. M. (Eds.). (1994). Mini-series: School violence. *School Psychology Review, 28*(2).

Gilman, D.A. and Knoll, S. (1984). Increasing instructional time: What are the priorities and how do they affect the alternatives? *NASSP Bulletin, 68*, 41–44.

Glasnapp, D. R., Poggio, J. P. & Ory, J. C. (1978). End-of-course and long-term retention outcomes for mastery and non-mastery learning paradigms. *Psychology in the Schools, 15,* 595–603.

Glass, G. V. & Smith, M. L. (1978). *Meta-analysis of research on the relationship of class size and achievement.* San Francisco: Far West Laboratory for Educational Research and Development.

Goldman, J. J., (1983). Flexible modular scheduling: Results of evaluations in its second decade. *Urban Education, 18*(2), 191–228.

Gorman, B. W. (1971). *Secondary education: The high school America needs.* New York: Random House.

Grinsel, J. G. (1989). Flexible scheduling: A second chance? *American Secondary Education, 18*(2), 29–31.

Gunter, M. A., Estes, T. & Schwab J. (1990). *Instruction: A models approach.* Boston: Allyn and Bacon.

Guralnik, D. B. (Ed.). (1974). *Webster's new world dictionary of the American language.* Cleveland & New York: William Collins & World Publishing Co. Inc.

Guskey, T. R. (1986). Staff development and the process of teacher change. *Educational Researcher, 15*(5), 5–12.

Hunter, M. C. (1976). *Improved Instruction.* El Segundo, CA: TIP Publications.

Hunter, M. C. (1982). *Mastery teaching.* El Segundo, CA: TIP Publications.

Johnson, D. W. & Johnson, R. T. (1987). *Learning together and alone: Cooperative, competitive, and individualistic* (2nd ed.). Englewood Cliffs, NJ: Prentice-Hall.

Johnson, D. W., Johnson, R. T., & Holubec, E. J. (1990). *Circles of learning: Cooperation in the classroom* (3rd ed.). Edina, MN: Interaction Book Company.

Joyce, B. (1992). *Models of teaching.* Boston: Allyn and Bacon. Joyce, B. & Showers, B. (1988). *Student achievement through staff development.* New York: Longman.

Justiz, M. J. (1984, March). It's time to make every minute count. *Phi Delta Kappan,* pp. 483–485.

Kagan, S. (1990). *Cooperative learning: Resources for teachers.* San Juan Capistrano, CA: Resources for Teachers, Inc.

Karweit, N. (1985). Should we lengthen the school term? *Educational Researcher, 14*(6), 9–15.

Kohn, A. (1991, February) Group grade grubbing versus cooperative learning. *Educational Leadership,* pp. 83–87.

Lehr, J. & Martin, C. (1994). *Schools without fear: Group activities for building communities.* Minneapolis: Educational Media Corporation.

Levin, H. M. & Hopfenberg, W. S. (1991, January). Don't remediate: Accelerate! *Principal,* pp. 11–13.

Lieberman, A. & Miller, L. (1992). Professional development of teachers. In M. Alkin (Ed.) *Encyclopedia of educational research* (pp. 1045–1053). New York: MacMillan.

Little, J. W. (1981, January). *School success and staff development: The role of staff development in urban desegregated schools.* Washington, DC: National Institute of Education. (ERIC Document Reproduction Service No ED 206 745)

Little, J. W. (1981, April). *The power of the organizational setting: School norms and staff development.* Paper presented at the annual meeting of the American Educational Research Association, Los Angeles, CA. (ERIC Document Reproduction Service No ED 221 918)

Loucks-Horsley, S., Harding, C. K., Arbuckle, M. A., Murray, L. B., Dubea, C., & Williams, M. K. (1987). *Continuing to learn: A guidebook for teacher development.* Andover, MA: Regional Laboratory for Educational Improvement of the Northeast & Islands.

Louis, K. & Sieber, S. (1979). *Bureaucracy and the dispersed organization.* Norwood, NJ: Ablex.

Lyon, M. A. & Gettinger, M. (1985). Differences in student performance on knowledge, comprehension, and application tasks: Implications for school learning. *Journal of Educational Psychology, 77,* 12–19.

McLaughlin, M. W. (1987). Learning from experience: Lessons from policy implementation. *Educational Evaluation and Policy Analysis, 9*(2), 171–178.

National Commission on Excellence in Education. (1984). *A nation at risk.* Cambridge, MA: USA Research.

National Center for Education Statistics. (1993). *Digest of education statistics.* Washington, DC: U.S. Department of Education, Office of Educational Research and Improvement.

National Education Commission on Time and Learning. (1994). *Prisoners of time: Report of the National Education Commission on Time and Learning.* Washington, DC: U.S. Government Printing Office.

National Education Goals Panel. (1994). *The national education goals report: Building a nation of learners.* Washington, DC: U.S. Government Printing Office.

Reis, S. M. & Renzulli, J. S. (1992, October). Using curriculum compacting to challenge the above-average. *Educational Leadership,* pp 51–57.

Rettig, M. (1994). *Directory of high school scheduling models in Virginia: 1994–95 school year.* A report of the "Study of innovative high school scheduling in Virginia". Harrisonburg, VA: James Madison University. (Point your Gopher to JMU's server at vax1.acs.jmu.edu; select "Faculty Publications" (choice #5); select "Directory of High School Scheduling Models in Virginia.")

Rosenbaum, S. & Louis, K. (1979). *Stability and change: Innovation in an educational context.* Cambridge, MA: ABT Associates.

Rossmiller, R.A. (1983). Time-on-Task: A Look at What Erodes Time For Instruction. *NASSP Bulletin, 67*, 45–49.

Seifert, E. H. & Beck, J. J., Jr. (1984). Relationships between task time and learning gains in secondary schools. *Journal of Educational Research, 78*, 5–10.

Semb, G. B., Ellis, J. A., & Araujo, J. (1993). Long-term memory for knowledge learned in school. *Journal of Educational Psychology, 85*, 305–316.

Shaw, V. (1992). *Communitybuilding in the classroom.* San Juan Capistrano, CA: Kagan Cooperative Learning.

Sizer, T. (1992, 1984). *Horace's compromise: The dilemma of the American high school.* Boston: Houghton Mifflin.

Slavin, R. E. (1980). Cooperative learning. *Review of Educational Research, 50*, 315–342.

Slavin, R. E. (1988). Cooperative learning and student achievement. *Educational Leadership, 50*(2), 31–33.

Slavin, R. E. (1990). *Cooperative learning: Theory, research, and practice.* Englewood Cliffs, NJ: Prentice-Hall.

Sommerfeld, M. (1994, May 11). Longer year, day proposed for schooling. *Education Week*, pp. 1, 12.

Trump, J. L. (1959). *Images of the future: A new approach to the secondary school.* Washington, DC: National Association of Secondary Principals.

## COOPERATIVE LEARNING

Adams, D., Carlson, H., & Hamm, M. (1990). *Cooperative learning & educational media: Collaborating with technology and each other.* Englewood Cliffs, NJ: Educational Technology Publications.

Adams, D. & Hamm, M. (1990). *Cooperative learning: Critical thinking and collaboration across the curriculum.* Springfield, IL: C.C. Thomas.

Andrini, B. (1991). *Cooperative learning in mathematics.* San Juan Capistrano, CA: Resources for Teachers, Inc.

Bernagozi, T. (1991). The whole class hated Anthony. *Learning, 20*, 61–63.

Bouton, C. & Garth, R. Y. (Eds.). (1983). *Learning in groups.* San Francisco: Jossey-Bass.

Brubacher, M., Payne, R. & Kemp, R. (Eds.). (1990). *Perspectives on small group learning: Theory and practice.* Oakville, Ontario: Rubicon Publishers.

Cohen, E. G. (1986). *Designing groupwork: Strategies for the heterogeneous classroom.* New York: Teachers College Press.

Cohen, E. G. (1991). Cooperative science lesson plans, *Cooperative Learning, 11*, 46–53.

Davidson, N. (Ed.) (1990). *Cooperative learning in mathematics: A handbook for teachers.* Menlo Park, CA: Addison-Wesley Publishing Company.

Davidson, N. & Kroll, D. L. (1991). An overview of research on cooperative learning related to mathematics. *Journal for Research in Mathematics Education, 22*, 362–365.

DeVries, D., Slavin, R., Gennessey, G., Edwards, K., & Lombardo, N. (1980). *Teams-Games-Tournaments: The team learning approach*. Englewood Cliffs, NJ: Educational Technology Publications.

Dishon, D. & O'Leary, P. (1985). *A guidebook for cooperative learning: A technique for creating more effective schools*. Holmes Beach, FL: Learning Publications.

Dreikurs, R., Grunwald, B. B., & Pepper, F. C. (1982). *Maintaining sanity in the classroom: Classroom management techniques*. New York: Harper & Row.

Dunn, S. E. & Wilson, R. (1991). Cooperative learning in the physical education classroom, *Journal of Physical Education, Recreation and Dance, 62*, 22–28.

Herman, P. M. (1991). Cooperative learning. Spelling groups. *Learning, 19*, 66–67.

Hill, W. F. (1977). *Learning through discussion: Guide for leaders and members of discussion groups*. Newbury Park, CA: Sage Publications, Inc.

Johnson, D. W. & Johnson, F. P. (1987). *Joining together: Group theory and group skills* (3rd ed.). Englewood Cliffs, NJ: Prentice-Hall.

Johnson, D. W. & Johnson, R. T. (1987). *Learning together and alone: Cooperative, competitive, and individualistic learning* (2nd ed.). Englewood Cliffs, NJ: Prentice-Hall.

Johnson, D. W. & Johnson, R. T. (1987). *A Meta-analysis of cooperative, competitive and individualistic goal structures*. Hillsdale, NJ: Lawrence Erlbaum.

Johnson, D. W. & Johnson, R. T. (1989). *Cooperation and competition: Theory and research*. Edina MN: Interactive Book Company.

Johnson, D. W. & Johnson, R. T. (1992, October). What to say to advocates for the gifted. *Educational Leadership*, pp. 44–47.

Johnson, D. W., Johnson, R. T., & Holubec, E. J. (1990). *Circles of learning: Cooperation in the classroom* (3rd ed.). Edina, MN: Interaction Book Company.

Johnson, D. W., Johnson, R. T., & Smith, K. A. (1991). *Active learning: Cooperation in the college classroom*. Edina, MN: Interaction Book Co.

Johnson, R. T., Johnson, D. W., & Holubec, E. J. (Eds). (1987). *Structuring cooperative learning: Lesson plans for teachers*. Edina, MN: Interaction Book Company.

Kagan, S. (1990). *Cooperative learning: Resources for teachers*. San Juan Capistrano, CA: Resources for Teachers, Inc.

Kagan, S. (1990). *Same-Different: A cooperative learning communication building structure*. San Juan Capistrano, CA: Resources for Teachers, Inc.

Kluge, L. (1990). *Cooperative learning*. Arlington, VA Educational Research Service.

Kohn, A. (1991, February) Group grade grubbing versus cooperative learning. *Educational Leadership*, pp. 83–87.

Lyman, L. & Foyle, H. C. (1990). *Cooperative grouping for interactive learning: Students, teachers, and administrators*. Washington, DC: NEA Professional Library.

Matthews, M. (1992, October). Gifted students talk about cooperative learning. *Educational Leadership*, pp. 48–50.

Nastasi, B. K. & Clements, D. H. (1991). Research on cooperative learning: Implications for practice. *School Psychology Review, 20 ,* 110–131.

Richburg, R. W. & Nelson, B. J. (1991). Where in western Europe would you like to live?: A cooperative lesson for world geography. *Social Studies, 82,* 97–106.

Rybak, S. (1992). *Cooperative learning throughout the curriculum: Together we learn better*. Carthage, IL: Good Apple, Inc.

Schniedwind, N. & Davidson, E. (1987). *Cooperative learning, cooperative lives. A sourcebook of learning activities for building a peaceful world*. Sommerville, MA: Circle Books.

Sharan, S. (ed.). (1990). *Cooperative learning: Theory and research*. New York: Praeger.

Sharan, S., Hare, P., Webb, C. & Hertz-Lazarowitz, R. (eds.). (1980). *Cooperation in education*. Provo, UT: Brigham Young University Press.

Sharan, S., Kussell, P., Hertz-Lazarowitz, R., Bejarano, Y., Raviv, S., & Sharan, Y. (1984). *Cooperative learning in the classroom: Research in desegregated schools*. New York: Erlbaum.

Sharan, Y. & Sharan, S. (1987, November) Training teachers for cooperative learning. *Educational Leadership*, pp. 20–25.

Shaw, V. (1992). *Communitybuilding in the classroom*, San Juan Capistrano, CA: Kagan Cooperative Learning.

Slavin, R. E. (1980). Cooperative learning. *Review of Educational Research, 50,* 315–342.

Slavin, R. E. (1983). *Cooperative learning*. New York: Longman.

Slavin, R. E. (1988, October). Cooperative learning and student achievement. *Educational Leadership*, pp. 31–33.

Slavin, R. E. (1990). *Cooperative learning: Theory, research, and practice*. Englewood Cliffs, NJ: Prentice-Hall.

Slavin, R. E. (1991, February). Synthesis of research of cooperative learning. *Educational Leadership*, pp. 71–82.

Slavin, R. E. (1991). *Student team learning: A practical guide* to cooperative learning (3rd ed.). Washington, DC: National Education Association.

Slavin, R., Sharan, S., Kagan, S., Lazarowitz, R., Webb, C., & Schmuck, R. (eds.). (1985). *Learning to cooperate, cooperating to learn*. New York: Plenum Press.

Stone, J. M. (1991). *Cooperative learning and language arts: A multi-structural approach*. San Juan Capistrano, CA: Resources for Teachers, Inc.

Sutton, G. O. (1992). Cooperative learning works in mathematics. *Mathematics Teacher, 85*, 63–66.

## PAIDEIA SEMINAR

Adler, M. J. (1982). A great American teacher tells—step by step—how to teach great ideas. *American School Board Journal, 169*, 30–32.

Adler, M. J. (1982). *The Paideia proposal: an educational manifesto*. New York: MacMillan.

Adler, M. J. (1982). The Paideia proposal: Rediscovering the essence of education. *American School Board Journal, 169*, 17–20.

Adler, M. J. (1982). A revolution in education. *American Educator: The Professional Journal of the American Federation of Teachers, 6*, 20–24.

Adler, M. J. (1983). Understanding the U. S. A. *Journal of Teacher Education, 34*, 35–37.

Adler, M. J. (1984). *The Paideia program: an educational syllabus*. New York: MacMillan.

Adler, M. J., & Mayer, M. S. (1958). *The revolution in education*. Chicago: University of Chicago Press.

Brazil, R. D. (1992). *A covenant of change. The Paideia manual: A guide to the re-training of America's teaching force*. (ERIC Document Reproduction Service No. ED 358 505)

Davis, O. L., Jr. (1982). A conversation with Mortimer Adler. *Educational Leadership, 39*, 579–80.

Gray, D. (1984, March). Whatever became of Paideia? (and how do you pronounce it?). *Educational Leadership*, pp. 56–57.

Gregory, M. W. (1984). A response to Mortimer Adler's "Paideia Proposal." *Journal of General Education, 36*, 70–78.

Levine-Brown, P., et al. (1993, May). *The Paideia Program*. Materials presented at the Annual International Conference of the National Institute for Staff and Organizational Development on Teaching Excellence and Conference of Administrators, Austin, TX. (ERIC Document Reproduction Service No. ED 365 394)

Palmer, A. J. (1984). The fine arts and the Paideia Proposal. *Tennessee Education, 13*, 4–9.

Ravitch, D. et al. (1983). The Paideia Proposal: A symposium. *Harvard Educational Review, 53*, 377–411.

Socha, T. J. (1985). The Paideia Proposal: Implications and challenges for communication instruction. *Iowa Journal of Speech Communication, 17*, 35–44.

Spear, K. (1984). The "Paideia Proposal": The problem of means and ends in general education. *Journal of General Education, 36*, 79–86.

## SIMULATIONS

Birt, D. (1975). *Games and simulations in history.* London: Longman.

Blaga, J. (1979). Simulations: An evaluation. *High School Journal, 63*(1), 30–35.

Bright, G. W. (1989). Teaching mathematics with technology: Probability simulations. *Arithmetic-Teacher, 36*(9), 16–18.

Charles, C. L. (1973). *Learning with games: an analysis of social studies educational games and simulations.* Boulder, CO: Social Science Education Consortium.

Cruickshank, D. R. (1980, Winter). Classroom games and simulations. *Theory into Practice,* pp. 75–80.

Ellington, H. (1981). *Games and simulations in science education.* London: K. Page.

Greenblat, C. S. (1988). *Designing games and simulations: an illustrated handbook.* Newbury Park, CA: Sage Publications.

Heitzmann, W. R. (1983). *Educational games and simulations* (rev. ed.). Washington, D. C.: NEA Professional Library, National Education Association.

Helm, G. R. (1987). Relationships—Decisions through the life cycle: A course to stimulate thinking skills. *Illinois-Teacher-of-Home-Economics, 30*(4), 127–28, 133.

Horn, R. E. (Ed.). (1977). *The guide to simulations/games for education and training* (3rd ed.). Cranford, N.J.: Didactic Systems.

Jones, K. (1982). *Simulations in language teaching.* New York: Cambridge University Press.

Jones, K. (1987). *Simulations: a handbook for teachers and trainers* (2nd ed.). London: Kogan Page.

Jones, K. (1991). *Icebreakers: a sourcebook of games, exercises and simulations.* San Diego, CA: Pfeiffer & Co.

Lamy, S. L. (1991). *Teaching global awareness with simulations and games: grades 6–12.* Denver, CO: Center for Teaching International Relations, University of Denver.

Lewis, D. R. (1974). *Educational games and simulations in economics, 134,* (rev. ed.). New York: Joint Council on Economic Education.

Shay, C. (1980). Simulations in the classroom: An appraisal. *Educational Technology, 20*(11), 26–31.

Stepien, W. and Gallagher, S. (1993). Problem-based learning: As authentic as it gets. *Educational Leadership, 50*(7), 25–28.

Stinson, J. (1993). Technology outlook on math and science: Conversations with experts. *Media-and-Methods, 29*(4), 24–27.

Thomas, J. H., Smith, S. C., and Hall, J. S. (1973). *Polling and survey research.* Arlington, VA: National School Public Relations Association.

Zeleny, L. (1974). *How to use simulations* (How to Do It Series, Number 26). (ERIC Document Reproduction Service No. ED 088 755)

## INSTRUCTIONAL TECHNOLOGY

Barron, A. E. & Orwig, G. W. (1993). *New technologies for education: A beginner's guide.* Englewood, CO: Libraries Unlimited.

Bryan, M. (1991). *Introduction to Macintosh system 7.* Alameda, CA: Sybex.

Flake, J. L., McClintock, C. E., & Turner, S. (1990). *Fundamentals of computer education.* (2nd ed.). Belmont, CA: Wadsworth.

Fraase, M. (1993). *The Mac internet tour guide: Cruising the internet the easy way.* Chapel Hill, NC: Ventana Press.

Heinich, R., Molenda, M., & Russell, J. D. (1989). *Instructional Media and the new technologies of instruction.* (3rd ed.). New York: MacMillan.

Lockard, J., Abrams, P. D., & Many, W. A. (1994). *Microcomputers for twenty-first century educators.* (3rd ed.). New York: HarperCollins.

Poole, B. J. (1995). *Education for an information age.* Madison, WI: Brown & Benchmark.

Semrau, P. & Boyer, B. A. (1994). *Using interactive video in education.* Boston: Allyn & Bacon.

Simonson, M. R. & Thompson, A. (1990). *Educational computing foundations.* (2nd ed.). New York: MacMillan.

Teague, F., Rogers, D. W., & Tipling, R. N. (1994). *Technology and media: Instructional applications.* Dubuque, IA: Kendall/Hunt.

Valmont, W. J. (1995). *Creating videos for school use.* Boston: Allyn & Bacon.

Van Horn, R. (1991). *Advanced technology in education.* Pacific Grove, CA: Brooks/Cole.

Volker, R. & Simonson, M. (1995). *Technology for teachers.* (6th ed.). Dubuque, IA: Kendall/Hunt.

# Appendix A

# Evaluation Matrix

## EVALUATION MATRIX FOR SELECTING AN ALTERNATIVE HIGH SCHOOL SCHEDULE

Choose five or six of the listed factors in the left column that are most important to your school. Compare the various scheduling options across the top and mark those which best address the factors you have identified. One may use a plus (+), zero (0) or minus (–) in each block of the matrix.

| Is this a schedule that offers: | Periods in a day | Day 1/ Day 2 | 4/4 Semester | 60 60 60 | 75 75 30 | 75–15 75–15 | Various Terms |
|---|---|---|---|---|---|---|---|
| opportunities for students to repeat courses? | | | | | | | |
| opportunities for students to accelerate? | | | | | | | |
| flexibility? | | | | | | | |
| teacher team planning? | | | | | | | |
| teacher extended blocks of time for planning? | | | | | | | |

| Is this a schedule that offers: | Periods in a day | Day 1/ Day 2 | 4/4 Semester | 60 60 60 | 75 75 30 | 75–15 75–15 | Various Terms |
|---|---|---|---|---|---|---|---|
| inexpensive implementation? | | | | | | | |
| enhanced vocational and/or Tech Prep opportunities? | | | | | | | |
| students an increased number of credits? | | | | | | | |
| students an increased number of course choices? | | | | | | | |
| students extended time for learning or for enrichment? | | | | | | | |
| easy implementation? | | | | | | | |
| support for student success? | | | | | | | |

| Is this a schedule that offers: | Periods in a day | Day 1/ Day 2 | 4/4 Semester | 60 60 60 | 75 75 30 | 75–15 75–15 | Various Terms |
|---|---|---|---|---|---|---|---|
| "family-like" support for students? | | | | | | | |
| different formats to satisfy course needs or teacher preferences? | | | | | | | |
| reduced teacher record-keeping? | | | | | | | |
| possibilities for improved student discipline? | | | | | | | |
| improved utilization of itinerant teachers? | | | | | | | |
| reduced number of preparations assigned to teachers | | | | | | | |

| Is this a schedule that offers: | Periods in a day | Day 1/ Day 2 | 4/4 Semester | 60 60 60 | 75 75 30 | 75–15 75–15 | Various Terms |
|---|---|---|---|---|---|---|---|
| reduced number of classes taught per day/term for teachers | | | | | | | |
| reduced number of students assigned teachers per term | | | | | | | |
| few political problems? | | | | | | | |
| | | | | | | | |
| | | | | | | | |
| | | | | | | | |
| | | | | | | | |

# APPENDIX B

# PLANNING CHECKLIST FOR ALTERNATIVE SCHEDULING FOR HIGH SCHOOLS

## BEGIN PLANNING A YEAR IN ADVANCE

Step 1    Identify programmatic, instructional, student achievement, or other issues that need to be addressed at the local school level.

Step 2    Determine how alternative scheduling might be used to assist in solving those problems.

Step 3    Advise superintendent and/or appropriate persons of intent to form a study group.

Step 4    Appoint a research and study group made up of parent, student, and teacher leaders to explore alternative schedules. Use outside consultants from both within and out of the system who have studied or implemented alternative schedules.

Step 5    Visit schools with alternative schedules and interview teachers and students to determine strengths and weaknesses of each schedule.

Step 6    Develop a consensus through the study group to move ahead in pursuing alternative scheduling.

Step 7    Inform superintendent and appropriate persons in instructional services of interest in changing schedules.

Seek support from instructional services in planning and trouble shooting issues pertaining to that department.

Step 8     Inform parent community of intent to pursue alternative scheduling. This should be done in writing through newsletter or a direct letter.

Step 9     Inform students and involve groups of students in discussion of impact of schedule change.

Step 10    Review study committee to insure cross department representation and different perspectives; solicit long term involvement of parents and students. Committee should reach consensus on possible scheduling models with variations.

Step 11    Ask the extended study group of steering committee (1) to establish a time line and (2) identify and reach consensus on best schedule for school needs based on data collected in Steps 1–5.

Step 12    Define instructional advantages of schedule for entire school and individual departments. How might this schedule improve student achievement?

Step 13    Identify the disadvantages for the school and each department.

Step 14    Examine the impact on vocational education center programs.

Step 15    Determine how this schedule will affect space and resources.

Step 16    Examine the impact relative to part-time teaching positions.

Step 17    Examine impact on transportation.

Step 18    Develop a staff development instructional plan based on the new schedule before implementation and one to continue at least through the first-year of implementation for both individual departments and the total school.

Step 19    Determine computer programming needs, if any.

Step 20    Determine how this schedule will have an impact on teacher productivity.

Step 21    Develop a time line and list of tasks to be done for implementation, including communication to various groups.

Step 22    Develop a plan for ongoing monitoring during the first year.

Adapted from memorandum prepared by:

Janie R. Smith, Director
Office of High School Instruction
  and K-12 Curriculum Services
Fairfax County Schools
Walnut Hill Center
7423 Camp Alger Avenue
Falls Church, VA 22042

# APPENDIX C

# INDICATORS OF ACHIEVEMENT FOR HIGH SCHOOL RESTRUCTURING EFFORTS

The purpose of the following list of achievement indicators is to provide ideas for data collection as part of the evaluation process for high school block scheduling efforts. For each indicator several means of data collection have been suggested. This list was prepared by a group of educators interested in carefully evaluating new schedules and their effects; it should be considered a partial list. Indicators have been divided into two categories: enabling and final. We suggest that the achievement of enabling indicators may lead to the achievement of the final indicators. This distinction is fuzzy at best. Comments or additions should be directed to Michael D. Rettig, *Study of Innovative High School Scheduling in Virginia*, Department of Secondary Education, James Madison University, Harrisonburg.

## ENABLING ACHIEVEMENT INDICATORS

| *ACHIEVEMENT INDICATOR* | *MEANS OF DATA COLLECTION* |
|---|---|
| *Student Attention* | |
| On Task Behavior | Sampling by observation |
| | Teacher & Student Surveys or Interviews |
| | |
| *Instructional Practices* | |
| Activity | Sampling by Observation |
| Variety | Teacher & Student Surveys or Interviews |
| Appropriate for Content | |
| Appropriate for Learners | |
| | |
| *Student Behavior/Discipline* | |
| Expulsion | School Records |
| OSS | Number of referrals, ISS, OSS, etc. |
| ISS | Percent of school population |
| Referrals | Percent of teachers referring |
| Detention | |
| Guidance Interventions | |
| | |
| *Homework* | |
| Quantity Assigned | Teacher & Student Surveys or Interviews |
| Completed | Teacher Records or Survey |
| Time Spent | Student and Parent Surveys |
| | |
| *Student Attendance and Tardies* | School Records |
| | |
| *Teacher Attendance* | School Records |
| | |
| *Field Trips* | School Records of Pull-outs from Class |
| | Teacher & Student Surveys or Interviews |
| | |
| *Interruptions* | PA Announcement Log |
| | Monthly Record of Bell Schedule Alterations for Assemblies, etc. |
| | |
| *Use of Community Resources* | Log |
| | Teacher, Student, & Parent Surveys or Interviews |
| | |
| *Library Media* | |
| Circulation | Library Records |
| Library Use During Day | Library Schedule/Sign-up |
| | Teacher & Student Surveys or Interviews |

| ACHIEVEMENT INDICATOR | MEANS OF DATA COLLECTION |
|---|---|
| *Student/Teacher Relationships* | Teacher, Student, & Parent Surveys or Interviews |
| *Student & Teacher Stress* | Teacher, Student, & Parent Surveys or Interviews |
| *Time per Course* | Calculation (period length x days) |
| *Time for Total Instruction* | Calculation (period length x days x courses) |
| *Presence of Other Practices*<br>Authentic Assessment<br>Use of Technology<br>Teaming<br>Heterogenous Grouping<br>Elimination of Study Hall<br>Inclusion | Teacher & Student Surveys or Interviews |
| *Summer School Enrollment* | School Records |
| *Gifted Education*<br>Number of Referrals<br>Number Eligible<br>Student needs met | <br>Gifted Eligibility Committee Records<br>Gifted Eligibility Committee Records<br>Teacher, Student, & Parent Surveys or Interviews |
| *Special Education*<br>Number of Referrals<br>Number Eligible<br>Student needs met | <br>Child Study Committee Records<br>Eligibility Committee Records<br>Teacher, Student, & Parent Surveys or Interviews |
| *Advanced Placement*<br>Number of courses offered<br>Number of students enrolled<br>Percent of school population enrolled | <br>Schedule<br><br>School Records<br><br>School Records |

| *ACHIEVEMENT INDICATOR* | *MEANS OF DATA COLLECTION* |
|---|---|
| *Dual-Enrollment* | |
| Number of courses offered | Schedule |
| Number of students enrolled | School Records |
| Percent of school population enrolled | School Records |
| *Parent Involvement* | |
| Open House Attendance | Attendance Counts |
| Volunteering | Logs, sign-in sheets |
| Parent Conference Attendance | Attendance Counts |
| Staff/Teacher Contact | Logs, Teacher Surveys or Interviews |
| Homework Hotline | Electronic Counts of Usage |
| Parent Info Network | Electronic Counts of Usage |

## FINAL ACHIEVEMENT INDICATORS

| *ACHIEVEMENT INDICATOR* | *MEANS OF DATA COLLECTION* |
|---|---|
| *Grades* | School Records |
| Distribution | |
| Number of failures | |
| *Credits Earned* | |
| Disaggregate by subject | School Records |
| Cumulative over HS years | School Records |
| *Athletic Eligibility* | |
| Percent of population meeting Requirements | School Records |
| Percent of eligible students losing eligibility during the year | |
| *Content Mastery* | |
| End of Course Tests | Score Distributions |
| End of Year Tests | Pass Rates |
| Final Exams | |

| *ACHIEVEMENT INDICATOR* | *MEANS OF DATA COLLECTION* |
|---|---|
| *Drop Out Rate* | |
| Percent yearly | School Records |
| Graduation Rate | School Records |
| *Standardized Tests* | |
| Achievement Tests (TAP, ITBS, CAT, etc.) | Scores |
| State Competency Tests Scores,(LPT in VA, TASS in TX, etc.) | Percent of non-passers |
| College Entrance (PSAT, SAT, ACT) | Scores, Percent of population taking the test |
| *Advanced Placement* | |
| Percent of population taking AP exams | School Records |
| Percent of student enrolled in AP courses taking the exam | School Records |
| Percent scoring 3 or higher | AP Scores (by course or school population) |
| *Dual-Enrollment* | |
| College Credits Earned | School Records |
| Grades | School Records |
| *Excellence Indicators* | Places, Prizes, etc. |
| Merit Scholars | |
| Quiz Bowl | |
| Latin Exam | |
| Vocational/Music/Art | |
| *Follow Up Graduation* | |
| College Entrance | Follow-up Surveys |
| College Completion | |
| Employment | |

Note: It may be advisable to consider the disaggregation of data for various indicators based upon any or all of the following characteristics:

Grade Level
Subject
Teacher
Race/Ethnicity
Economic Level        Free/Reduced Lunch
Gender
Academic/Voc.
At-Risk               Bottom 25%
Special Ed.

Revised: April 14, 1995